LIVERPOOL
ECHOES

© Richard Whittington-Egan 2002

Published by The Bluecoat Press, Liverpool
Book design by March Design, Liverpool
Printed by MFP

ISBN 1 904438 04 0

RICHARD WHITTINGTON-EGAN

LIVERPOOL
ECHOES

The Bluecoat Press

CONTENTS

HISTORIC ECHOES

LITERARY ECHOES

THESPIAN ECHOES

MELODIOUS ECHOES

PERSONAL ECHOES

PROLOGUE

LIVERPOOL – MY HOME

Liverpool is no longer, physically, my home. I do not live there. I have not lived there for over forty years. And yet, in a way, I have never left it. I have carried my birthplace with me in my head and heart all my life long – in France, Italy, Germany, Austria, Switzerland, London and New York.

Of course, *my* Liverpool is somewhat different from *your* Liverpool of today. Mark you, everybody's Liverpool is different – a place of one's own, its shape defined and settled by your particular experience, your personal recognition of one of the many, many aspects of the chameleonic city on the water.

My life began in Mossley Hill, in the shade of the Victorian merchant princes' tree-bowered, sandstone castles. It moved, in the 1920s, to 140 Upper Parliament Street, whence I was wheeled daily to take the air in Falkner Square's locked and railinged private gardens. In the 1930s, I was at 34 Prince's Park Mansions, where I remember my regular defiance of Ponti, the Italian caretaker, who used to shake his fist at me, and Bill, his churlish-seeming general factotum, who, despite a wooden or injured leg, would give me chase. It was there that I landed myself in severe trouble by clambering out of the nursery window and walking the length of the precipitous parapet that formed a narrow ledge extending along the back, overlooking Prince's Park, of the topmost part of the building.

In 1941, I was quartered temporarily in a small house at the corner of Queen's Drive and Dovedale Road, and it was there that I knew the terror – and pride – of living through the Great May Blitz, when Hitler's Luftwaffe stole the lives of hundreds and hundreds of Liverpool men, women, and children, but failed to break the city's spirit. It was from a different house, an old family home, Hazelwood, 55 Queen's Drive, that I joined the army and went off to war.

In the late 1940s and 1950s, I was at 35 Arundel Avenue, just round the corner from where my friend Tony Rose's grandmother, Mrs Nicholaides, lived in Hartington Road at its junction with Croxteth Grove. Thereafter, I was at 7 Percy Street, in the heart of Liverpool's Bohemian quarter, where I came to know the artists Bob Percival, Ronald Scarland, Frank Lamb and James Cliffe, the sculptress Eve Tompsett, and the versatile musician and wit, Friz Spiegl. Later I was to meet up with that very individualistic, not to say idiosyncratic, Liverpool author, Frank Shaw, initially crossing swords with him, and, ultimately, becoming good friends.

Finally, before force of circumstance despatched me, non-return, to London, I dwelt supremely happily at 12 Sunnyside, that enchanted and enchanting enclave within Prince's Park, the dignified brother and sister, the

Smiths of Smith's (Carpets, of Williamson Square), residing in full Victorian splendour next door.

All these last forty-five years I have drawn alien air as breath. The exile is a hostage to misfortune. That misfortune is life-long loss, *and the awareness of it*. The exile – like James Joyce – remembers everything. Joyce carried in his head a detailed street by street, alley and *cul-de-sac*, map of Dublin. He knew every shop and pub and nook and crevice, so that if, by some unthinkable universal catastrophe, Dublin had been razed, he had within his remembered knowledge all that was needed to build it up again – which, indeed, he did, writing *Ulysses* in Zurich.

Revisiting Liverpool, I find myself in a strange city. Homeless, after all these years, relying on hotels. My ain folk all gone. It is an odd feeling. It lends a strange new slant to the old Negro spiritual, *Goin' home … Goin' home*. As my father used to say, "You can't go back". He was right.

Corners that I knew and loved have crumbled into dust; been blown away. Shiny new buildings, symphonies in glass and sunlight, have arisen; some of them very good. Alas! There are also concrete eggboxes, and scattered others of that architectural ilk. Long celebrated for its meticulous vandalism, Liverpool has systematically swept away most of the monuments of its historic past. Indeed, the Bluecoat Chambers was only saved from a like fate by the persistence and civic influence of the late Robert Gladstone. Sadly, there was no one to curb their destructive enthusiasm when they flattened and ruined the historic God's Acre around St James' Mount, at the Cathedral's feet. The gravestones of famous and plain folk alike were undiscriminatingly torn up and knocked down. It was, and is, not only a scandal, but a total breach of good taste. Similarly, one by one, the old Victorian churches that stood in grace and dignity on either side of the Prince's Road Boulevard, where the trees are heavy with dust and the once-sparkling sand is punctuated by tracts of weedy grass, have been picked off by the wreckers.

Old wartime scars have healed. Fresh green fields have grown up over erstwhile streets of Jack-the-Ripper gloom and menace. Clean winds of change have scoured from the city map Ascot, Athlone, Skirving and Latimer Streets, where, in the 1880s, those two redoubtable Hibernian *immigrées*, jewels from the Emerald Isle, Catty Flannagan and Maggie Higgins, despatched their kith and kin with arsenic water from soaked flypapers for the insurance money. I remember the scene of one of the crimes well, for my friend, Pat Baines, lived next to their house in Latimer Street. The late Pat Baines. Remembered faces, as well as places, have vanished.

As I step out of Lime Street Station, I feel as if I myself have joined the ghosts. Change, if not decay, all around I see. The Washington, the Imperial, the Victoria, historic Lime Street hostelries, have gone. Whilom rip-roaring Lime Street itself has become a dreary desert of comparative respectability.

While, on the other hand, the Adelphi Hotel, where I tend to put up when I am back in town, has lost, or perhaps, and hopefully, has only mislaid, its former distinguishedly exclusive ethos.

The Exchange Hotel, and Exchange and Central stations, are all closed. The Bear's Paw, a favourite rendezvous, is no more. The blinds have descended for ever upon Henderson's and Bunny's. The Tatler News Theatre has long vanished from Church Street. So has the Prince of Wales from Clayton Square. The murky romance has vanished from Scotland Road, where wilde thyme blows in the place of the cobbles. The One o'clock Gun is silent. The splendid Gothic Sailors' Home, with its wonderful cast-iron galleries – gone. The Pier Head is no longer the Pier Head as I knew it, but the reclamation of the adjacent docks and warehouses, and their transformation into a riverside place of pleasure and painless instruction, is an absolutely superb piece of improving modern development.

But, for better or worse, the simple truth is that I just can't leave Liverpool alone. The sun has long ago set upon my resident days, but its invoked remembered blaze still irradiates these greyer times, and, through the thickening haze, shafts of high-noon light will go on picking out figures, events, little capsules of irresistible atmosphere.

I still see with awful clarity, Tommy, the young – sixty years ago! – man who looked after the two ravens, raucous and red-meat-shredding, then occupying the first cage on the left in the Sefton Park aviary. I see, too, the little green-painted, wooden refreshment hut, predecessor of the present brick-built monstrosity that stands upon its site, and round the corner the archery ground where the Mersey Bowmen – my mother, a toxophilite, was one of them – directed their arrows at the bright, round targets. Neither must one forget the Vesuvian cave, a sort of replicated eighteenth century garden grotto beside the brooding pool, where ghosts and goblins dwelt, and where we Sefton Park children dared one another to venture into its dark and cold interior alone.

Then, a boulder's throw from the beautiful Iron Bridge, there was the Palm House. Magnificent. Surrounded by life-sized statues of famous men – Darwin, Mercator, Christopher Columbus. The scent and warmth that greeted you as you opened the door, the towering palms, the banana trees, the spiral iron staircase twisting 70 feet up to the roof, and, of course, the sweetly seductive statue of Highland Mary.

I especially recall the huge boulder, an erratic, the geologists would call it, standing at the foot of the hill leading up to the Palm House, and the coldness of it against the palm of my hand on that October night in 1957 when my friend Tony Robinson and I were walking in the park, and the Russian Sputnik, the man-made satellite which inaugurated the Space Age, was orbiting high in the sky above us. How amazed we would have been then had we known that four years later, in July 1961, at a reception at the

Hyde Park Hotel, in London, I would be patted on the head by Major Yuri Alexeyevitch Gagarin, who, in the April of that year, had been the first man in space, and, on that same occasion, shake hands with the prime minister, Harold Macmillan! Seven years after that, on 27 March 1968, Gagarin was to die at the age of 34, when the obsolete MiG 15 jet trainer he was flying lost height and crashed into the ground 40 miles north of Moscow. A national hero, he is buried in the Kremlin wall.

Liverpool's parks seem to me exceptionally lovely. I was first wheeled round Prince's Park by my nanny, Ethel Blundell, in my pram. I remember, later, Judy the donkey's gravestone, and seeing the old men playing ollies on the olly pitch, which was not far from the Swiss chalet boathouse at the end of the lake. Coming out of the park, one used to see old George the cabby, with his invariable billycock, his horse and cab standing patiently outside Prince's Park Mansions, and hear his triumphant clip-clopping away when someone hired them. Horse and man have long since clip-clopped into eternity.

A favourite childhood place was Calderstones Park, outside the main entrance to which the Calder Stones then still stood in their circular railed enclosure. Amid the park's luxuriant plantations the young imagination saw skin-clad, cudgel-bearing prehistoric figures moving stealthily, or crouched, ready to launch a stone-tipped arrow, or execute a club-wielding spring from beneath the ha-ha.

Another much-loved haunt was quaint, old-world, bosky Otterspool Park, with its little zoo, and the wild, tangled, Jericho-bounded shoreline beyond, before it was tamed to the decorous, laid-out, concrete-and-flower-bedded neatness of the splendid Mersey-side sweep of Otterspool Promenade. How different from the lonely Cast-Iron Shore, where in the winter's evening dusk we swore to hear the banshees wailing, and our hearts would pound as we crept, as inconspicuously as possible, down the narrow, high-walled lane that approached it, where Jack the Ripper was said to lurk and Spring-Heeled Jack would surely leap.

Considerably more grand than the Otterspool Zoo was the Liverpool Zoo, in Elmswood Road, Mossley Hill, with its little folly tower and its most celebrated resident, Micky the chimpanzee. I knew him first when my father took me to the garage on the outskirts of Liverpool – was it Prescot? – where he was kept as a pet before being hailed off into resented captivity. I mourned his undeserved death by bullets after his escape – 'running amok' as it was sensationally described – put the locals into a blind panic.

The parish of the chimes of beautiful, hill-crowning Mossley Hill Church is one of my most dearly cherished parts of Liverpool. I have the fondest memories of Sudley, now a musuem, but once Great Aunt Emma's home, where, as a girl, my mother used to play tennis on the sunken lawn, below the bank where Great Aunt Emma would sit watching. Down the hill, along

Rose Lane to the Plaza, on Allerton Road. Into the marbled coolness of the foyer, with the plashing indoor fountain, the fat goldfish, and big, ornamental, tropic shell. How many afternoons of my youth did I spend within those alluring portals, sitting in the listening dark, crunching my way through a mammoth bag of multi-coloured sugared popcorn, watching Katharine Hepburn in *The Little Minister*, getting to know Hollywood in its Joan Crawford, Clark Gable, Jean Harlow, Humphrey Bogarde high noon, before the Plaza, like Hollywood itself, vanished into limbo.

There was, I remember, behind the Plaza, a dairy farm, where I used to love to watch the cows being milked. I think it was Capstick's Farm. The recollection of the name is reinforced because, many years later, I was told by Chief Detective Superintendent John Capstick, of Scotland Yard, 'Charlie Artful', the man who caught Peter Griffiths, the Blackburn baby killer, and whom I came to know well in my Fleet Street days, that he thought that the Allerton farm belonged to relatives of his. Actually, his father had owned a dairy farm in Chapel Avenue, Walton, and as a lad he used to earn a few coppers by running a milk round. The deliveries he made included, appropriately enough, the local police station and Walton Gaol. John Capstick's family lived later in Hesswell Road, Aintree.

Long before the Beatles usurped it and hymned it into musical immortality, Penny Lane was my stamping ground. I connect it with two classic Liverpool murder cases. It was the tram junction where William Herbert Wallace, the alleged Anfield uxoricide, caught a car for non-existent Menlove Gardens East, and it was there that I used to chat in his hairdresser's shop with Mr Bioletti, the son of James Bioletti, who gave evidence about the cosmetic use of arsenic by ladies in the Maybrick murder trial.

Which brings back another memory. A golden summer's evening walk with my young – then – mother to Battlecrease House, in Riversdale Road, and on past Wokes' the chemist's, on the corner of Aigburth and Beechwood Roads, where Mrs Maybrick bought flypapers, and the old Aigburth Hotel, where the inquest was held on James Maybrick, its site now occupied by a vandal's delight, the Kingsman public-house. I might just mention that James and Florence Maybrick were friends of my grandparents. They used to come to dinner to their house and would invite them back to Battlecrease. My grandparents were also in the party that went with Mr and Mrs Maybrick in the horse bus they had hired to the 1889 Grand National. It was on the course at Aintree that James and Florence had the tremendous row over the attention that she was paying to Alfred Brierley which some believed to have been the precipitant of the subsequent demise of James.

I grow old. I grow old. Time lengthens and the memories unfold. Long-forgotten scenes start vividly back into focus; images like those magic lantern pictures of one's childhood. Images that dissolve and draw you back into them. Were they ever really there? Was I? And yet I *know* I hunted tigers in the thickets of Prince's Park – did I not tear my leggings on the railings doing so, and land up in rare trouble with my Nanny? – and buffalo and Indians in and out the boscage by the waters of Sefton Park Lake.

Clearly I see, in the mind's backward glancing eye, the *Jolly Roger,* the pirate ship, long since sunk, anchored in the water alongside Wendy's hut, and the statue of Peter Pan in Sefton Park, and I seem to recall being present at the celebratory inauguration, the day of the pageant, with the Lord Mayor and all the local big wigs in attendance. That must have been around 1929 or 1930, I would guess.

Another childhood vignette. Burbo House, Blundellsands, and the very special home-made lemonade, served to us, ice-cold, amid the grassy-tussocked sand hills, when, as infant school children at Bellerive Convent, we were taken there by the nuns on a feast day outing.

Then there were visits to Waterloo, where the ice cream man on the shore cried his wares: "Hokey Pokey a penny a lump. That's the stuff to make you jump!" And invitations to tea at what had been my maternal great-grandparents' home, 11 Beach Lawn, occupied by then in solitary state by my Great Aunt Peggy, served by Cook and an enormous retinue of maids, and where Martin, the coachman, who used to drive my great-grandparents, with a pair of running Dalmatians beside the carriage wheels, now worked more tamely as a handyman. I used to love to sit by the window of the first-floor drawing-room, watching the big ships sailing past, fully lit up at dusk, heading for the Mersey Bar, and so close on the nearby river that you felt that you could almost touch them. I can never catch the scent of that old-fashioned flower called 'cherry pie' without its calling up a vista of my great-grandparents' huge and beautiful Victorian garden and its sparkling greenhouses.

There were other trips, 'over the water', aboard the ferry-boats, *Royal Daffodil* and *Royal Iris*, to Seacombe, Wallasey and New Brighton. With memories of the Ham-and-Egg Parade, the donkey rides, and the one-legged man who used to dive off the pier for pennies, whose plaintive "Don't forget the diver", was immortalised in Liverpool comedian Tommy Handley's radio show *ITMA* (It's That Man Again).

Very exciting, too, was a trip on the overhead railway, riding, 16 feet up in the air through the summer sunshine, from the Dingle to Seaforth Sands. What small boy could fail to treasure such an out-of-the-ordinary experience? Strange are the twists of fate. More than two decades later, in December 1956, through the blackness of a winter's night of ice-edged wind, I was to make that same journey – but with a chilling difference. I was reporting 'live' for the BBC from the swaying carriage in the night sky, the very last Dingle to Seaforth Sands run, that the 63-years-old Overhead Railway would ever make. A sentimental journey indeed.

I remember being taken to see the flower clock at Woolton, which, by the way, really did seem to be a village then, with a village pond, which, the last time I saw it, had been transmogrified into a facultative car park. In those days there was no through road opposite the tram's terminus. A long wall ran across on the other side of the road. As a child I was especially fascinated by the golden elephant's head adorning the outer wall of one of the village inns.

Gateacre and Childwall were very remote and rural when I was a boy. There was a busy blacksmith's forge beside Gateacre Grange. Sparks flew from the anvil, the hammer blows rang out like bells, and the hiss and stench of burning hoof as the red-hot shoe was applied are unforgettable, unforgotten. Down Gateacre Brow I would go, past the Bear and Staff to where the Black Bull lay behind its fine monkey puzzle, strike off in the direction of Childwall, paying my respects to Cuckoo Lane and the curious roadside stone cross, and come thus to Childwall Church, where the grave of the late Victorian poet, Sir William Watson, an extremely rumbustious and amusingly eccentric character, has been to me a constant object of pilgrimage.

Here, too, is the picuresque Childwall Abbey Hotel. I remember it when it really was a hotel. For the great theatrical stars of the past, it was always a favourite place to stay, and there was a window upon the glass pane of which many, Sir Henry Irving among them, scratched their names with diamonds. Irving was fond of smoking a cigar in the old room facing the garden. Ellen Terry is said to have been very happy when roaming through the lovely old garden, with its really beautiful ancient bowling green.

On memory's mercurial wings I travel back townwards, past the once-thick woods on Woolton Road, past evocatively named Gipsy Lane, where I scanned repeatedly but never once spotted hair nor hide of a real, live Gypsy, past Bishop Eton Monastery, where there was a wonderful life-sized crucifix in the grounds, and the Convent of the Poor Clare nuns, where, unlike good Victorian children, they are heard, but not seen. They live their prayerful days and lives away behind a blind-faced grille. Self-chosen religious exiles. Of the tall-towered, vaguely gothic waterworks – or Dudlow Pumping Station someone once told me to call it – a Woolton Road landmark throughout my Liverpool life, there is no longer a trace. Levelled like everything else, I presume.

I miss, in Upper Parliament Street, all its network of little offshoot streets – Amberley, Kimberley, and Verulam – and the milk-bottling premises, on the lefthand side at the Smithdown Road end, where you could watch the wonder of circling machinery, tended by white-clad milkmaidens, through the 'specially installed big, plate-glass window. I miss, too, Anthony Buck's pharmacy, a Victorian relic with its iron-stemmed, red-globed gas-lamp, on the Sandon Street corner of Upper Parliament Street. In my day the pharmacist was Tom Ashworth. Sadly gone, up in flames, is the Rialto, the first cinema that I ever went to. Happily, I am still able to find the old Church of Humanity in the lower reaches of Upper Parliament Street, though it has gone these fifty years and more by another name, and fundamentally changed the identity of its purpose.

I remember nostalgically the Twenty Three Club in Hope Street, where I lunched with such friends as Barrie Hall, concerts manager, and Sir (then plain) John Pritchard, conductor, both of the Philharmonic Hall, Miss Alexis Zaina, Liverpool University lecturer in Italian, Dr Frohlich, the distinguished pioneering physicist, also from the University, and Dr FB Julian, physician and poet, from Rodney Street, and author of *Ovid in Arcady*, or, as I teased him, 'Avid in Orcady'.

Two Liverpool lanes haunt me.

Edge Lane, where phantoms flit between the dark trunks of the leafless trees, and disport amid the bare flower-beds and locked greenhouses of brooding winter in the Botanic Gardens, and the shade of the old beaver-hatted Mole of Mason Street, Joseph Williamson, reputedly still stomps about his tunnels deep in the subterranean sandstone.

Lark Lane, with the painted white clock face on the wall outside the horologist's shop; the black and white building which has done duty as antique shop and up-market eating-house; the tobacconist and newsagent's shop deeply bedded in the early years of the twentieth century; the old-fashioned chandler's shop, with its wonderful potpourri of cleanly house and home caressing smells; the old police station where they kept Mrs Maybrick for a while, and the hidden backwater jewel, Hadassah Grove. And, for me personally, the house with the pointed turret, on the right near the gates into Sefton Park, has especial sentimental significance, for it was here, in what is today a place of stylish bistros, that, getting on for a hundred years ago, was the dame school in which my mother learned the three Rs.

Vanished from the lower slopes of Mount Pleasant, and sorely missed, is Hunt's Hotel, a curious nineteenth century oasis, with stone-flagged back garden, aviary, fig tree, and omnipresent nasturtiums, where a comfortable room was always put at the disposal of the visitant returning exile.

One of the old features of my Liverpool which I very much miss are the vanished bookshops that I knew in my youth, and from which I obtained many of the volumes which formed the basis of what has since grown into a library of some 20,000 volumes. There was Jameson's in Market Street, with its long trestle-tables of secondhand books; Elly's in the basement in the corner of the elbow of Sweeting Street; Henry Young's in South Castle Street; Martin McGoff's in Moorefields, Mr Peters' shop in Victoria Street, which, after his death, his wife ran from a house in St James' Road; and there was thin-faced, fine-boned, clerically-aspected Mr Waterston's shop in Berry Street, with its vast collection of theological volumes threatening to suffocate the secular stock! I always enjoyed hunting through the shelves at the Newington Bookshop, whose jolly proprietress offered me a signed copy of the first edition of Oscar Wilde's *The Happy Prince*, for £10, which, at the time, seemed to me an enormous sum, which I could not afford. It would now be worth anything between £800 and £1,000.

A very tender memory is of the lovely grey seal with soft, sad eyes, that swam gracefully in its big glass tank in the aquarium at the Museum, in William Brown Street.

I should, I suppose, know better, but like one of those inextinguishable divas of the past who was forever making just one more 'last appearance', I keep coming back from the Reichenbach Falls to make a Sherlockian last, last bow.

And so it is, my patient reader, that seven Liverpool books, and I do not care to recall how many years, on, the old literary trouper begs your kind indulgence as he returns once more to the old familiar stage, feeling that I am in some sense, in some small way, giving back to Liverpool the life by Liverpool given.

MURDEROUS
ECHOES

THE CAFFERATA POISONING CASE

There is, or was within living memory, a dark old house situated in the Vauxhall Road area of the fair city of Liverpool. The house, like many another in that quarter, had fallen upon evil times. It had seen change and decay. It flaked and peeled like some sick animal in a neglected zoo.

But the darkness of that house was not entirely a matter of mouldering masonry and soot-grimed bricks. It came as much from the inside as the outside. For dark deeds had been done there, and it was, I believe, the legacy of those deeds, staining its atmosphere as surely as the smokes and fogs of a hundred years had stained its brickwork, that imparted to it the forbidding air with which it always seemed enwrapped.

The plain fact is that that old house was once the lair of a secret poisoner. Within those walls had dwelt merciless cunning, and therein had been enacted scenes of great cruelty and anguish, culminating in what it was the custom of those times to designate, 'murder most foul'.

Certainly there had been nothing sinister about the place in the year 1854, when Mrs Ann James arrived from the fresh-blown pastures of her native Devonshire, healthy, happy, and full of hope and ambition, to take up residence there. A clever, capable woman, Mrs James had rapidly transformed her new home into a thriving place of business. On the ground-floor she opened up a grocery shop, and a large room where meals and refreshments were served and several of the upstairs rooms were let to lodgers. Soon, the enterprising Mrs James found herself salting away a tidy nest-egg of savings.

Success brought in its wake a sizeable train of relatives. In next to no time Mrs James was joined by her married sister, Eliza Townsend. With her came her invalid husband and their three sons. Next to arrive were Ann James' married niece and her husband, a japanner by trade and Cafferata by name.

And then there were eight …

Nine, actually, for there hove upon the scene now a gentleman named Thomas Winslow. A former ironworker, he started off in the somewhat crowded James household as an upstairs lodger, but achieved rapid promotion – first, as *major-domo* of the lodging side of the business, and subsequently and additionally as manager of the grocery shop.

Predictably, this led to some degree of ill-feeling among the Jamesian relatives. They did not take to Winslow. They liked even less what they regarded as the disproportionate influence which he seemed to be exercising over Mrs James. It soon became a house divided: the Townsends and the Cafferatas on the one hand, Winslow on the other, and poor Mrs James fair and square in the middle.

The Townsend-Cafferata faction sustained a swingeing blow when, first, Mr Townsend, and then, in rapid succession, Eliza Townsend and two of her three sons, died.

That left only one Townsend – young Martin, a bit of a nuisance, forever joining, and having to be bought out of, the Army, but not rating as a very significant arms-bearing adversary in the internecine war – and the two Cafferatas.

Even by the high standards of Victorian mortality rates, the occurrence of four deaths in one family in so short a span of time was suspicious. In the light of later events, the arteries of suspicion harden into virtual certainty of the operation of compound foul play.

In the January of 1860, Mrs James herself was laid low by several mysterious attacks of illness, during one of which Mr Winslow somehow persuaded her to sign an authority, which he had written out, for him to withdraw the £130 which she had amassed in the savings bank. He also went to the Gas Company, where she had four gas shares valued at £200, and tried to get them entered in his name. On being told that this could not be done without a proper transfer, or by will, he arranged for the solicitor of the Gas Company to see Mrs James, and draw up such a will. In this document the business and the stock-in-trade were bequeathed to Winslow, and it was directed that the remainder of the property should be divided equally between Mrs Cafferata and Martin Townsend.

On 5 February, Mrs James suffered so severe an attack of the mystery illness that Dr Cameron, Physician to the Southern Hospital, was summoned. Three weeks later, Thomas Winslow wrote to Mrs Cafferata, who was away in Manchester, telling her that she must come at once if she wished to see her aunt alive. She came, and, for a fortnight, slept in the same bed with Aunt Ann in the back-parlour. During that time she could not help noticing how exemplarily attentive Winslow was, showing great interest in Mrs James' fluctuating condition, and insisting upon bringing all her meals to her himself.

Very gradually, the invalid seemed to improve. Then, on 29 March, came a severe relapse, and Dr Cameron was hastily sent for. Again, his patient got gradually better. But further and worse relapses followed, with the worried doctor in attendance, on May 8th and 25th.

And, indeed, there were by now very tangible grounds for worry. Four times in less than four months he had been urgently summoned. Always the symptoms were the same – the patient in great distress, suffering from violent purging and vomiting. This time as he came out of the hushed sickroom he felt absolutely certain of it – a secret poisoner was at work in that house. Someone was trying to destroy Mrs James. When he left, the doctor had certain samples and specimens in his bag. He was going to have them analysed. Then he would know if he was right.

He had his answer on 10 June. The analyst had found indisputable traces of antimony.

Dr Cameron acted swiftly. He communicated with the police and with them, he went to his patient's home. The police took possession of all the medicine bottles and a number of cups that were in the patient's room, and Dr Cameron had Mrs James removed to the Southern Hospital, out of harm's way. Sadly it was too late, for there, on 24 June, she died.

A post-mortem revealed the presence of cancer in the intestine, and the pathologist gave cancer as the cause of death, but added that death had been accelerated by the administration of continual small doses of antimony.

On the basis of this evidence, Thomas Winslow was arrested. He vehemently protested his innocence, accusing the Cafferatas of having poisoned Mrs James.

His trial opened at Liverpool on 20 August 1860. Testimony that he had been trying to obtain antimony was given by a Mrs Ann Foley, a woman who had once worked for Mrs James. She said that Winslow had given her tuppence and told her to go and buy some antimony, "for the dog". But the chemist would not let her have it.

More damaging was the evidence of a boy, Thomas Maguire, who had also lodged at Mrs James' house. He said that he had purchased a white powder from a bottle labelled 'Ant.' at William Miller's chemist's shop in Tithebarn Street, and had given it to Winslow. He had several times seen Winslow cutting bread in the kitchen for the mistress, take a white powder in a paper from his pocket, and sprinkle it on the bread before he buttered it.

In his charge to the jury, the trial judge, Baron Martin, told them that if the prisoner administered antimony with the intention of killing, and the deceased's death from a natural disease was thus accelerated, that was murder, but they must not convict unless the evidence satisfied their minds of his guilt.

Apparently it did not. Winslow's defence lawyers must have done their job well, for it took the jury only a few minutes to bring in a verdict of Not Guilty. So, officially at least, the Liverpool Poisoning Mystery remained just that – a mystery.

But if not Winslow, who? The Cafferatas? Young Martin Townsend?

The old dark house has kept its secret, but if stones could speak, I am pretty sure of the name that they would whisper …

DEATH IN THE TEMPEST MANICURE LOUNGE

Among sundry surviving quaint nooks and corners of old Liverpool, there linger still in the Tithebarn Street area two narrow, dagger-thrust-straight passageways, really more like alleys, known by the ancient name of 'hey' – Hackins Hey and Tempest Hey, respectively. It is with the latter, named in commemorative tribute to the early nineteenth century family of Plumbe Tempest, owners of considerable properties in these parts, of that we are presently concerned. For it was here, in the year 1946, that a somewhat curious establishment known as Bobby's Gents' Manicure Lounge, run by a shady lady by the name of Mrs Ella Staunton, became the scene of a singularly grisly, not to say lethal, incident.

Born in 1905, Ella Valentine French had in her youth been eye-catchingly lovely, slim with a delicate complexion and generously tumbling cascades of Titian hair. A beauty queen at 15, a ballroom dancing champion at 22, Ella had gone on to travel the world as a dancer and manicurist, with spells as salesgirl in an exclusive New York gown shop, and lazing away halcyon holiday hours on the sun-drenched Carribean beaches of Cuba.

In 1934, at the age of 29, she had married Thomas Staunton, of Crosby, importing to the altar with her a child of a previous, unsanctified, liaison. The marriage with Staunton was short-lived – four years – and unblessed with progeny. Not too long after the separation, Ella elected to throw in her lot with that of a Dutch naval captain. Whether or not that union would have prospered there is no knowing, for in the early days of the Second World War the gallant captain went down with his ship.

It was, indeed, during those first months of the war that Ella decided to go into business. She and a friend and partner, Gladys Henderson, set up shop in Rumford Street – a premises which was rapidly identified by the sharp-eyed Liverpool constabulary as what was vernacularly spoken of as a 'knocking shop', to wit, a brothel. They set about collecting the necessary evidence in earnest. The condemnatory dossier waxed fatter and fatter. Then … Mrs Henderson was killed in one of the terrible air raids of the 1940 May Blitz, and the authorities decided to proceed no further with the ripening investigation. Ella Staunton was off the hook.

However, having had a taste of easy money, by May 1946, Ella was once again reaping the fringe benefits of sporadic prostitution. She had opened another business premises, within a stone's throw of Rumford Street, Bobby's Gents' Manicure Lounge, situated in a basement in Tempest Hey. But fresh tidings of bawdy behaviour in Mrs Staunton's premises had come to the ears of the police, and on the afternoon of 20 May 1946, a surveillance of her suspect basement was initiated.

Arrangements had been made with the owner of the small engineering workshop which occupied the ground floor immediately above the suspect manicure lounge, and this was to be the vantage point from which, peering through a ventilation grille exposed below a lifted portion of floorboard, a pair of peeping 'Jacks' could keep a watchful eye on the antics in Bobby's subterranean lair.

It was at 4.15pm on that Monday afternoon that Detective Constables Anderson and Ballam took up their position and commenced observations. Voices from below they could hear clearly, but their view through the spy-hole was prescribed, restricted. They could see only part of the salon, albeit that part where Ella greeted her clients, sat them down on arrival, and offered them a hospitable drink. What they could not see were the interiors of the curtained alcoves, into one of which, in due course, the client was ushered. If, however, the proprietress followed the client into the alcove bearing with her a basin of water, the assumption must be, they decided, that this was a visit for legitimate cosmetic purposes.

As Anderson and Ballam steadfastly looked and listened, they could no longer see Mrs Staunton and the man whom she had just admitted, but they could hear a peculiar, disturbing sort of noise which they recognised as that of a distinctly unpleasant struggle going on. They began to feel uneasy.

"It sounds like he's giving her a good hiding," said Ballam.

They agreed that they had better check out exactly what was going on down there. They dashed over to the connecting staircase, practically tumbling down it into the basement and hammered on the salon door. There was no response. No one came to open it.

What they did then was to hasten up the street to Exchange Station, from where they telephoned the establishment. Again, no response. The line was engaged. So they made their way back to Tempest Hey, where they arrived just in time to see a man leaving Bobby's Lounge, closing the door behind him.

They approached the man and, identifying themselves as police officers, asked him to provide some identification. He thereupon produced a medical card, bearing the name Thomas Hendren and the address 9 Roe Street, Birkenhead. As Anderson was knocking again at the salon door, Hendren told him that he was wasting his time.

"There's a man in there. She won't answer for a quarter of an hour or twenty minutes," he said, adding with a smirk, "You know what Ella is. She's a prostitute."

This was not news to the detectives, although when, later, it all came out, it was a considerable shock to her relatives, and greeted with shock, horror, and disbelief by the neighbours in respectable Ullet Road, where she lived.

Having supplied the detectives with his personal details, and saying that he was in rather a hurry to get back to Birkenhead, Hendren was permitted to go on his way.

Determined now to find out just what mischief was afoot in Bobby's salon, Anderson and Ballam returned once more to Exchange Station to put through another phone call. Still engaged. Back they trudged to Tempest Hey and began knocking really thunderously on the door of the manicure lounge.

It was then, at about 4.50pm that they discovered to their embarrassment that the door was not locked. It had been open all the time! They pushed their way in and stepped into a narrow passage, the carpet of which, they noticed, was quite severely displaced and rumpled up. As they entered the lounge itself, they stopped abruptly. Just inside the doorway, eerily illuminated by the light of a large standard lamp, lay a woman's body. She was supine. Her head was covered with blood. There was a length of electric light flex knotted round her neck. It was Ella Staunton.

The walls and carpet of that cellar of death were spattered with blood. In a small kitchen opening off the lounge they found a bloodstained box-opener, shaped like a miniature pickaxe.

This was surely a unique case. The detectives had missed by a hair's breadth actually witnessing the murder. Leaving Anderson to keep guard over the corpse, Ballam rushed off to telephone through to police headquarters and to send for an ambulance.

A post-mortem carried out later that night brought a surprise discovery. It had been generally assumed that Ella Staunton had been strangled or had died as the result of injuries inflicted by the box-opener. Not so. The pathologist found that death had resulted from a wound to the heart, most likely brought about by a stabbing with a knife.

In view of the unexpected turn which events had taken, Mr Tomas Hendren's credentials and activities presented with a whole new and possibly sinister significance. A rapid riffling through official documents had revealed that the 31-year-old man was 'less than a good 'un'. Light fingers were his particular affliction. They had indeed provided him with a record. He had been arrested on 3 May 1946, and charged with stealing property from the Birkenhead factory where he worked. He was remanded on bail with further charges pending.

These concerned thefts perpetrated in his own home, where he lived with his parents. He had forced open a savings box which he had found in his sister's room, stealing money from it, and taking also a quantity of National Savings Certificates. It was his mother who had discovered this latest of his turpitudes, and her errant son had left home after being warned that if he did not restore the stolen property his aggrieved sister would press charges against him.

The usual mitigations were trundled out by his anxiety-ridden mother, who stated that, formerly a ship's baker, he had always been well-behaved and law-abiding, but because of illness he had had to leave his last ship. That was in January 1945. Since then he seemed to be unable to hold down a job, and things had gone from bad to worse when his fiancée, a Miss Johnston, a post office worker in Salford, had broken off her engagement to him in the spring of the same year. It transpired that the young woman suspected him of having given her a dose of venereal disease.

Severely depressed, Hendren had, in June 1945, been found by his mother with his head in the gas oven. In a second bid to take his own life he had swallowed 120 Aspirins. Convicted of attempted suicide, he had served a short sentence in Walton. Released under medical supervision, he had remained unemployed until he found the factory job from which he had recently been dismissed for theft.

Facing what she regarded as a painful duty, his mother informed the police that her son had in his possession a frightening-looking nine-inch knife. He had told her that it had been given to him by a Mexican who he had met during one of his voyages. It was his habit to carry this formidable weapon about with him.

There was by now little doubt in the minds of the police that the man they had allowed to slip through their hands as he left the murder scene was the killer. But where was he now? He had not been seen at his Roe Street home since storming out after a family argument eleven days ago.

The first clue came from a Liverpool taxi driver. He said that at around five o'clock on the evening of 20 May he had picked up a man matching Hendren's description – 5ft 9in tall; well set-up shoulders; small, clean-shaven, thin-featured face; brown eyes; fair hair, thin on top; wearing a brown check suit, brown trilby hat, black shoes – at The Ocean Club, in Lord Street. The fare had at first said that he wanted to go to Birkenhead. Then he had changed his mind and asked to be driven to Huyton railway station. He had insisted on their going there via Wavertree, saying that he wanted to buy a raincoat there.

"I told him that he'd do better buying one in the city centre," said the cabby, "but he said he wanted a second-hand one."

The passenger went into a gent's outfitters in Wavertree and purchased a cheap macintosh. Checking at the shop later, detectives made the significant discovery that the clothes coupons surrendered for the mac were in the name of Staunton.

The police scoured Huyton, but found neither sign nor clue as to the fugitive's whereabouts.

Then, another lucky break. Hendren telephoned his sister in Llandudno. The call was traced to a telephone box in St Helens, and the hunt was switched to that town. The foreman at St Helens' Shaw Street railway station remembered that a man who had struck him as being in a state of considerable agitation had asked him the times of the trains to Leeds.

"I told him 6.20am and 9am, and his next question was, 'Where's the porters' room?' I told him he could not stay on the station all night, and with that he walked off the platform."

Next morning a porter found papers bearing Hendren's name stuffed away behind a toilet bowl.

A message had gone out to the police at Salford warning them that the wanted man might try to pay a visit to his former fiancée.

It was 6am when two Salford policeman entering the public toilets in Albert Park and found a man sitting in a cubicle. Suspicions aroused, they asked him to identify himself. He said his name was Johnston – the name, it will be remembered, of Hendren's fiancée – and explained that he was on his way home after spending the night with a woman.

"I believe that your name is not Johnston but Thomas Hendren," one of the officers, Sergeant Vaughan, told him.

Hendren immediately dropped all pretence.

"Yes, Sergeant," he admitted. "They want me for Ella."

Arrested and searched, he was found to have a number of items, including a fountain-pen, a cigarette lighter, and a wallet, which had belonged to Mrs Staunton.

"I took them out of her handbag after I had done her with the box-opener," Hendren told the detectives.

The existence of the box-opener had deliberately not been mentioned in any of the newspaper reports.

When the police escort arrived at Manchester to take him back to Liverpool, Hendren told them, "All I want to say is that I did it".

And in the course of the journey to the Liverpool bridewell he confided to Detective Superintendent TA Smith:

> She's had plenty out of me – over a hundred pounds in the five years I've known her. When I asked her to lend me a couple of quid, she wouldn't. So it happened. I got about ten pounds out of her handbag, a five-pound note and five ones. I bought a box-opener in Lewis' that morning. I thought of breaking in somewhere.

His trial for murder opened at Liverpool Assizes on 27 June 1946, before the formidable Mr Justice Oliver, whom I had often seen in action. An old friend of mine, Mr Basil Nield, KC, MP, defended, and Mr HI Nelson, KC appeared for the prosecution. Hendren was smiling as he stepped up into the dock at St George's Hall and pleaded not guilty.

The defence was that at the time of Ella Staunton's murder the prisoner was insane. Mr Nield called several of Hendren's relatives to testify to his flaring temper, and to his love for reading comics as witness to his immaturity. The, to me unconvincing, cause of his alleged insanity was said to date from his wartime service in the Merchant Navy. The ship on which he had been serving was one of the last to leave Singapore at the time of the Japanese invasion, and Hendren had been one of those ordered to go ashore to help to bury the dead. There had, however, been too many corpses for burial to be possible in the very short time available, so the bodies had been piled up so as to create a human bonfire, which had been set alight after spraying with petrol. The resultant stench of the repugnant conflagration had been overwhelmingly sickening and, Hendren had told his parents, the experience had haunted him ever since.

The tale did not convince Mr Nelson either. He pointed out that, far from being insane, Hendren had shown admirable presence of mind in his purchase of a raincoat to conceal the bloodstains on his suit.

Moreover, neither were the prison medical officers, who had examined the prisoner while he was awaiting trial and failed to discover the smallest symptom of insanity, convinced.

The jury, however, was convinced … of Hendren's guilt.

Thomas Hendren was executed at Walton Gaol on 17 July 1946. What the gas stove and the bottle of Aspirins had failed to do was achieved mercifully swiftly at the practised hands of another of my friends, the late Mr Hangman Pierrepoint.

THE SKELETON OF BRANDY COVE

One day, in the year 1919, a quiet, very ordinary-looking little man sat down in the Compton Hotel in Liverpool and wrote a letter to the girl he called 'Wifie', and loved with all his broken heart:

I gave myself to you long ago, but you never seemed to care after the first few weeks … I gave you my name and my love, and you trifled with both.

There are, I suspect, few people in Liverpool now who remember the old Compton Hotel. It stood in Church Street, just opposite where St Peter's Church stood until its demolition in 1923, and where Woolworths stands today. Even eighty-odd years ago it was something of a 'relic', perpetuating in its name the glory that was Compton House – the vast building which has been described as 'a romance in brick and stone'.

The story of the great Victorian store known as Compton House began humbly, about the year 1832, when two enterprising young Liverpool men, James Redcliffe Jeffery and James Morrish, opened a small draper's shop on the corner of Church Street and Basnett Street. The bold affrontery conveyed by its *avant-garde* air, flatteringly combined with the tact and politeness displayed to its customers, and its outstanding business efficiency, speedily built up a first class reputation for the shop, together with a solid body of loyal and satisfied clients.

In what seemed no time at all, the premises extended itself, adding department after department, where you could buy anything from a kitchen saucepan or an elegant ornamental clock, to a horse's saddle, household furniture or a travelling trunk, to the finest ladies' millinery, and the best quality gentlemen's clothing. One after another, adjoining premises were eaten up, new departments added, until the original little draper's shop had swollen into a huge department store with a frontage that occupied the entire block from Basnett Street to Tarleton Street, and stretched as far back as Williamson Square.

Then, on 1 December 1865, it all went up in smoke – literally. A shop-boy's carelessly jettisoned lucifer burnt the whole place to the ground. Since James Morrish had, in 1860, retired from the business, taking with him the tidy fortune that was his share, to James Jeffery, the sole owner, fell the daunting task of rebuilding. He set to work with iron will and steely strength of purpose, and amazingly, by 1867 Compton House had arisen again out of the ashes. But alas, the economic climate had changed, and the expenses of running the new Compton House amounted to more than double those which had been required for the smooth working of its predecessor, and after a Gargantuan struggle for survival, the final shutters were put up in March 1876.

Sadly, not long thereafter, James Jeffery, a man broken in health and spirit, faded away like a ghost – but his giant brick and mortar shadow was still cast over the Liverpool of 1919, and the Compton Hotel occupied the upper part of the old building.

The leaves of the calendar turn. Forty-two years flicker by. The scene changes. It is the year 1961. The month of December. We are in the Coroner's Court at Gowerton, Glamorgan. Gleaming, strangely white in the dusky twilight of late afternoon, there lie on the polished surface of an oaken table a pathetic little heap of human bones. For nearly eight hours the coroner and his seven-man jury have been trying to find the answer to a grim riddle. Was it possible that here, in that small bundle of crumbling bones, lay the answer to a question which for forty-two years had mystified the whole of Britain? – Where is Mamie Stuart?

Today, the question that most people would ask is: *Who* was Mamie Stuart? But back in 1920, everybody knew the name of the 26-year-old ex-chorus girl who seemed to have dissolved into thin air.

Mamie, the daughter of James Stuart, master mariner, of Sunderland, had met, on 3 July 1917, a 37-year-old marine surveyor, Everard George Shotton, of Penarth, Cardiff. The couple fell in love and, on 25 March 1918, were married at South Shields register office.

There was, although Mamie did not know it at the time, just one – or rather, two – small flies in the ointment. Shotton already had a wife, whom he had married twelve years before at Newport, Monmouthshire, and a small son. In blissful ignorance of these impedimenta, Mamie bore her new husband home to Sunderland, and triumphantly introduced him to her family.

It was in February 1919, that George and Mamie Shotton went to live in Swansea, where they took furnished rooms in the house of a couple named Hearn, at 28 Trafalgar Terrace.

Five months later, on 19 July, Mr Shotton left Trafalgar Terrace, explaining that his job was taking him away from Swansea for a while. And on 22 July, Mr and Mrs Hearn saw Mamie off from Victoria Street railway station. She was, she told them, going to spend a short holiday with her parents in Sunderland.

The Hearns never saw her again. Mrs Hearn had a letter from her from Sunderland in September 1919, and that, so far as they were concerned, was the last of Mamie Shotton.

In fact, Mamie returned to Swansea on 5 November 1919. Shotton met her train, which arrived from Sunderland shortly before midnight, and took her to the furnished house which he had rented for six months. Situated close to the village of Newton, in a pretty seaside area called the Mumbles, five and a half miles south-west of Swansea, it was a detached two-storey villa, standing on the top of a hill commanding a magnificent view of Swansea Bay, and was named Ty-Llanwydd, which means 'The Abode of Peace'.

Exactly a week after her arrival, Mamie wrote a letter to her sister, Mrs Brass. That same day she also sent a letter-card to her mother and father, posted at Swansea, 5.15pm, on 12 November. But when, a few days later, they wrote back to her at Ty-Llanwydd, their letter was returned to them by the Post Office, marked 'House closed'. Puzzled, the Stuarts prompt;y despatched a reply-paid telegram to their daughter. When this, too, was returned, marked 'House closed', puzzlement turned to alarm.

Then, just before Christmas 1919, a telegram was delivered at the Stuarts' Sunderland home. It had been handed in at Swansea, purported to come from Mamie, and brought them 'the compliments of the season'.

The New Year arrived. Still no news. January … February … then, in March 1920, came the first confirmation of the Stuart family's steadily increasing fears. The manager of the Grosvenor Hotel at Swansea asked the police to examine a portmanteau which had been left for some months unclaimed at his hotel. When they opened it, they found that it contained a second, mutilated, portmanteau, in which were two dresses, cut to shreds, a pair of lady's boots, also cut to pieces, some small items of personal jewellery, a Bible, a rosary and a manicure set. It contained, too, a fragment of paper on which was written a Sunderland address.

Inquiries at Sunderland had soon established that the address was that of Captain and Mrs Stuart, and when the police went to see them, the Stuarts told them that the whereabouts of their daughter, Mamie, had been a mystery since the previous December.

The mystery was further complicated by the circumstance that, although the portmanteau found at the Grosvenor contained clothing which had undoubtedly belonged to the missing girl, it could in no way be associated with her, for, so far as the manager could remember, the bag had been left behind by a man who had stayed at the hotel by himself.

Mid-March brought another sinister pointer. A local charwoman, a Mrs Bevan, engaged to clean up Ty-Llanwydd in preparation for new tenants, discovered a mildewed, brown-leather handbag behind the wash-stand in the front bedroom. In it was a sugar ration-card in the name of Mamie Stuart, together with cash amounting to about two pounds.

Weighing all these clues and circumstances, Chief Inspector William Draper of Scotland Yard, who had been called in to help the local force with the investigation, made no bones about the fact that he felt certain that what they were dealing with was a case of murder.

He was equally sure that George Shotton, who by this time was safely back in the arms of his family, living with his legal wife and child at an isolated house named Grey Holme, at Caswell Bay, about a mile and a half from Newton, knew the answers to the many questions which plagued him.

Shotton, dapper, of medium height, with a shock of frizzy, jet-black hair, deep-brown, piercing eyes, and a dark face, which lit up on occasions with an unusually attractive smile, was all surface charm and co-operation. Yes, he had known Mamie. Yes, well – very well. And yes, (those dark eyes of his downcast in candid shame), they had lived together. Married her? Oh, no. How could he? He had a wife and child already, hadn't he? (Frank, disingenuous look.)

> When did I last see her? Let me think. It would have been about the fifth or sixth of December – in Oxford Street, Swansea. We'd had a quarrel, you know. Separated. Finished.

Plausible. But the police were not satisfied. They began to dig. Slowly, meticulously, they uncovered the facts of the bitter-sweet romance between the gay, vivacious Mamie, and the dour, suspicious, and apparently violent man whom she had 'married'. From the lips of friends, family and acquaintances, from the mute testimony of letters, the picture of a stormy, jealousy-riven relationship emerged. Mrs Hearn remembered:

> On one occasion Mamie Shotton made a very strange remark to me. She said, "If I am ever missing, do your very utmost to find me, won't you?"

Then there was a letter from Mamie to her parents:

> *If you don't hear from me, please wire to Mrs Hearn and see if she knows anything about me. The man is not all there. I don't think I will live with him very long. I am very much afraid of him. My life is not worth living.*

That was in July 1919.

And there were letters from Shotton. He had obviously begun to suspect that his 'own little darling' was being unfaithful to him – as indeed she was.

Letter from Mamie to her boyfriend:

> *My dearest Dalbert – Awfully sorry, old Boy, for not writing to you sooner, only you must know how very careful I have got to be … I am leaving Cardiff, I think, tomorrow, so if you wire my fare to Sunderland I will leave straightaway and be with you very shortly, and we will make up for lost time … My old man seems to know quite a lot … but what the eyes don't see,*

the heart can't grieve … Am just dying to see you and feel your
dear arms around me.

Convinced now that Shotton was their man, the police nevertheless went through the motions of circulating Mamie's description all over Britain.

> Age 26. Of very attractive appearance. Height 5ft 3in or 4in. Well built. Profusion of dark brown hair, worn bobbed. Dark grey eyes. Four faint teeth marks on right cheek, the result of a dog-bite when a child.

But, secretly, they were looking for a corpse.

They searched every last inch of Ty-Llanwydd, and several times dug over the garden which surrounded it. They searched and dug up much of the adjacent countryside, too. They found nothing. Even so, on 29 May 1920, Shotton was arrested – and charged with bigamy.

By now he was admitting that he was the man who left the portmanteau at the Grosvenor Hotel:

> After we had finally parted I went back to Ty-Llanwydd and found a whole lot of her things all screwed up on the floor. I put them in a small attaché-case and took them to my office, and afterwards to the Grosvenor Hotel, and left them there.

He duly appeared at Glamorgan Assizes in July. His defence that it was not him, but someone impersonating him, who had married Mamie at South Shields, failed to impress the jury, and on 27 July 1920, he was sentenced to eighteen months' hard labour by Mr Justice Avory.

And that, had it not been for a millionth-chance twist of fate on a November day forty-one years later, would have been the end of the story.

On Sunday 5 November 1961, the precise anniversary of the day that Mamie Stuart travelled for the last time from Sunderland to Swansea, three young pot-holers, John Gerke, Graham Jones and Colin MacNamara, were exploring a disused lead mine sunk into the cliff top at Brandy Cove, on the Gower coast of Glamorgan.

And there, in the dank and darkness of a bat-infested cavern at the base of an old air-shaft, 50 feet underground, they stumbled upon the secret tomb – and the perfect murder. There they found Mamie Stuart.

The lady had been sawn not in half, but into three. Her skeleton lay hidden behind artfully placed boulders and a three-inch-thick stone slab. Around the bones were swaddled the rotted remains of a sack. Nearby lay a black butterfly comb, a tuft of brown hair still attached to it, and two rings – a broad, gold wedding-ring, and an engagement-ring set with three stones.

At Cardiff's forensic science laboratory, Home Office pathologist Dr William Reginald James and Dr John Lewis Griffiths reassembled the bones into the skeleton of a woman: age between 24 and 28; estimated height 5ft 3in. Transparencies of the skull, projected on to photographs of Mamie taken during her theatrical career, showed indisputable corresponding features between the two.

Most of those who had actually known Mamie were either dead or doddering, but an elderly woman, Elsie Evans, who had been her intimate friend, was able to identify her rings. In all, 20 witnesses told their stories to the coroner and his jury.

The strangest tale of all was that of an 83-year-old retired postman, William Symons. He said that one afternoon in 1919, he had seen Mr Shotton struggling with a heavy sack outside Ty-Llanwydd. Shotton had glanced up and his eye caught a glimpse of the brass buttons on Symons' blue uniform.

"Oh, God!," he had exclaimed. "For a minute I though you were a policeman."

Symons had offered to help carry the sack to Shotton's yellow van, which was standing outside the gate. "No, no, no," said Shotton, who then put the sack in the van himself, and drove off in the direction of Brandy Cove.

It did not take the jury long to reach their verdict: that the skeleton was that of Mamie Stuart, that she was murdered, and that the evidence pointed to George Shotton being her murderer.

But as it turned out, Shotton was beyond the jurisdiction of that, or any other earthly court. It had taken a three-week, country-wide search, involving Interpol, Scotland Yard and nine police forces to track him down to Bristol's Southmead Hospital, where, on 30 April 1958, aged 78 and penniless, he had died.

For nearly three years his body had lain in Grave Number 000405 in Arno's Vale Cemetery, Bristol. It is a weed-grown, unmarked grave. No headstone. No inscription. His only epitaph the words spoken by Mrs Edna Collins, the woman in whose home in Coronation Road, Bristol, he was during his last years a paying guest: 'He was such a perfect gentleman.'

Mamie Stuart's epitaph was spoken by Mr DR James, a poetic Welsh coroner:

> They found her, between highland and lowland, in a
> coign of a cliff; by a silver sea, without a grave,
> uncoffined, unknelled and unknown.

But now her pathetic little ghost has risen to attain a kind of immortality as one of the legends in the murder-will-out folklore of crime.

In case you had not guessed, the ghost of Everard George Shotton hovers about the vanished writing-room in the old Compton Hotel.

THE CASE OF THE FRIGHTENED WITNESSES

Marie Milne, June Bury, George McClaughlin, I remember their names like a litany – a trinity of shady characters, who, acting for once as upright citizens, helped to put the rope round the necks of two callous killers, Alfred Burns and Edward Devlin. Long after all that remained of the murderers lay buried behind prison walls, their evil influence lived on. That, at any rate, is what four – if we include old Tom Emery the blameless cabby – frightened people for whom friendly Liverpool became a place of bristling menace, believed.

The first attack was on George McClaughlin. It came from a man in a prison yard, armed with a length of lead pipe. A few days later, another prisoner tried to stab him with a pair of scissors. In a different prison, a gang of fellow-prisoners armed with shears went for him in the basket shop. After he had been released from jail, the attacks still went on. Married, and with a child, McClaughlin was severely beaten up in the street. For many a long day he walked in terror.

Next, Marie Milne. The underworld whisper at the time of the trial was that eight men in Borstal, friends of Burns and Devlin, had drawn lots. The man who drew the shortest match had to break out. His mission: to slit Chinese Marie's throat. Before he could do so, he was caught and taken back to Borstal. But still, when it was all over and Burns and Devlin condemned to die, she was far from safe. Coming home one night from a dance at the Rialto Ballroom, she was dragged into a dark alley off Parliament Street by three men, who gave her a kicking that needed 36 stitches to repair her injuries. And threatening letters kept dropping through her letter-box. One contained the sinisterly tinkered-with words of a popular song:

> *Some enchanted evening*
> *I was looking for a stranger*
> *And that stranger was you.*

After that, when Marie Milne went out she always rode everywhere by taxi.

June Bury took what she regarded as her first revenge beating in the Lighthouse all-night café. She was attacked for the second time in Manchester. She came back to Liverpool and was set upon twice more. When she came out of hospital, she fled to Manchester, and whilst in Piccadilly she was beaten up yet again. That did it. She left for London, to lose herself amongst the capital's anonymous hordes.

Even so, relatively small a bit-part player as Tom Emery, the taxi driver, who had been hailed by the murderers to drive them to the vicinity of their target, did not go unremembered. Although in 1956 he was 76 years old, he was brutally attacked in a dark street, beaten and slashed. For some time thereafter he gave up night-time driving, when the best money was to be made, and, plumping for discretion rather than valour, stuck to working day shifts.

A few months after the trial, Mrs Joan Downing, who had been only a minor witness, received a threatening letter warning her: *It is no use telling the police. Your number is up.* Thoroughly upset, she went into hiding, and while she was away, someone, the avengers, she believed, set fire to her house.

Such was the general level of alarm, that, mother of two, Mrs Joan Dudley, also a very minor witness, who lived not far from Mrs Downing, in another of those Manchester streets where the pale sunlight is trapped in the orange-red brickwork, was firmly convinced that she was a victim of the Burns and Devlin avengers. Their vengeance, she thought, caught up with her in Blackpool, 12 days before Christmas 1955, when she accepted a lift in a car. Five minutes later, she was lying dumped in the roadway. She had been shot. Happily, she did not die.

Did Burns and Devlin really manage, through a gang of their friends, to stretch out the arm of vengeance from their graves, or were the threatening letters really no more than unpleasant hoaxes, and the reported slashing, shooting, fire-raising, and beatings which befell the frightened witnesses mere flexings of the long arm of coincidence? That is the one abiding, unsolved mystery of the Burns and Devlin case.

It all began one summer's evening fifty-one years ago in Cranborne Road, off Smithdown Road, when little Mrs Beatrice Alice Rimmer turned the key in the lock of her house, Number 7, and stepped through the front-door into eternity.

It had been a really pleasant Sunday. Mrs Rimmer had been on her usual weekend visit to her son, Thomas, and his wife's home in Madryn Street, Toxteth. Those trips were always enjoyable, but since the recent arrival of her new baby grandson, the weekly Sunday visit had been even better. It was about a quarter to ten when Tom, who had walked down High Park Street with his mother, waved her off on the Number 27 bus, telling her he would call round to see her the following evening.

Small and plumpish, there must have been something about the 54-year-old widow. Perhaps it was that she managed to look stylish in her yellow floral-patterned frock, loose-fitting brown coat, and winsomely old-fashioned looking, dark-coloured straw hat, carrying an umbrella and a bunch of flowers in her neatly-gloved hands. Anyway, she had certainly impressed herself on the memory of Henry Bentley, the bus conductor. He distinctly recalled her alighting at the top of Lodge Lane, outside the Pavilion Theatre. He was the last person we know of to see Mrs Rimmer alive.

The next evening – Monday 20 August 1951 – Tom went over, as he had promised, to his mother's house. As a rule, she went out on Monday evenings to play whist at the Sefton Park Conservative Club. He was hoping to catch her before she left. Tom Rimmer was just approaching his mother's door when her next-door neighbour, Jack Grossman, appeared. He was, he said, a bit concerned. No one had caught sight or sound of Mrs Rimmer all day. That was unusual … and look … there was her milk untouched on the door-step, and the morning paper still sticking out of the letter-box. Tom, who up to a few months before had been a policeman in the Liverpool Force, felt a familiar, worrying sense of suspicion switch on; a distinct fear that something might be seriously amiss. He knocked several times at the front-door. No response. With mounting unease, he bent down, pushed the newspaper in and the flap of the letter-box up, and peered through. The passage-like hallway inside was dark. He could just make out something that looked like a bundle of discarded clothing on the floor. Definitely alarmed now, he ran round to the back entry, dragged himself up over the rear wall, and dropped down into the back yard. He saw that the kitchen window had been broken. Punching out the remaining jags of glass with his elbow, he clambered through into the ominously silent house. It was in the hall-passage, just behind the front-door, that he made the discovery that he had begun to dread. His mother was lying there, white, ice-cold in a far-spread pool of congealed blood, and the flowers which he and his wife had given her the previous day lay beside her like a wilting funeral wreath.

He raised the alarm. His old colleagues arrived. The murder investigation machine creaked into familiar gear. Not that there was much to go on. The police surgeon on call put in an appearance at 10.30pm, made his grisly calculations, and placed the time of death as – delayed for a few hours after the actual attack – around 2am. At 11.30pm my old friend Dr JB Firth turned up, and set to work immediately carrying out a meticulous examination of the body and its surroundings. He reckoned that it had taken between twenty and thirty separate blows to produce the fifteen wounds which he found, mostly on the left side, on the head. Some of those wounds were clean-edged, others ragged, yet others were stellar-shaped. These diversities suggested to him that two different weapons had been used, one sharp-edged, the other blunt, perhaps a heavy torch. There seemed a likelihood that two assailants had been involved in the perpetration of the brutal savagery. Death had been caused by a combination of shock, a skull fracture, and loss of blood. A part of the skull, about two inches in diameter, was exposed. It had been a horribly lingering death, life slowly ebbing away in that dim passageway with the sluggish, but inexorable, draining of blood.

Detective Superintendent Hector Taylor, acting head of the Liverpool CID during the absence on holiday in Ireland of Chief Superintendent Herbert Balmer, and his team of detectives, worked heroically to try to break the case before the boss returned.

An appeal was put out asking anyone who had visited Mrs Rimmer's home in the past three months to come forward, and a mammoth search for the murder weapons extended even to the Edgar Allan Poe-ish scouring of the place of the dead – the ancient acreage of Smithdown Road Cemetery. Neither appeal nor scour produced any useful result.

Bert Balmer, whom I knew well, and upon whom in those days I would often pop in for a chat, was a formidable police officer, who spared neither himself nor anybody else once he got his teeth into a case. Returning from holiday, he at once took charge of the murder hunt. Now it so happened that at this very time there had been a spate of house-breaking and burglary in the Cranborne Road area. The police thought that they had struck gold on 4 September, when they found silver – stolen articles stashed away in a disused bakery in Spofforth Road. Two youths were triumphantly arrested, but, to Balmer's intense disappointment, proved on further investigation to have no connection with the Cranborne Road affair. Relying on that strange, powerful instinct which long-in-the-tooth veteran detectives develop, Balmer got it into his head that one or other of his 'regulars' stowed safely away in Walton Gaol might know something and might be persuaded to 'sing'.

And his hunch paid off. The songbird proved to be a 19-year-old Liverpool lad, name of George McClaughlin, just starting an 18-month sentence for breaking into his aunt's home, at 109 Cranborne Road. George's *curriculum vitæ* was not good. He had first come into what you might call disadvantageous contact with the police at the tender age of nine. Since then, he had notched up forty thieving convictions. As a change from breaking-in, he had broken out of an approved school, been recaptured and shunted off for Borstal training. His latest desertion had been from the Army, and immediately prior to being admitted to free board and lodging in Walton, he had been living rough in Liverpool, stealing for the wherewithal to keep body and soul together, and spending long hours of slow falling crumbs and bitter teas in the city's seedy all-night cafés. It was, indeed, in one of these out-at-elbow establishments – Bill's, at the top of Paddington – that George met Ted.

Ted, to give him his full style and title, Edward Devlin, a dapperly apparrelled, 'all-about', 22-year-old Mancunian, of externally superior, but morally identical, calibre to the shabby George, was a similarly shiftless and shifty character, convinced that the world owed him a living. He operated from a comfortable base at his mother's house, in Leinster Street, Hulme, Manchester, whence, mischief-bound, he ranged regularly forth bent on larcenous business. He had been at it since he was 13 and had, in the ensuing near-decade, matured into, to use a contradiction in terms, a pretty respectable villain. He had just emerged from doing half a stretch (six months) in Strangeways.

The two fell to talking about 'specs' for possible profitable jobs. McClaughlin reckoned he knew a peach. In Cranborne Road, where his aunt lived, there was a widow at Number 7. The talk was that her husband had left her well provided for. She didn't go out to work and seemed to be able to fork out easily for everything she wanted. According to local gossip, she had a fair old sum of cash hidden away in the house. The meet between George and Ted had taken place on 27 July. They teamed up again the next day, and went out together to Cranborne Road to "case the old woman's job up", as George elegantly expressed it.

Having belligerently declared, "I'm no squealer", McClaughlin proceeded to furnish his jail visitor police officer with the lowdown that built up the retributory case against Mrs Rimmer's killers. On the Thursday before August Bank Holiday, he had had another meet with Ted, this time at the Continental Café, off Lime Street. Ted had arrived with a companion, whom he introduced as Alfie. Like Ted, Alfie fancied his chances, all done up dandiacal in a smart brown pin-stripe. George Alfred Burns, 21 years old, was also a native of Manchester, living there with his widowed mother in Medlock Street. And, like Ted and George, into crime, he was a young man prepared to work very hard at not working for a living.

Waiting on the plotting trinity at the Continental was 21-year-old June Bury, a young woman who divided her life between Liverpool and Manchester, where she had met Ted Devlin. Working as a waitress was a bit of a novelty for her. Mostly she used her charms and favours to extract money from men. Currently she was living with a Lothario by the name of Stan Rubin, in Canning Street, but she still nurtured a soft spot for Ted, with whom, previously, she had, for a while, shared a bed. Now, as plans for the Cranborne Road screwing were perfected, a rôle in them was found for June. George would give Ted and Alfie a leg up over the back wall. They would force the kitchen-window catch, and one of them would then climb through into the house, and open the back door for the other. June, meanwhile, would knock at the front-door, and when Mrs Rimmer opened it, keep her talking there while the others came through at her from behind.

The plan foundered when George was caught and sentenced for breaking into his aunt's house, further up Cranborne Road. He was in Walton serving the early days of his 18-month sentence when the screwing and its concomitant disaster took place.

June Bury was traced back to Manchester. She swore that in the end she had refused to take part in the robbery. She had last seen Burns and Devlin in Manchester on Friday 17 August, when they told her that they were going to Liverpool. She had absolutely no idea what they had got up to that weekend, but she knew of a girl who probably did. She did not know her surname – she only knew her as Chinese Marie.

Within three days, the detectives had tracked Marie Milne down in

Liverpool. Aged 17, half-Malayan, she lived with her mother at the Great George's Place end of Upper Parliament Street. She was, like June Bury, a waitress and facultatively part-time prostitute, often to be seen picking up men outside the Rialto Cinema and on Princes Avenue. Superintendent Balmer never revealed what in the way of bargaining passed between him and Marie Milne, but the upshot was that she agreed to tell him everything she knew, and to give evidence in court. In exchange, she seems to have been granted immunity from prosecution in regard to any connection with the Rimmer murder. As a result of the statement made by Miss Milne, the police felt that they had sufficient evidence in hand to justify charging Burns and Devlin with the murder. All they had to do now was to find them.

Detective Constable Leslie Skinner, of Liverpool CID, who, like Bert Balmer, happened to be a very good friend of mine in my old journalistic days in Liverpool, was strolling along Stretford Road, Manchester, with Detective Constable Lynch, of the Manchester CID, when the latter recognised one of two men walking towards them as Devlin. The detectives watched the men disappear into a milk-bar, followed them in, and arrested Devlin. He was taken back to Liverpool by car, and charged at Allerton police station. During the journey from Manchester Devlin asked: "Have the girls been talking? Have you seen June and the Chinese bit?"

When it came to hunting down Alfie Burns, it proved very easy. He was already under lock and key in Manchester's Strangeways Prison, having been picked up as an abscondee from borstal.

Burns and Devlin were reunited, standing side by side in the dock in the court of Stipendiary Magistrate, Arthur McFarland, at Dale Street, where I used to spend quite a bit of time in those days and saw a fair number of Liverpool's criminous celebrities on the first stage of their journeys – sometimes to the gallows. I was present there at the Burns and Devlin committal proceedings, and remember how insolent Devlin's attitude and behaviour were, whispering and sniggering to his companion in the dock. I never saw two people on a serious charge so unaffected by the circumstances in which they found themselves. I was later to see them at their trial. I expected that after the long weeks in custody there would be quite a change in their demeanour, but not a bit of it. They were still as cocky as ever. Neither the solemn atmosphere of the Assize Court, nor the impressive presence of the scarlet-and-ermined Red Judge, seemed to impinge upon them. I think they saw themselves as gangster heroes – just like in the films.

It was while these two dangerous young men were awaiting trial that things started to become very frightening for McClaughlin and the two girls; especially for Chinese Marie, whose testimony would be crucial for the prosecution. All three received threats, threats which, in view of the quarters from which they were coming, the recipients took extremely seriously. In fact, June and Marie went into hiding. I shall never forget Marie Milne's terrified face peering through the crack of a half-opened door the night that I tracked her to her secret hideaway to interview her. Even McClaughlin, in jail, was not safe, for criminals of the calibre of Burns and Devlin had friends and tentacles that found prison bars no barrier. And when I managed to find and talk with Tom Emery, the elderly taxi driver who had taken the murderers to Smithdown Road in his cab, I saw that the poor man was in a state of some terror, despite his insistence that he had not seen the faces of, and could not therefore identify, his sinister fares. But, be it to their eternal credit, the resolve of all the frightened witnesses stayed firm.

The prosecution solicitor, Mr JR Bishop, and those for the defence – Mr Harry Livermore for Devlin, and Mr Joseph Norton for Burns – set to work on their respective preparations. The full version of the story was now about to unfold.

On 3 August, Burns and Devlin had met June Bury by arrangement at the Rainbow Café, in Islington, and she had brought Marie Milne along with her. That night the four of them went down to the coffee stall at the Pier Head, and on from there to the Lighthouse Café, another all-night joint, where they remained until 7am. June had by then taken the decision to finish with Stan Rubin and move on, in the game of musical beds, to Ted Devlin. So the quartet hailed another taxi and set off for 39 Canning Street, where June peremptorily packed up her relationship with an angry Stan, packed a suitcase, and left. Another taxi ferried them to 2 Verulam Street, where Burns paid 25 shillings up front for a room for Marie and himself for a week. And on that Saturday night (4 August), Devlin and June selected an hotel on Mount Pleasant as their somewhat seedy love-nest. On the Sunday the two couples went off to Manchester, where they spent the day, the girls returning that same night to Liverpool, June Bury having, before their departure, refused absolutely to play any part in the projected robbery. Marie Milne, however, agreed to act as look-out for the two men when they broke into the house.

At 4.45pm on Friday 17 August, Chinese Marie kept a date with Burns and Devlin outside the Rialto Cinema, at the corner of Upper Parliament and Berkley Streets, and the trio went along and had a meal at the Green Dragon Chinese Restaurant, in Leece Street.

On the Saturday, the three met again at 3.30pm on Lewis' corner.

So we come to the fatal Sunday, 19 August. June Bury had remained in Manchester. McClaughlin was in Walton Gaol. Burns, Devlin and Milne foregathered at the usual spot outside the Rialto in the early afternoon. At around 2.15pm they took a taxi to Smithdown Road, having it put them down outside Sefton General Hospital, at a point just about a 100 yards beyond the Smithdown Road junction with Cranborne Road. They walked those 100 yards back, and Burns told Marie: "This is where you wait for us at six o'clock tonight." And, pointing up the road, "That's where Mrs Rimmer lives." Then they caught a bus back into town.

Punctually at six o'clock, Marie was duly standing at the blitzed site spot by the Webster Road junction with Smithdown Road, where Burns had told her to be. She waited there until 6.30pm. No sign of Burns or Devlin, so she went back to the Rialto. The two men turned up by the taxi rank there, and took her into nearby Wilkie's Café, where the three of them dawdled, watching the evening slowly die, its lengthening shadows gradually merging with the descending clouds of darkness to weave that summer's day's shroud. Laggard-seeming night at long last fallen, it was at a quarter to ten that the villainous three emerged, blinking from the café's garish bright light, into the blindfolding dark, and boarded a bus that carried them up Upper Parliament Street and, veering right, down Smithdown Road to the corner of Cranborne Road, and an appointment with Fate.

Quoting now the subsequent evidence of Marie Milne, Burns and Devlin told her to wait on the corner there for five minutes, to allow them time to get into the house from the back. She was then to go to "the house four houses past the entry", and knock at the front-door. Once inside, she was to stand between the old lady and her front-door to make sure that she could not get out to look for help. This, she said, she did not do. What she did, was wait on the corner until half-past ten, then got a tram back to the Rialto. There she had met up again with Burns and Devlin, and, as the three of them walked down Upper Parliament Street, she had noticed that they both had blood on their clothes, and saw that Ted had a heavily bloodied handkerchief wrapped around his hand. She had also heard Devlin ask Burns: "Will the old lady live?" To which Burns replied: "To hell with the old woman; we'll be out of Liverpool before long, and we'll take little Marie with us."

We can, I think, never know for sure the detailed course of events between the time that the two men left Chinese Marie on the corner and met up with her again back at the Rialto. Only three people knew the whole truth; one of them was dead, the other two had a vested interest in peddling their own particular versions of how they had not been anywhere near Cranborne Road that night, let alone murdered Mrs Rimmer.

What the forensic evidence indicated was that Mrs Rimmer had been attacked in the hall, the moment she entered the house. There was blood on the wall behind the front-door, and a great deal more between the front-door and the door leading to the sitting-room. Dr Firth noted that the formation of the blood splashes was indicative of the unfortunate woman's having received many of the injuries to her head as she lay on the floor. Her blood was Group A. He had found bloodstains on both Burns' and Devlin's clothing. Those on Burns', however, belonged to Group B. Those on Devlin's proved too slight for classification.

Burns and Devlin were put up before Mr Justice Finnemore at Liverpool Assizes, at that time held in St George's Hall, on 19 February 1952. The trial lasted ten days. Devlin was defended by Miss Rose Heilbron, Burns by Sir Noel Goldie, KC. Mr Basil Nield, KC led the prosecution. Both Miss Heilbron and Mr Nield were later to become High Court judges. Sir Basil, I came to know well. Dame Rose Heilbron I first met in her and her husband's flat in Verulam Buildings, just after her elevation to the Bench.

The defence case was beguilingly simple. Pure denial. No one – that is, of course, the prosecution witness, Marie Milne, apart – had actually seen either of the accused in the vicinity of, or to enter or leave, Mrs Rimmer's house. No one had witnessed the murder. No murder weapon or weapons had been discovered. The prosecution was, therefore, again Marie Milne's testimony apart, relying entirely on circumstantial evidence – which, incidentally, despite popular misconception to the contrary, can very often be the best. An alibi defence was offered. Devlin stated:

> Round the time of the murder I was doing screwing jobs
> at Manchester, Hulme, Deansgate and other places … I
> was probably screwing a gaff on August the nineteenth.

And Sir Noel Goldie brought forward Burns' supportive claim that he and Devlin had been robbing the factory warehouse of Messrs Sun Blinds Ltd, in Great Jackson Street, Manchester, on the night of 19 August.

Devlin, called by his counsel, swore in the witness-box that he had never met George McClaughlin, and described how he, Burns, and a Manchester man named Allan Campbell, carried out a robbery at Messrs Sun Blinds Ltd, on the night of Sunday 19 August 1951.

Burns was also put in the witness-box by his counsel. He told of how he had gone to a football match, he thought at Maine Road, on the afternoon of Saturday 17 August. He said that he and Devlin had spent that night at his (Burns') mother's. At about 11am on the Sunday, they had "shot off" to a Mrs Downing's house, and then went on a lunch-time pub crawl. That evening, he, Devlin, and Allan Campbell, were at the Ship Inn. At about 11.30pm, they went to Great Jackson Street and carried out the robbery. He and Devlin had then returned to spend the night at Burns' mother's house in Medlock Street. Unfortunately for the prisoners, despite Allan Campbell's brave testamentary perjury, it could be shown that the details of the date of the break-in at Sun Blinds Ltd, in respect of which he was currently serving eighteen months, had somehow slipped his mind, for it had actually taken place on the night of the 18th, and not the 19th, of August.

February 27th. Verdict Day.

As dawn broke over the city a queue was beginning to form outside St George's Hall. By 7am, the queue had snaked to an inordinate coiling length. With a rattle of keys and bolts, the doors opened at ten o'clock. Two hundred trial-goers were disappointed. Finnemore J summed up for four-and-a-half-hours. At 4.15 the jury retired. Outside, the paving-stones of St George's Plateau were hidden beneath a quivering formicate mass. Those were the dramatic days of hanging, and the shadow of the noose exercised a powerful morbid fascination. A sussuration, almost an audible groan, swept along and over the teeming black ants. At 5.30pm the jury had returned, with a guilty verdict.

Appeals, petitions, special applications, dragged on over a period of eight weeks since they had been sentenced. It all came to a full stop at nine o'clock on 25 April 1952, a morning of spring sunshine. Burns and Devlin, standing side by side on the Walton scaffold, paid the debt they owed for the cruel taking of Mrs Beatrice Alice Rimmer's life. It was my friend Pierrepoint who acted as society's debt collector. He was assisted by Syd Dernley. And it is Dernley who, in his reminiscences, has given us a last glimpse of the two hard men, and how, when it came to it, they who had so easily meted out death to the little old widow, faced it themselves. Devlin spun round to meet his executioners as they came into the condemned cell to fetch him. Once described as 'handsome in a hard sort of way', he did not look hard, nor did he look handsome, now. He was white as a sheet, his face and brow creased with deep lines. He was clearly terrified. He put up no resistance. Burns, the former couldn't-care-less tough guy, no longer existed. Also white as a sheet, and looking like a frightened lad, staring wide-eyed at the pinioned figure of his friend, white hood already over his head, noose around his neck, he walked meekly out on to the trap. Pierrepoint threw the lever. With neither prior protestation of innocence, nor final confession of guilt, Burns and Devlin were plunged into the Great Silence.

THE TERRIBLE DESPATCH OF JOHN CONWAY

When, as happens from time to time, someone – perhaps my shirt-maker or a shop-assistant who is obligingly calculating the correct size of bow-tie which I require – runs a tape-measure round my neck, I usually inform them, in jocular vein, that the last person who did that was the public hangman! This invariably produces a dutiful loud guffaw at what they think is a very ropy – in several senses – little joke.

Although offered as a jovial conversational gambit, it happens to be sober truth, for the former official hangman, the late lamented Albert Pierrepoint, did on one occasion, in a spirit of grisly gallows humour, pass his tape-measure round my neck. We had become acquainted at the time when another friend of mine, Joe Gaute, an editorial director of Messrs George G Harrap & Co, was arranging the acceptance of Pierrepoint's memoirs, *Executioner: Pierrepoint*, subsequently published in 1974, and my criminous advice had been sought in connection with one or two small points in the text.

The hangman, like the muffin-man, is an extinct, a vanished, figure. Some say good. Some say bad. Some, remembering the Moors Murderers, Brady and Hindley, and the Wests, of Cromwell Street, Gloucester, are not so sure.

As a matter of fact, I got to know Pierrepoint quite well, and found him, as you might expect, a somewhat unusual man.

Albert was a Yorkshire lad, born in the village of Clayton, near Bradford, about the year 1905. He came of a family which, like the Sansons, the headsmen – master operatives of the guillotine – of France, boasted a tradition of providing their country's executioners.

Albert's father – Henry Albert Pierrepoint – and his Uncle Tom – Thomas William Pierrepoint – had both been well-qualified, long-serving hangmen before him, and Albert approached his work as a craft, a calling, a 'sacred vocation'. He firmly believed that he had been chosen by a 'higher power' for the task which he undertook, and that he had been put on earth especially to do it. Thus, he spared himself no pains in learning to carry out what he was truly convinced became in his hands the most humane and dignified method of meting out death.

In the course of twenty-five years, he had performed more judicial hangings than any other British executioner. His celebrated clients included such classic murderers as Heath, Haigh, and Christie, the controversial figures Timothy Evans, Derek Bentley, and Ruth Ellis, and Liverpool's infamous George 'Cameo' Kelly and Burns and Devlin. Each of them had, in the old-time hangman's phraseology, been 'turned off' with a dedicated craftsman's skill and pride, the appropriate drop calculated with the utmost care, the knot of the noose deftly positioned at the jaw's left angle, so as to break the neck neatly between the second and third cervical vertebrae and sever the spinal cord. What had at all costs to be avoided was the slow strangulation, asphyxiation, which would result from failure to dislocate the neck. Equally, it was vitally important to get the equation between the weight of the prisoner and the length of the drop allocated right, or the unfortunate man's despatch could turn into a very terrible disaster. What happened to John Conway at the hands of Mr Hangman Berry at Kirkdale Prison, in Liverpool, in 1891, would have appalled Pierrepoint.

Conway, also known by the name of Owen Gilbin, was a dark-bearded, 62-year-old stoker, or, as it was described in moments of aspiration, marine or ship's fireman. He was also the local delegate for his trade union, and it was to the office which he occupied in that capacity that he lured, and there murdered, 9-year-old Nicholas Martin. He had then stuffed the body into a carpet-bag, taken a cab to the riverside, and flung the bag into the water of one of the docks, where it was found floating on 16 May 1891. As well as the boy's mutilated body, the bag contained a knife and a saw, which proved to be the murder weapons.

The bag was traced to Conway, and witnesses came forward to testify to the police to having seen Conway and the boy together shortly before the time of the gruesome discovery. But why he had committed this dreadful crime was – and remained – a complete mystery. Certainly, there was nothing in the man's previous record indicative of any quarrelsome, let alone murderous, tendency. Moreover, he himself was at an absolute loss to explain his uncharacteristic action.

He did, however, on the day before his execution, admit to Father Bonte, the priest who attended him in the condemned cell, to having done the deed:

> In confessing my guilt I protest that my motive was not outrage. Such a thought I never in all my life entertained. Drink has been my ruin, not lust. I was impelled to the crime while under the influence of drink, by a fit of murderous mania, and a morbid curiosity to observe the process of dying. A moment after the commission of the crime I experienced the deepest sorrow of it, and would have done anything in the world to undo it.

Conway, Berry tells us, was a very superstitious man. He was a great believer in omens and witchcraft and all sorts of supernatural powers. He got it firmly into his head that if one really good man could be persuaded to pray for him, he would be saved from the gallows. For the efficacy of his own prayers he had scant regard, thinking that they would avail him nothing and that he was not fit to receive the last sacraments of his church.

The morning of the execution dawned. James Berry had done his vital calculation. The prisoner weighed 11st 2lb and stood 5ft 7in high. That meant a drop of 4ft 6in.

And that was when Berry found himself in conflict with the prison medical officer, Dr James Barr.

"The drop should be six feet nine inches," pronounced the doctor.

That was according to the 'official scale'. What he was referring to were the conclusions reached by the Aberdare Committee. This was a body which, as a result of the public concern about such 'incidents' as Berry's failure, after three attempts, to hang John Lee at Exeter Gaol, in February 1885, Berry's bungled hanging of Moses Shrimpton at Worcester, in May 1885, when his omission to take into account the weakness of the prisoner's neck muscles resulted in his head being torn clean from his shoulders, and the like decapitation of Robert Goodale, a 15-stone giant of a man, hanged by Berry, in what became known as the 'Goodale Mess', at Norwich, in November 1885.

By what route the committee reached its conclusions in the matter of recommended weight/distance of drop ratios is not clear. What is, however, apparent is that favourable ear was given to the purely theoretical views of the medical men rather than to the practical advisings of the experienced hangman, and after the Governor of Kirkdale had lent his support to Dr Barr's demand for a longer drop, Berry, very reluctantly gave way to the doctor.

"All right, I'll do it as you like, but if it pulls his head off, I'll never hang another."

Actually, he had secretly reduced the drop by nine or ten inches. He adjusted the white cap. The prisoner's pale lips whispered the words, "Lord have mercy on my soul," followed by, "Oh, my God! Oh, my God!"

Berry pulled the lever.

Conway dropped from sight, as with a tremendous boom the two heavy wooden sides of the trap-door struck the stonework. Then, in the reverberant silence, a sinister sound came echoing up from the pit. The splashing of blood on the brick floor. Berry peered over into the blackness below and saw that the man's head was held to the body by the merest fragment of ragged neck muscle.

In high dudgeon and disgust, Berry left the prison immediately. He was informed that he would not be required at the inquest, nor would he be allowed to give evidence. The coroner told the jury that the governor of the prison had testified that everything had gone off as usual at Conway's execution, and Dr Barr had also stated that it had been "carried out in the usual way".

"Was there no hitch at all?" asked the coroner.

"No, so far as the execution was concerned," replied Barr.

The plain truth is that the Aberdare Committee had come down heavily on the side of risking decapitation rather than strangulation.

Angry and resentful, Berry resigned his position as Number One Hangman after the Conway débâcle.

Strangely enough, my paternal great-grandfather, Dr Richard Whittington-Egan, attended, in his capacity as Irish Crown Pathologist, an even more alarming hanging mishap at Dublin.

The case in point was that of an unfortunate Irishman, a native of Kildare, named Andrew Carr. A good-looking, well set-up, manly fellow, very sunburnt and pronouncedly hirsuit, with dark brown hair, beard, whiskers and moustache, he had joined the Army at an early age, seen rapid promotion to colour-sergeant, and served with the 87th Regiment for twenty-five years.

It was while Carr's regiment was quartered in Tullamore that he had first met Margaret Murphy. She was one of the five daughters of a farmer resident in that neighbourhood. An improper intimacy had developed between them, and when Carr was ordered abroad for foreign service, the girl, finding herself disgraced and rejected by her family, made her way to Dublin, where she became an outcast, taking to the streets, and sinking lower and lower.

It would be about the year 1860 that she became an inmate of one of the terrible dens in Bull Lane, situated at the rear of the Four Courts in a network of similar purlieus. Two years later, when the 87th Regiment returned from India, Carr went to live with Margaret in a hovel kept by a woman named Brien. He remained with her for a week. Then a quarrel took place and, vowing, it is alleged, that he would have vengeance on her, Carr left Margaret and returned to the regiment. For some reason which was never revealed, he was reduced to the ranks, and it was as a private that, at the age of 42, he took his discharge on a pension of eight pence a day.

That was in May 1870. He returned at once to Dublin, where he sought and found Margaret. She was living at 14 Bull Lane. Here, as long as the money lasted, Carr lived with her, a life of drink and vice, punctuated by vicious drunken quarrels.

On the morning of Thursday 16 June 1870, Carr handed Margaret sixteen shillings, which was all that he had left. And she, finding that his means were gone, went blatantly to work making the acquaintance of other soldiers. Hardly surprisingly, this led to several violent quarrels in the course of the day, and by the evening they were both far gone in drink and dark and threatening words were bandied between them.

It was between 10.40pm and 10.50pm that evening that Police Constable William Arthurs, while passing on his beat up Pill Lane, was accosted by a man "slightly under the influence of drink", who told him: "I'm just after murdering a woman in a house in Bull Lane by cutting her throat, and if you don't believe what I say, look at my hands."

The constable looked. Sure enough, the man's fingers were liberally smeared with blood. Blood was also seeping from a cut in his left wrist. The man told him: "This cut I gave my wrist with the razor with which I cut her throat."

Constable Arthurs took the man – it was, of course, Andrew Carr – to Green Street police station. The constable, together with Constable Johnston, then made his way round to check at the house where the murder had allegedly been committed.

It was the first building on the left-hand side of the street, the ruin of one of those well-built, old-fashioned houses, erected perhaps a century before in the days when Bull Lane, now the terrain of the depraved and the lawless, was inhabited by respectable citizens. The place was in a terrible state of dilapidation. Every window from the cellar to the attic had been smashed, or had the sashes entirely removed. The banisters were wrenched off, and large portions of the old, greasy panelled woodwork of which the walls of the staircase were composed, had been removed, apparently for fuel. The whole house was in darkness.

The constables clambered gingerly up the rickety stairs, which were covered with layers of mud, brought in by midnight wanderers, brawlers, and the troops of bullies who haunted such dens of infamy to plunder and beat any drunken fool who might have been lured after nightfall into Bull Lane. Upstairs, the walls were covered with slimy filth, and the doors of every room – from which the old paint had long ago peeled off – were falling from their hinges, their broken panels showing the violent assaults to which they had been subjected. Everywhere was pervaded by a nauseous, fetid stench, which proceeded from the poisonous fumes of the noxious abominations which had been allowed to collect in the back yard.

The miserable top floor back room in which the murder had been committed, did not contain a particle of furniture, except two old wooden stools, and on the mantelshelf a few old cracked cups and saucers and empty bottles. The bars of an ancient grate were burned out from long use, and the dirty, slime-covered walls showed in several places where candles had been stuck against them. There was, too, a heap of old straw, ground into filthy chaff, and in a corner a tattered mattress black with grime, together with a few strips of old carpet.

In the centre of all this, in a pool of clotted gore, there lay the body of a young woman, her head nearly divided from her body by the desperate gash in her throat made by the open razor that lay in the blood beside her, her long brown hair protruding from beneath a gypsy straw hat, trimmed with blue ribbon and artificial flowers, saturated with blood, as was also the white dress trimmed with blue that she wore – the cheap finery recently purchased with the money given to her by he who had taken her life.

Carr was duly charged with murder.

At one o'clock in the morning my great-grandfather went along to the house in Bull Lane and examined the body, which, I see from his notes, he found lying on its back, the head turned over to the left shoulder, the lower limbs drawn up and apart, the arms extended by the side, the right hand clenched on a white handkerchief, bloodstained. There were no wounds on the hands, but there was some blood on them. The left eye was blackened, but not from recent injury. On the right side of the neck and forepart of the throat was a wound extending from the middle line behind, round to the anterior edge of the sterno-mastoid muscle of the left side, a few fibres of which were divided. This wound divided all the muscles, nerves, and blood vessels down to the spine, which had been in several places chipped by the weapon. The great blood vessels on the left side were uninjured. This wound was the cause of death, which must have been immediate, and it was not a self-inflicted wound.

The city coroner, Dr NC Whyte, held an inquest at Mr Crinion's public-house in Pill Lane. Carr was brought up in police custody by cab from the Green Street station house. He was wearing a plaid shooting coat, and the lower part of his trousers and Blucher boots were smeared with clotted blood. He looked most dejected.

Carr was committed for trial, found guilty and sentenced to death. The hanging was scheduled to take place at Richmond bridewell – the Dublin male prison in the parish of Rathmines, later re-named Mountjoy – at 8am on Thursday 28 July 1870. One of the windows looking out over the exercise yard was taken away and the bars removed. This window was to serve as a doorway to the rude scaffold platform of deal which had been built out some 22 feet up over the yard at the rear of the prison. The executioner, a man who sheltered behind the anonymity of the black crape mask which he wore covering his face, and obviously did not know his job, launched the prisoner on a 14-foot drop down the outside wall of the gaol. With a dreadful snapping sound, Carr's head, still shrouded in the white cap, was wrenched from his body, and both fell, spouting blood, to the rapidly incarnadined shingle of the yard, where body and head rolled over and over and for fully three minutes the wretched man's headless trunk continued to quiver and twitch in a horrible, obscene mockery of still-living flesh.

My great-grandfather wrote:

> The last earthly thing Carr saw was the full-leafed tree with the top of Greenmount Brewery and its tall, smoking chimney.

Great-grandfather knew, too, the identity of the masked executioner.

> 'The Finisher' of the Law was a tailor, an Englishman.
> His name was Fallon. He put on the crape on the stairs.
> He ran out of the jail immediately after the execution. It
> is hoped, like Judas, to hang himself, and with more skill
> than he did Carr. He got £5, and as a volunteer was a
> legalized murderer.

That, I think, was a sentiment with which my friend Pierrepoint would have wholeheartedly agreed, for in the end his views on capital punishment underwent a quite extraordinary change.

Listen to his *Confessio*:

> The fruit of my experience has this bitter after-taste: that
> I do not now believe that any one of the hundreds of
> executions I carried out has in any way acted as a
> deterrent against future murder. Capital punishment, in
> my view, achieved nothing except revenge.

Pierrepoint resigned his position as Number One Hangman in 1956. Ten years before that he had become 'mine host' at a public-house at Hollinwood, between Oldham and Manchester, curiously named the 'Help the Poor Struggler' – wags were soon calling it the 'Help the Poor Strangler', and insisting that a notice was to be found inside reading: 'No hanging around this bar.'

Hanging was finally abolished in 1965. The last two men to hang were Peter Anthony Allen and Gwynne Owen Evans, the murderers of an inoffensive Cumberland laundryman. Evans was despatched at Strangeways Prison, Manchester, at 8am on 13 August 1964 – oddly enough by a hangman named Allen. And Peter Allen simultaneously dropped through the trap at Walton Gaol.

On my desk before me as I write lies an innocuous-looking piece of wood. But about it, in my imagination, there winds a procession of all those hooded figures who, over the years, dropped to their death on Liverpool's scaffold. They include among them George Sumner, or Ball, the Liverpool Sack Murderer; Lock Ah Tam, the Gentle Chinaman, who slew his family; George Kelly, the Cameo Cinema Killer; Alfred Burns and Edward Devlin, the murderous burglars who brutally did little Mrs Alice Rimmer to death. About it, too, flit the shades of those who might so easily have met their end in its shadow – Mrs Florence Elizabeth Maybrick and William Herbert Wallace. It is a portion of the hanging beam from Walton Gaol's now demolished gallows. It was presented to me by a reader of mine, a former warder at Walton, and a man who, more than once, had shared in the dread death watch of the last lingering hours of those whose fate or folly had brought them to the inescapable noose.

The Liverpool Pirates

This is a story which begins in the bright sunlight of a palm-fringed tropical island ... and ends in the forbidding gloom of the Liverpool Assize Court in St George's Hall.

It is a story which comes from the long-ago world of *The Onedin Line* – or, rather, its real-life equivalent. The world of the trade winds, the tall ships, laden with exotic spices and manned by the indomitable shellbacks.

It is a tale of mutiny and piracy and murder most foul on the high seas, that thrilled and chilled all Liverpool, and set the old sailormen gossiping in the Sailortown pubs and grog-shops, and thanking whatever sea gods may be that they hadn't shipped aboard the ill-fated barque, *Veronica*.

On 28 December 1902, the steamship, *Brunswick*, owned by the Liverpool shipping firm of Hugh Evans & Company and plying mainly between Lisbon and various South American ports, sighted landfall and was presently dropping anchor at Tutóia, off the small island of Cajueiro, which forms part of the bar of Parnalba River, where it flows into the Atlantic on the north coast of Brazil, 150 miles south of the equator. She was to pick up a cargo of cotton and hides from the Evans Company's warehouse there.

Since the island was now an uninhabited one, Chief Officer William Thomas Watson, peering through his spy glass, was surprised to see a ship's longboat, the name *Veronica* painted on its bow, lying alongside the jetty. This was unusual, for the island was seldom visited by other vessels.

He was even more surprised when five men, clearly in the last stages of exhaustion, frantically hailed him and signalled that they were seeking permission to come aboard. This was granted, and they pulled out to the *Brunswick,* and clambered up to the deck. They were taken below, given a good hot meal and clean clothes.

Their spokesman, a 28-year-old German, Gustav Rau, had a sorry tale to tell. He and his four shipmates – Otto Monsson and Harry Flohr, both German, Dirk Herlaar, a Dutchman who called himself Willem Smith, and Moses Thomas, a black American – were the only survivors of a crew of 12 – a motley crew, said to have been recruited from the dregs of the Gulf waterfront, and two of whom, Rau and Monsson, had smuggled loaded revolvers aboard with them – who had set out from Ship Island, in the Gulf of Mexico, on 11 October 1902, on the 1,100-ton, three-masted barque, *Veronica*, of St Brunswick, owned by Robert and John Henderson Thompson of Liverpool, with a cargo of timber, bound for Montevideo.

To begin with, said Rau, the voyage had gone well. Then, it was as if a hoodoo had fallen upon the vessel. First, on 25 October, one of the crew, a Swede, Gustav Johansen, had died of a fever at sea. Then, on 23 November, the first mate, Alexander MacLeod, fell from the main topsail-yard and was killed. Finally, on 20 December, the *Veronica* had caught fire, and the order was given "Abandon ship!"

The ship's two longboats were lowered. In one, was Captain Alexander Shaw, with Fred Abrahamson, Julius Parsson, Patrick Durran and Alexander Bravo. In the other, was Rau with his four companions.

Unfortunately, the two boats became separated, and Rau had no idea what had become of the captain and his party. After five days in an open boat, with only one cask of water and 11 ship's biscuits to sustain them, Rau and his men had reached Cajueiro.

The master of the *Brunswick*, Captain George Brown, agreed to take the men to Lisbon. And that would, in all probability, have been the end of the affair, had it not been for the strange behaviour of the black cook, who now made the most urgent request that he be berthed apart from the others.

That something was troubling Moses Thomas deeply, soon became evident. The calm of the tropical night was continually broken by his eerie howlings, groanings and lamentations. Nightmares, perhaps, brought on by his recent experiences? That notion was dispelled on the Monday (12 January 1903), when Thomas asked to see Captain Brown.

In consequence of what he told him, the captain communicated with the British consul at Lisbon, and was instructed to carry his five passengers on to Liverpool. The consul meanwhile got into contact with the Liverpool police, and when, on 28 January 1903, the *Brunswick* arrived here, she was boarded by detectives. After taking statements from Thomas and Flohr, who had by this time decided that the only sensible course open to him was to make full confession, to come clean, they arrested Rau, Monsson and Smith, and charged them with murder. Flohr subsequently turned King's Evidence.

The three accused promptly admitted that it was all true. Seven men had indeed been murdered. The ship had been set on fire – but it was not they who were guilty. It had all been the work of the black cook, Moses Thomas.

It was in May 1903, with the *Veronica's* longboat marooned low and dry as Exhibit A in the basement of St George's Hall, that, aloft in the Red Judge's Court, the true story of the last voyage of the *Veronica* emerged.

The log of the 13 days of horror and motiveless blood lust makes scarifying reading. It begins in the early hours of Monday 8 December 1902, when, at about 3am, Rau crept up behind Paddy Durran, the look-out, and felled him with a heavy iron belaying-pin. Flohr and Smith then crammed him, senseless, into the port locker.

This was the first act in a mutiny which had been smouldering in the mind of Gustav Rau from the day he walked up the gangplank. A savage, overbearing man of powerful personality, he had enlisted Monsson and Smith in his scheme, and Flohr, a somewhat weak and gentle-natured 18-year-old, had been terrorised into throwing in his lot with that of the menacing conspirators.

The mutineers' next victim was Alex MacLeod, who, Rau had said, had fallen to his death from the mast top. What actually happened was that MacLeod had come searching for the look-out man, Durran, who was by now the knocked-out man, reposing in the locker, and Rau struck the unsuspecting first mate down with his bloodstained belaying-pin, and flung him overboard.

Rau and Smith then made their way aft. Two shots. The second mate, Abrahamson, staggered, bleeding, from his cabin and lurched towards the captain's quarters. Captain Shaw was standing by the compass, looking at the topsails. Possibly because he was very deaf and his eyesight was no longer too good, he did not seem to realise what was going on. Rau, a frightening figure, revolver in one hand, belaying-pin in the other, shot him. The wounded captain managed to crawl into the chartroom, where he found Abrahamson. They bolted the door.

There was, at a later stage, some parley between Rau and the captain through the chartroom skylight.

"I'll give you my gold watch," pleaded Shaw. "Please save my life. I have got a wife and children, and I should like to see them again. If you will let me go I will take you to any port you want."

Rau spared him – for the moment.

Meanwhile, Monsson had killed Parsson, and thrown him into the sea. Durran, who had come to, tottered out of the port locker, and begged Rau for a drink of water.

"I'll give you a good drink," said Rau, who thereupon finished him off with his belaying-pin, and tossed him over the ship's rail into the 'drink'.

Now it was the cook's turn. Moses Thomas, only too well aware of the murderous business that had been going on, was cowering in abject terror in his cabin.

"Come out, you son-of-a-bitch," shouted Rau.

Thomas' only reply was to barricade his door.

The dark hours of the night dragged by for the quaking cook in a waking nightmare. About 7am, Rau renewed his attack. He beat thunderously at the cabin door.

"Come out, or I'll come in and kill you."

And Moses came forth – trembling.

Rau did not kill him. Instead, he ordered him to the galley to make some strong coffee. Rau was a practical man and knew that they all had to eat.

The next murders were committed on 14 December. Abrahamson and Captain Shaw were shot, and consigned to the cradle of the deep Atlantic. Rau pocketed Shaw's gold watch.

Now only seven men remained. Two more were to die. Johansen and Bravo.

Rau, now calling himself Captain Bungstarter, and his henchmen dressed themselves in the murdered officers' uniforms and strutted around the decks barking out orders.

On 20 December the *Veronica* was deliberately set on fire, and Rau and his four surviving fellow-mutineers cast off in the longboat, leaving her to sink to the sea bed.

On Christmas Day they reach Cajueiro … the first stage of their journey to the dry dock in St George's Hall.

The trial came on before Mr Justice Lawrance. Counsel for the Crown were Mr Alfred Tobin, KC and Liverpool's famous son and legal luminary, FE Smith, later Lord Birkenhead. The indictment contained counts of murder, conspiracy, fire-raising or arson, piracy and theft, but the charge proceeded on was that of the murder of Captain Alexander Shaw.

Young Flohr's evidence was used by the Crown successfully to support the testimony given by Moses Thomas.

There was little difficulty in establishing means and opportunity, but the matter of motive posed a most perplexing problem.

It has been suggested that poor food may have provoked a dissatisfaction, which, first voiced when, shortly after leaving Cajueiro, the *Veronica* was becalmed with sails idle in the Doldrums had given rise to feelings of frustration that had escalated over the lengthening days of the voyage into a murderous frame of mind. But there is not the slightest reason to think that the food was significantly worse than that in many other sailing ships of the time.

Bullying and brutality by the ship's officers has been provisionally put forward as a potential source of the trouble. Again, there is absolutely nothing to support such a contention, although the first mate, MacLeod, was known to be a tough customer who did not hesitate to knock a man down if he didn't jump to it smartly enough when given an order. But in the declining days of sail, that relic of the far from unusual ill-treatment of the shellbacks of earlier days still persisted.

More persuasive is the theoretical explanation that several plainly belligerently-inclined, ill-disciplined and resentful Germans, possessing firearms, got together and, the balance of their temperaments being affected by the fierce Caribbean heat, embarked upon a senseless killing *Fest*, just for the hell of it.

Certainly, murder for gain was totally out of the question, for none of the murdered men left much money for their killers to seize.

As Crown Counsel, Mr FE Smith, was later to hazard:

> This drama of the sea proves … that when men brood on
> trivial matters they may commit enormities so totally out
> of proportion to the provocation or hope of gain, that the

only rational explanation is that they must have been insane. Yet these men were sane. Why they began, no one may tell. Once started, fear and the desire to save their own wicked and worthless lives accounts for what followed, but the mutiny remains and must remain for ever an unsolved mystery of the sea.

All three mutineers were sentenced to death, but Monsson's sentence was later commuted to life imprisonment.

On 2 June 1903, Rau and Smith were launched on the lonely sea of death, hanging from the 'yard-arm' of the gallows at Walton Gaol.

Flohr slipped quietly out of Liverpool, and, no doubt, set sail for his native land.

Moses Thomas, having issued a writ for libel against a newspaper, which action was settled for £150 and costs, became engaged to the daughter of a well-to-do Ormskirk farmer. The farmer's horrified family made the girl break it off. Moses once more had recourse to the courts, suing for breach of promise, and receiving a substantial settlement. He then retired to the West Indies, a devout admirer of the English judicial system.

The Capture of Police Killer Kennedy

It is twenty minutes to midnight. A small group of police officers are clustered in the vicinity of a house on Copperas Hill. One of them detaches himself from the rest. He has spotted a man walking rapidly along adjacent St Andrew Street. Swiftly and silently, he follows him. Drawing closer to the hurrying figure, the collar of whose overcoat is turned up, trilby pulled well down, and whose left hand is strategically positioned so as to hide his face, his pursuer nonetheless recognises William Henry Kennedy, and approaching him says, "Come on, Bill. Now then, come on, Bill."

Fast as a striking cobra, Kennedy spins suddenly round, faces Detective Sergeant William Mattinson, of the Liverpool Police Force, pulls a revolver out of his right-hand pocket, thrusts the muzzle into his ribs, and hisses, "Stand back, Bill, or I'll shoot you."

No empty threat. Mattinson would not be the first policeman that Kennedy had killed.

Pluckily, the detective closes with him. There is a fierce struggle, in the course of which Mattinson is convinced that he hears a distinct click from the pistol. He manages, however, to wrench the gun from Kennedy's grasp, seizes him by the collar, and pushing and shoving, hustles him all the way back along St Andrew Street to Copperas Hill, where the others are waiting. They are Chief Inspector Roberts, of the Liverpool Force, and Inspector Albert Kirschner and Sergeant Duncan, of the Metropolitan Police, who have come from New Scotland Yard to Liverpool to arrest Kennedy.

At Warren Street bridewell, Kirschner tells Kennedy that he is being charged with having been connected with a man named Browne, now in custody, in the stealing of a Vauxhall motor-car from Tooting, in south London, the previous November.

Round about 4am, Kennedy is hied off to Police Headquarters in Dale Street, where he is lodged for what remains of the night in a cell. The following morning – Thursday 26 January 1928 – he is taken up to London. His wife is permitted to accompany him.

~

Let us now take a journey back in time to 27 September 1927.

In the early hours of that Tuesday morning, PC George William Gutteridge, of the Essex Constabulary, set out from Stapleford Abbotts, about half-way between Romford and Ongar, where he was stationed, in order, in the line of duty, to meet up at 3am with PC Sydney Taylor, of Lambourne End, at what was officially known as a 'conference point', outside Grove House, at Howe Green, a quiet, rural locality on the Romford-

Ongar road.

After their 'meet', the two constables parted at around 3.30am, both heading for their respective homes, Taylor pedalling off on his bicycle.

Shortly before 6am, PC Gutteridge's dead body was discovered by William Ward, who, driving a touring car, was delivering mail to all the little local post offices between Romford and Abridge.

At first, Ward had thought that Gutteridge had met with an accident, been knocked down by a passing car. Then, to his horror, he saw that he had been shot. He was lying, half propped in a sort of semi-sitting position against a bank at the side of the road leading to Passingford Bridge, some 400 yards from his home at Townley Cottages, Stapleford Abbotts. His helmet lay on the ground close beside him. So did his notebook, open at a blank page, and his pencil was firmly gripped in his right hand. Obviously, he had been about to take down the particulars of some person or persons. The fact that his torch was still in his pocket, and the road was an unlit one, suggested that he must have been about to write by the light presumably provided by a vehicle. And, indeed, there were plain marks of the wheels of a motor-car that had run up against the bank where Gutteridge must have been standing.

Dr Robert Woodhouse, of Romford, was called to the scene to examine the body. He arrived at about 9am, and opined that death had taken place between four and five hours previously. The constable had been shot four times. There were two bullet wounds in the left cheek, and with incredible brutality his killer had shot out both his eyes.

Police Constable Gutteridge was just 38 years old when he was murdered, married, with two young children, a boy and a girl. He was given an impressive funeral, two hundred uniformed colleagues, headed by the Chief Constable of Essex, marching four-a-breast in the cortège, and he was laid to rest in Warley Cemetery.

Why had he been thus callously gunned down? Who could have done it? Here was a mystery indeed – and, to be frank, there did not seem to be much chance of its being solved.

The investigating officers did, however, get a lucky break. They learned that at about 2.30am on the morning of the murder a blue Morris-Cowley car, registration number TW 6120, had been stolen from the garage of a Dr Edward Lovell, who lived in London Road, Billericay. And at seven o'clock that same morning, Albert M'Dougall, a clerk, who lived at 21 Foxley Road, Brixton, South London, found what was obviously an abandoned car by his house. It was a Morris-Cowley bearing the number plate TW 6120.

The car provided two clues. On its floor, under the front passenger seat, a spent cartridge case. On its running-board, at the driver's side, marks of human blood.

The clue of the empty cartridge case was eventually to prove of enormous importance. Brought by the Chief Constable of the CID, Frederick Wensley, to the attention of the Assistant Commissioner Crime, Major-General Sir Wyndham Childs, who was something of an expert in such matters, it was immediately recognised by him as a Mark IV bullet, made at the Royal Laboratory, Woolwich Arsenal.

He also knew that it was a leaden flat-nosed type of revolver ammunition, which, issued to the British Expeditionary Force when it left for France in 1914, had been claimed by the Germans to be an expanding bullet, violating the terms of the Hague Convention. In protest, the Germans had begun cutting the tops off their nickel-coated bullets, making them effectively dumdums. The practice only ceased when the Mark IV ammunition was withdrawn from the troops in France – and either re-made or destroyed.

Examining the cartridge case under a microscope, he saw that what had appeared to the naked eye to be a little blister on the copper cap, was actually an elevation of the copper above the normal level of the cap, composed of a large number of minute bead-like facets. Other elevations in the form of lines and striations were also present. What they meant was that the breech-shield – that is the part of the weapon which takes the shock of the discharge – of the gun that fired the cartridge, would have depressions corresponding to the elevations or excrescences on the cartridge case.

It transpired that a bullet taken from PC Gutteridge's head was a Mark IV, and the revolver which fired the shot was a Webley. But where on earth, Sir Wyndham wondered, had the murderer got hold of such obsolete ammunition?

In fact, two different types of obsolete ammunition had been used in the shooting of PC Gutteridge. The second was spherical lead bullets, loaded with black powder instead of cordite; a kind which had not been in use since 1897.

~

Four months passed. Then, one day, Wensley came into Childs' room again with the news that a man had been arrested from whom four revolvers, including two Webleys, had been taken.

The man was Frederick Guy Browne. He was the owner of the Globe Garage, at 7a Northcote Road, Battersea, where he combined legitimate work, repairing and so forth, with periodical profitable burglary and car theft.

Towards the end of December 1927, a letter had arrived at Scotland Yard. It was from an ex-convict who had known Browne, who, incidentally, could boast a very respectable criminal record, at Dartmoor. In it, the man said that he had been the driver of a car which had been the cause of a serious accident in Sheffield on 14 November. Browne had sold to a Sheffield butcher, Benjamin Stow, a Vauxhall car which he had stolen in Tooting.

The informant described Browne as a very dangerous man, adding that he had visited him the previous October at his garage near Clapham Junction, and seen hanging in the office there, a big Webley revolver. He had jestingly said to Browne and his assistant, Pat Kennedy:

"I hope you didn't shoot Gutteridge."

And received the reply:

"We've been expecting them coming for us every day. But if they do come, we can prove we were letting cars out of the garage at 6am. We did go down there for a car the day before this chap was murdered, and it's a good job we weren't there the same day."

Later, in November, at the informant's home in Sheffield, Browne stood in the corner of the kitchen, a large Webley in each hand, and said: "If they come to my garage I'll let them in, even if there's half a dozen or a dozen, but there's not one that goes out alive." He is also alleged to have said: "The police aren't so fond of pulling a car up at night after what we did to Gutteridge."

The police came to Browne's garage at 7.30pm on the night of 20 January 1928, and arrested him. He was initially held on the charge of stealing a car. After the discovery of two Webleys, one fully loaded with six Mark IV bullets, and the other with six rounds of the very old spherical, black powder ammunition, and examination by Childs confirmed that the breech-shield of one of the Webleys bore depressions which corresponded exactly with the elevations on the cap of the cartridge case taken from the Morris-Cowley, the charge was changed to one of murder.

Hearing on the grapevine of Browne's arrest, his friend Kennedy promptly took off for Liverpool, where, on Sunday 22 January, he and his wife, Pat, took a room in the house of David Staunton, at 119 Copperas Hill.

~

William Henry Kennedy was a man with a chequered career behind him. Born, thirty-six years before, in Ayrshire, of Irish parents, and taken as a lad to Liverpool, all his life he had affected the brogue of the Emerald Isle, and was used to answering to the name of Pat. Apprenticed to a compositor in Liverpool, he had the option of a good steady job with prospects 'in the print'. But, sadly, he lacked the vital ingredient of stability. He quit to join the Army, left the service with discredit in 1911, returned to Liverpool in 1913, and resumed his career as a compositor.

All might yet have been well, had it not been for a fatal flaw in his character, which seemed to make it impossible for him to conduct his affairs with anything remotely resembling honesty.

His criminal career was scarcely Rafflesian romantic – petty thefts, drunk and disorderly, indecent exposure, house-breaking and larceny. Several custodial sentences later, he went back into the Army, only to be discharged with ignominy. Again, Liverpool enjoyed the dubious benefit of his shady presence. He divided his time there between the practice of crime and the hawking of fruit.

A favourite watering-hole of his was Ye Cracke, in Rice Street. Joseph Thomas, the husband of the licensee, was an old friend of his, he and Kennedy having been out in South Africa together, bearing arms in the Boer War. As a matter of record, Kennedy had one of his last drinks in Liverpool at Ye Cracke, coming in there, according to Thomas, on either 23rd or 24th of January 1928.

According to his own account, it was in June or July 1927, when, after his latest release from prison in November 1926, he was working on a farm in Cheshire, that he had a letter from Fred Browne, whom he had got to know 'inside'. Browne wrote that he was opening up a garage in Battersea and invited him to come down as manager. He was glad to accept the job. In the course of his work he used to go out on occasion on motor rides with Browne. These trips would be in the nature of business journeys.

Sitting before Chief Inspector James Berrett at Scotland Yard at seven o'clock on the evening of 26 January, Kennedy was told that he was being detained with regard to the theft of a Vauxhall motor-car in Tooting, but, said Berrett: "I have been making inquiries for some time past respecting the murder of PC Gutteridge at Essex. Can you give me any information about the occurrence?"

Kennedy sat silent for a minute or so. Then said: "I may be able to tell you something, but let me consider. Can I see my wife?"

The two had been married only very recently. Kennedy had left London in December 1927, and gone off to West Kirby, where he had wed a young woman named Pat, with whom he had returned to London on 13 January 1928. He was still deeply entangled in the coils of love.

His wife was brought in to him. He turned to face her.

"When I was arrested in Liverpool yesterday I told you there was something more serious at the back of it. Well, there is. These officers are making inquiries about that policeman who was murdered in Essex."

She turned red … then pale.

"Why, you didn't murder him, did you?" she asked.

"No, I didn't, but I was there and know who did. If I'm charged with the murder and found guilty, I'll be hanged and you'll be a widow. On the other hand, if I'm charged and found guilty of being an accessory after the fact, I'll receive a severe sentence of penal servitude and be a long time from you. Will you wait for me?"

"Yes, love, I'll wait for you any time. Tell these gentlemen the truth of what took place."

"All right, I will."

What follows is his version of events as set out in his statement, the gospel according to Kennedy.

He well remembered, he said, the day of 26 September 1927. Browne had suggested that he should go with him to Billericay to help him steal a car.

They left the garage in Northcote Road together at half-past six, and went by train from Liverpool Street. They stole the Morris-Cowley from the doctor's garage. Browne decided that they would drive home by the byways, thus avoiding the main road to London. They sped through all sorts of lonely country lanes which led eventually to a kind of main road on the way to Ongar.

They had gone some distance along this road when they saw someone standing on the roadside bank, flashing his lamp, signalling them to stop. They drove on, but Kennedy heard a police whistle and told Browne to stop. He did so, and when the person came up to them they saw that it was indeed a policeman.

He asked Browne where he was going and where he came from. Browne said from Lea Bridge Road Garage, and that they had been called out to do some repairs.

The policeman asked if he had a card.

"No," said Browne

"Have you got a driver's licence?"

"No."

He then asked Browne: "Is the car yours?" And before he could answer Kennedy said: "No, the car is mine."

The policeman had then flashed his light in both their faces, and asked Kennedy if he knew the number of the car.

"Yes, TW 6120," he had replied.

"Very well, I'll take particulars," he said, putting his torch back in his pocket and pulling out his notebook.

The narrative now takes on a somewhat less than objective, less disinterested slant.

Says Kennedy:

> I heard a report, quickly followed by another one. I saw the policeman stagger back and fall over by the bank at the hedge. I said to Browne, "What have you done?" and then saw that he had a large Webley revolver in his hand. He said, "Get out quick." I immediately got out and went round to the policeman, who was lying on his back, and Browne came over and said, "I'll finish the bugger," and I said, "For God's sake don't shoot any more, the man's dying," as he was groaning. The policeman's eyes were open, and Browne, addressing him, said, "What are you looking at me like that for?" and, stooping down, shot him at close range through both eyes.

We can never know the true history of the events enacted on that lonely Essex road that awful autumn night, but it was Childs' opinion that:

> Browne first shot the constable, and Kennedy subsequently blew the poor fellow's eyes out as he lay on the ground.

Childs had noted when studying a photograph of the dead man's face that the skin was punctured with minute holes and that the cartridges which had been used to shoot out his eyes had contained a granular black powder. The granules made puncture holes. Such black powder cartridges were found in Kennedy's gun.

Browne and Kennedy, both professional criminals, were jointly charged with the murder of PC Gutteridge. They were tried before Mr Justice Avory, the 'Acid Drop', at the Old Bailey in April 1928. Both were found guilty. Browne was hanged at Pentonville and Kennedy at Wandsworth, at 9am on 31 May.

Transmuted under the powerful impulsions of romance into a poet, the plausible Billy Kennedy, as he signed himself to his newish bride, was constrained to pen, with tardily acquired wisdom:

The follies of youth
Are the sins of old age,
And the ill-fated fool
Passes out with the sage –
They both pay the price,
With death as sin's wage,
A crimson-hued blot
At the end of the page.

MYSTERIOUS
ECHOES

HUYTON'S HAUNTED HOUSE

Nightfall brought only terror to the Johnson family of Huyton. Lights burned all night in the living-room. Five frightened people, pale-faced and sleepless, huddled there … awake … listening …

Upstairs, shufflings and tappings sounded behind the locked doors of empty, deserted bedrooms. Eerie footsteps creaked across the landing. Light switches clicked on and off. Coats floated down the staircase, launched by invisible hands.

Their neat, semi-detached in Wimborne Road was, said the Johnsons, haunted. Haunted by an old woman in white, who glided through its rooms after dark. And they invited me to spend a night there with them to see for myself.

Here is what happened.

11.00pm – I arrive at the house. The Johnsons and eight friends are gathered in the living-room.

11.09pm – Accompanied by Mr Johnson, I go up to the attic, and then search all the upstairs rooms. They are empty. I lock each room after I have examined it, then seal every door and window with specially marked adhesive tape, to prevent trickery. As a further precaution, unknown to Mr Johnson, I stretch a network of black cotton across the stairs and landing. Anyone trying to play pranks will break these threads.

11.16pm – We return to the living-room. Settle down to wait.

11.35pm – Everyone in the room hears a low moan. "There she is," says Mrs Johnson.

Midnight – One of the neighbours who has come in to join the Johnsons, Mrs Nora Casey, says: "Listen! … Up above." We all hear a muffled, shuffling noise. A rustle of fear goes through the room. Then … silence.

12.09am – A loud crack from the staircase. Staircases often creak at night, BUT, at

12.31am – Distinct tappings from upstairs. Definitely due to someone … or something. I go upstairs and examine the seals and the threads. They are all intact.

Then there is a long period of silence.

1.30am – I suggest that we put out the living-room light. I open the door. Then, go out alone, and stand at the foot of the stairs.

1.50am – All quiet. I am standing halfway up the stairs. Suddenly … a piercing scream from the Johnsons' 14-year-old daughter, Ann – "There she is! There she is! Oh! I can see her." I dash down the stairs, experiencing a bone-chilling coldness by the living-room door. It is as if someone has left the door of a large refrigerator open. I grope for the electric light switch.

Ann's face is distorted with terror. She is crying. Her body is rigid. When she recovers she tells me: "I *saw* her standing behind you at the foot of the stairs. I had seen and experienced, apart from the coldness, nothing. But four other people claimed to have seen the apparition.

Mrs Letty Roberts told me: "I saw her. An old woman, standing right behind you. She had the face of a devil. It was horrible." She buried her face in her hands and began to cry.

Miss May Fagan said: "I saw a kind of grey shape hovering behind you on the stairs."

Mrs Nora Casey and Mrs Frances Fagan also saw the uncanny figure.

2.30am – Mr Johnson goes upstairs alone. He comes down hurriedly, after seeing, he tells us, the old woman vanish into a back bedroom.

We wait another two hours. There are no further incidents. And at 4.30am – I leave.

Now, before I tell you about the most extraordinary occurrences that took place on my second visit to the Johnsons', let me give you the background to the case.

First of all, the Johnsons themselves. Mr Gerard Johnson was a small, greying man of 45. He had been employed for sixteen years at nearby Lister Drive Power Station. His employers described him as "a man of normal intelligence and a sound worker." Mr Johnson himself told me: "Nothing like this has ever happened to me before." Eleanor, his wife, was a sensible, 41-year-old housewife. She never believed in ghosts. And there were the Johnsons' four daughters – Irene, 7, Kathleen, 10, Ann, 14 and Mary, 19.

Nothing could be less like the legendary 'haunted house' than the Johnsons' home. It was just an ordinary council house on a modern estate. Downstairs was a living-room, a kitchen and a bathroom. On the first floor, one front bedroom and two back bedrooms. At the top, a single, large attic. The house was built in 1937, on what was then a country field. The Johnsons were the fourth family to occupy it. Previously, they had had a flat at Speke. They spent seven years there before exchanging tenancies with a Mr and Mrs John Walker. "I wanted to get a place nearer my work," explained Mr Johnson.

The family moved into their new home on Friday 13 June 1958. At eleven o'clock on the night of Sunday 15 June, Mr and Mrs Johnson went to bed in the first-floor front bedroom.

Two o'clock in the morning is a funny sort of time to be woken up. Especially if it is the early hours of a Monday morning , and you are only too well aware that soon you will have to lever yourself out of bed to get your husband and children off to work and school. And even more so if you are dog-tired after having only moved into your house the Friday before, and you still haven't got everything straight.

That is why Eleanor Johnson thought at first that she was just having a bad dream when she saw that face – 'like a shrivelled skull, greeny-purplish, like a Halloween turnip'. She made that sort of double-take effort we all make to wake ourselves up, just as the crocodile's jaws are closing, or the spear is plunging into our breast. As she became more wide awake, she was aware, in the thin, pale light that seeped in through the window, of the same old furniture from home, but looking now in their new, strange bedroom somehow alien and unfamiliar, and the old woman with the evil face, still there, standing by the bed.

Mrs Johnson told me: "She was tiny, barely five feet tall, very bent, like an old hawthorn tree, and leaning on a stick. She was wearing a white night-gown. There was a grey shawl round her bony shoulders, and her long grey hair was done in two scrawny plaits. It was her face that terrified me. She seemed to be cackling evilly into my husband's face. He was fast asleep. Didn't stir. I went cold as ice … then hot as fire. I shook my husband and whispered, 'Look what's standing over you'. But Gerry didn't see anything. As he turned to look, she glided to the fireplace and vanished."

Mr Johnson told his wife what pretty well any other husband would have told her – "You must have been dreaming". And drifted straight off to sleep again. But next day– Monday 16 June – he had second thoughts. Next night it was his turn.

Again the Johnsons retired at eleven o'clock.

This time Mrs Johnson was safely asleep, but her husband was still at that half-and-half stage when you see a jumble of figures and pictures.

Mr Johnson told me:

> I was just drifting off when I felt something tucking the clothes in. I knew it couldn't be my wife because she was on the inside of the bed. Anyway, she was asleep. Then the doorknob started rattling. I jumped out and switched on the light, but the room was empty. I looked out on the landing. No one there either. But as soon as I got back into bed, stealthy footsteps started moving about outside. They went on till dawn.

The ghost had murdered sleep that night for Gerry Johnson.

The following night, three of the sisters, Mary, Kathleen and Irene, had the frightening experience of seeing the doorknob of their room slowly moving from side to side. "Dad, somebody's trying the door," Mary shouted. Mr Johnson raced upstairs. There was no one on the landing, or in any of the rooms.

"The Ghost", as they now called it, seemed determined to impress the entire family. The last of them to receive a visitation was 14-year-old Ann. She slept alone in one of the back bedrooms. On Thursday 19 June, she felt a bit quaky when she went up to her room around 10.30pm. She had been in bed roughly ten minutes when she felt a tap on her shoulder.

Ann Johnson told me:

> I turned over and saw an old lady standing by me. Her face was very old and crinkly, and she had a very nasty laugh on her. I was scared stiff. I buried my head under the clothes. Then I plucked up courage, leapt out of bed, and ran to my mother's room. As I ran, a big wind seemed to be drawing me back. I looked over my shoulder – once. The old woman was beckoning me with a spidery finger to follow her up to the attic.

Attics, like cellars, can be pretty spooky places, especially the attics of creepy old Victorian houses. But the Johnsons' house was not a bit like that. Its main feature was a bay-window behind a straggly privet hedge. Hardly a moated grange. But there is always something peculiarly horrible about a ghost in a modern setting, something offensively incongruous about a supernatural presence beside a custom-built kitchen unit, on a factory floor, in a supermarket … or a plain little council house in Huyton.

It was exactly one week after her first sighting of the ghost, that Ann had an even more frightening experience. Her parents were out watching television at a friend's house. She went up to bed at 10.30pm. Feeling a bit nervous, she left her bedroom light on. She was glad when she heard her parents arriving back, but simultaneously her light went out. When her father brought up a fresh bulb, he found there was nothing wrong with the old one.

Ann told me:

> I had just shut my eyes when the light went off again. I looked up and saw the same old woman laughing into my face. I couldn't speak. I turned my head away. That was when I saw a second figure, at the foot of the bed. It was a man, neither old nor young, with dark, glittering eyes set in a white face that seemed hideously battered, as if someone had been knocking him about with a spade. I saw his hands sliding up and down the bed rail. Then the old woman grabbed a holy picture off the chest of drawers beside my bed. She hurled it to the floor and, extending one arm, started to push the chest of drawers towards the door. It seemed to glide along a couple of inches off the ground. My door, which had been open, banged to, and the chest, which had glided about seven

feet, thumped down and jammed against it. I was trapped with the two figures. I screamed and screamed as loudly as I could.

Downstairs, Mr Johnson heard his daughter's shrieks. He had to use his shoulder before he could get into the room.

I tried to push Ann's door open. It wouldn't budge. It was like fighting a strong wind. In the end, I managed to force the chest of drawers which was blocking it out of the way. Ann was lying unconscious on the bed.

This was too much for the Johnsons. So far they had kept things to themselves. Now, at their wits' end, they decided it was time to ask for help. They sent for a priest and a doctor. They also summoned the police.

First to arrive was Father Arthur Brady, Roman Catholic priest of St Dominic's Church, Huyton. I questioned Father Brady and he told me:

I found the child frightened and trembling. I blessed the rooms. I think a supernatural visitation is quite possible. The family was obviously terribly frightened, and I didn't feel it was a conspiracy.

And the family doctor told me:

I examined Ann. She was suffering from severe and genuine shock. The parents struck me as quite normal people. I have an open mind on the whole matter.

The police came, tramped around the house. They found nothing.

But still the haunting went on. By now desperately afraid, the family decided to sleep together in the living-room. The doors of the upstairs rooms were locked. No one ventured up there after dark.

A Huyton council estate was a warm and friendly place, and the neighbours rallied round. They came in at night and kept vigil with the fear-stricken Johnsons. And they saw things, too. The man with the glittering eyes did not put in another appearance, but the old woman made sure that Mr Johnson had a good look at her. She came down to the kitchen for this purpose. It was the witching hour of 3.30am when he was making a pot of tea to sustain them all. He was standing by the cooker when he felt a cold wind on his back. He turned and saw her gliding out of the bathroom door towards him. He ran like a red-shank into the living-room.

Mr Alexander Keys, a friend, was there that night, and he wanted to go to the lavatory. He wasn't a bit scared – he was a tough ex-boxer and ex-RN – but he had the fright of his life when he went out of the living-room.

> She was standing in the corner by the kitchen stove, grinning like a death's head.

Mrs Frances Fagan, a 57-year-old mother of twelve, did not see her: but she heard her, making "a queer muttering, as though somebody very old was in a wicked temper."

The previous tenants were traced. Mr and Mrs John Walker had lived at the house in Wimborne Road for a year, and were glad to leave. Their dog, they said, would never go upstairs. In May 1958, just before the Johnsons moved in, Mrs Walker saw a little old lady with a shawl over her head standing by her bed.

As it happens, Ann, in her early teens, was the ideal age for a classic poltergeist infestation, and although the disturbances seemed to start around her mother, it was Ann, as time went on, who was the most upset by the other-worldly ructions.

Throughout July things got worse. The house was filled with weird knockings, footsteps and tappings. The apparition appeared again and again to all the family.

At the beginning of August, events took a new turn. The noises, previously heard only at night, started occurring in the daytime, too. By the end of the month, the Johnsons were nearing the end of their tether.

It was at the beginning of September that I paid my first visit to the house. Three days later, I spent a second night there. And this time I took a photographer with me.

Here is the log of the second night's events.

11.30pm – We arrive at the Johnsons' and search the house from top to bottom. Everything appears to be in order. Empty rooms. No wires, loose boards, or mechanical devices. All windows firmly secured. Doors locked and sealed.

11.50pm – We descend to the living-room, where we join the Johnsons and a party of their neighbours.

Midnight – All quiet. We sit in the living-room … waiting …

12.50am – Nothing has happened. We extinguish the light. Immediately there is a loud bump from upstairs. Then silence.

1.16am – Ann agrees to go up to the bedroom where she first saw the old woman. Her father, my photographer, Bill Mealey, and I go up with her. We stand there in the dark. The minutes drag by. After about a quarter of an hour, Ann starts to breathe heavily. Then screams: "There! There! By the door." I strain my eyes in the blackness. See nothing. But the atmosphere is stiff with expectancy. The next few seconds are chaotic. Ann sobs, "She's gone now," and collapses, half-fainting, in her father's arms.

1.40am – Back in the living-room Ann and her father both claim to have seen the phantom. And Bill Mealey reports: "When the girl screamed, I first tried to photograph the thing. The flash would not work on three exposures, although all connections between the camera and electronic flash mechanism were plugged in correctly and the 'ready-to-fire' warning light indicated 'fully charged'. With no attention to flash or camera, it worked after Ann said, 'She's gone now', and I photographed the girl without trouble."

2.10am – Observations resumed. Mealey and I take up positions on the first-floor landing. We hear a sort of 'plop' in the back bedroom. We burst in and find four coats, which I had seen shortly before hanging from pegs on the wall, folded in a neat pile in the centre of the floor. I can personally vouch for the fact that no living human being had been into that room after my previous examination of it.

Two hours tick slowly by in the darkness. Nothing to report.

4.45am – One of the neighbours goes out to the lavatory. As she comes back, she switches off the light. Seconds later, there is a click. The light comes on by itself.

5.50am – Dawn is breaking. We leave.

There was never at any time any suggestion that the Johnsons were faking it all for notoriety or personal gain. They were so very obviously frightened to death and bitterly disappointed by their new home. In the end, the family went in desperation to the council, and, although councils do not officially believe in ghosts, seeing the Johnsons' plainly genuine distress, they found themselves able to arrange another move for them.

I am pleased to be able to report that the ghost did not go with them, nor, from that day to this, has she ever been seen again.

LIVERPOOL GANGS AND GARROTTERS

One of my earliest criminous memories is of my mother telling me of her father's telling her of the Liverpool garrotters, and how they were put down by a fierce old gentleman called Mr Justice Day and his cat.

I remember looking up the word 'garrotters' in *Chambers' Dictionary* and finding that garrotting was a Spanish mode of putting criminals to death, originally by strangling them with a string around the throat, tightened by twisting a stick. *Garrote* is the Spanish word for a stick or cudgel. Later, the method was refined by the introduction of a brass collar, tightened by a screw, whose point was driven through to enter the spinal marrow.

What on earth, I wondered, could such barbarities have to do with latish nineteenth century Liverpool? But wait ... a subsidiary definition in my indispensable *Wörterbuch*: 'To garrotte: suddenly to render insensible by semi-strangulation in order to rob.'

There was, it seems, a severe outbreak in the Liverpool streets in the latter part of the 1880s of what we would today call by the infinitely less romantic and evocative, Americanised term of 'mugging', but which our grandparents' more refined ear and taste christened rather more exotically, garrotting. But, on the rose by any other name principle in reverse, there was absolutely nothing remotely romantic about being seized by a villainous scouser, half-throttled, and thus painfully separated from your purse or wallet.

And that is where, in 1886, the luminant Mr Justice John Charles Frederick Sigismund de Haren Day made his salvatory entrance on the darkling scene. The widely accredited intelligence at the time was that the garrottings were being carried out by a band of ruffians who called themselves the High Rip Gang.

Some doubt has subsequently been cast on this. Sir William Nott-Bower, Head Constable of Liverpool from 1881 to 1902, who, in his memoirs* recalls that Liverpool in his time was, in parts, a dangerous city. There were streets, particularly in the vicinity of Scotland Road, which were unsafe for respectable people to enter, and where the police habitually patrolled in pairs.

'This condition of affairs caused much concern and anxiety,' he confessed, 'and unfortunately some genius invented an absolutely unfounded cause for it.'

Sir William is referring to the suggestion that the large number of crimes in the Scotland Road area was due to a gang known as the Organization or, alternatively, the High Rip Gang, which existed for the purpose of plunder

---

* *Fifty-Two Years a Policeman. Sir William Nott-Bower, KCVO, (Edward Arnold, 1926).*

and violence, and the execution of vengeance on all who ventured to give evidence against them.

He fulminates:

> All this created considerable, and entirely unjustifiable, alarm … There was never the very faintest shadow of foundation for the suggestions made … But letters from all sorts of irresponsible persons, Press comment, and a certain sort of public opinion assumed the impossible, and accepted the fact of a High Rip Gang.

So … Sir William was a sceptic. Why? Because: 'It was impossible, for such a gang could not have existed without the Police ever *hearing* of it.'

My friend of many years, the lawyer and author, James Morton, who is a leading authority on gangs and gangland, past and present, national and international, has this to say:

> Whether there was such a gang [as the High Rip Gang] may be open to question, but there were certainly a great number of robberies with violence and woundings in the list for the [Liverpool] November Assizes of 1886 presided over by Mr Justice Day.*

John Day had been elevated to the High Court Bench in June 1882, at the age of 56. Nursing a profound distrust for 'the theories of penology built upon Lombroso and criminal anthropology', he placed his faith in deterring criminals from further offence against God – he was a zealous Roman Catholic – and society, by means of severe sentences coupled with the use of the lash known as the 'cat-o'-nine-tails'. His pity – he was not a cruel, sadistic, or unmerciful man – was always directed towards the victim. He regarded it as his duty to avenge the weak and innocent.

He was not, however, one of those remote judges of that ilk which enquires: "What is a Beatle?" When, at the time of the 1886 Assize, he came to Liverpool, he was not content to relax amid the judicial luxuries provided at Newsham House, the Judges' Lodgings, at Newsham Park, but decided instead that it was necessary for him to see for himself something of the night haunts and habits in their normal environment of the kind of social pests who were to appear before him. Accordingly, he requested Sir William Nott-Bower to arrange such a tour for him, and the other Judge of Assize then in Liverpool, Mr Justice Grantham, said that he would like to come along, too.

Gangland, Volume 2. James Morton. (Little, Brown, 1994).

So, on the following evening, timing the excursion for after the public-houses had disgorged their rough habitués into the streets, the two judges, and Day's son, Frank, who was his Marshal for that Assize, escorted by the Head Constable, Chief Inspector Robertson, and another detective, sallied forth on an educational foray that included on its itinerary visits to such ill-famed nocturnal *loci* as the Loose Box and the Long Jigger. Both judges said that what they had seen that night was a revelation to them, and could not fail to be a help in the future discharge of their judicial duties.

The expedition does not, however, seem to have exerted any immediate influence over Mr Justice Day's normal sentencing procedure. Its mode went like this.

"I shall not sentence you to a long period of imprisonment."

The thug in the dock would give a self-satisfied grin of relief. The old boy was going to be lenient like Hopwood.

Mr Hopwood was the Recorder of Liverpool at the time. He was renowned for his leniency, a factor which Mr Justice Day determined to counter by a deliberate policy of harsh sentencing, in the hope of stamping out, or, at the very least, drastically reducing, the prevailing social evil.

A piece of doggerel of the period enshrines a 'High Ripper's' view:

Oh, Mr Hopwood, what shall I do?
They've sent me to Assizes,
And I wanted to go to you,
For though I may only get the sentence of a 'Day',
Oh, Mr Hopwood, the cat may spoil my stay.

To return to the smirking thug in the dock.

Mr Justice Day continued addressing him: "I consider you a case in which the rate-payers' money would be expended to no good purpose; and so I shall not send you to penal servitude."

The thug would by now be jubilant.

"But I shall sentence you to twelve months' hard labour, with twenty-five strokes of the cat when you go in, and another twenty-five when you come out."

Total collapse of thug.

"Show your back to your dissolute friends when you come out."

In one case where the prisoner fell on his knees pleading for mercy, Day told him: "Get up, you cowardly rascal, and take your punishment like a man."

The policy, of inflicting a short term of imprisonment, balanced by the maximum allowance of the cat, sometimes misfired, the prison doctor declaring the man medically unfit to receive so many lashes. Observing this, Day made sure that a medical examination preceded his promulgation of sentence. What happened in practice was that the actual sentencing of those found guilty would be put back to the last day of the Assizes. It has been calculated that over a period of fourteen years, Day inflicted 3,766 lashes of the cat on 137 criminals.

Well, *did* the High Rip Gang exist?

There is no doubt that the *Daily Telegraph* believed that it did, for that newspaper reported in its issue of 15 November 1886, that two 19-year-old lads, said to be High Rips, had received fifteen years' penal servitude apiece for stabbing a member of the rival Logwood Gang. It also reported that one man had had to be given police protection because he had refused to let the High Rips use a goods shed belonging to the Lancashire and Yorkshire Railway Company, to which he held the keys.

Certainly Elizabeth O'Brien, an old lady of 86, who was interviewed in 1960, was in no doubt as to the gang's existence. Her recollections were quoted in the *Liverpool Echo* of 19 October 1960:

> There were women in the High Rippers who identified themselves with a flower or plume in the hair. They were more vicious than men.

She also remembered that the only person who could exercise any sort of control over the High Rippers was a policeman known by the nickname of 'Pins'. When he approached, the gang would scatter, with loud warning shouts of, "Pins is coming!" A quaint piece of social history folklore, from a woman who would have been a child of nine when Mr Justice Day was dealing with the gang – and doing it his way!

James Morton tells how, in the early part of the twentieth century, it was at one time estimated that fifty per cent of Liverpool's Chinese community was actively engaged in the manufacture of opium.

At that time, too, there were formidable gangs who were 'hard at it' committing dock crimes of various kinds, including the 'rolling' of half-seas over sailormen. Paradise Street, Back George Street, and Park Lane, were gangland territory, and sailors were being lured out of such safe ports as the Sailors' Home and the YMCA with dangled carrots of shebeens and invitations tendered to the naughty parlours of willing girls. They would end up, not garrotted, but probably senseless, and certainly money-wad-less, in a dark alley.

The Throstle Gang had a strikingly pretty girl – once, so underworld rumour had it, a model in London – whose brevet it was to float seductively through Liverpool hotel bars, picking up target men. As she languorously wafted them back to her flat with her – "Just a short stroll away, dear. No need for a cab," – she would stop in Benson Street and ask her companion of the night to light her cigarette for her. That was the signal, and the waiting

Throstles would descend, Assyrians coming down like a wolf on the fold, to 'marmalise' the out-of-luck, would-be Lothario.

But Liverpool gang-buster, Bert Balmer, had on this occasion had the girl and her dupe followed, and he and his fellow-officers of the law proceeded to set about the marmalisers. The Throstles got up to seven years apiece: the girl, alleging that the men had forced her into the scam, got away with a twelve months' sentence.

As a young officer back in 1937, Balmer had to deal with a serious outbreak of protection racketeering. A gang led by a villain who, like Ronnie Kray, called himself the Colonel, and numbering two tough Australian fist-wielders in its ranks, was indulging in threatening behaviour at the racecourse. The Colonel and his squad had been playing rough games at the Grand National meeting, and Balmer and his boys found two bookmakers who had been very badly slashed. At first, the wounded bookies refused to talk, saying it was their own fault, and that they should have paid up. But Balmer wasn't on for that. He extracted the identity of the man who had put the finger on them. It was, of course, the Colonel. Balmer went after him, and following a terrific struggle in which his coat was slashed to pieces, made an arrest. The Colonel, demoted, went down for four years.

Doing their sums in 1948, statisticians came up with an amazing figure. It was reckoned that there had been a grand total of 200 juvenile gangs in Liverpool across the decades, and that there were still dozens in 1950, among which was the Peanut Gang, which derived its name from the fact that its members began their disreputable career by splitting open bags of peanuts on the docks before, to quote James Morton:

> ... they graduated to splitting open the heads of seamen decoyed into alleys off Lime Street for their wage packets.

Never make the mistake of failing to take a gang seriously just because its members are still of the age when they should be being read nursery rhymes. One very successful gang of housebreakers was led by an eight-year-old armed with a blowlamp!

The Brodie Gang is a name from the past to conjure with. It numbered in its ranks a wife who was, sexual discrimination in reverse, known as the 'Strong Arm Man'. Her aggressive tendencies having got the better of her, she took umbrage at, and a razor to, a witness whose evidence she did not at all care for. She wound up serving four years for her exercise in practical criticism. With her enforced retirement as Her Majesty's guest, the Brodies lost heart, and the once strong and healthy gang just withered away.

Another celebrated old Liverpool gang was the Swallows. All the members had a swallow tattooed on their wrists. This big, well organised gang went out of business, along with a great many others, after the conviction and hanging of George 'Cameo Killer' Kelly at Walton in 1950.

Today there are assuredly new – and very likely fiercer – gangs, drug-connected, woven into the warp and woof of Liverpool life, but I take leave to doubt that, however much more efficiently they may operate, however much more terror they may succeed in inspiring, they will never gather about them the quasi-romantic nostalgia which, however wrong-headedly, invests the old Liverpool gangs of yesteryear.

A Georgian Puzzle in Venanation

"Sir, let me tell you, the noblest prospect which a Scotchman ever sees, is the high road that leads him to England."

So declared the peerless fashioner of fine fancy phrases and maker of stout dictionaries, Dr Samuel Johnson.

And in 1875, the year after Dr Johnson's death, suiting the action to the precept, Charles Angus, the ambitious, 18-year-old son of a barber of Stranraer, headed south across the border to seek his fortune among the Sassenachs.

Georgian Liverpool, where he found himself, was a place of excitement and promise. It bustled with activity. Sedan-chairs bearing the well-to-do through the streets. The rattling mails spanking, with flying hooves and steaming horses, into the coaching inns of Dale Street. The brawling Sailortown taverns and the fragrant coffee-houses. Places like the Slaughterhouse, officially George Bennett's superior wine and spirit purveying premises, with its inner sanctum, the Rat Pit. The massive warehouses of the Goree. Vessels from all four quarters of the globe, laden with tea and spices, teak and jute, cloves and rubber, cleave the waters of the Mersey, and drop anchor along its waterfront. And, riding the choppy river amid the forest of tall-ship masts, the dark outlines of the slavers, holds filled with innocent merchandise, but soon, on the middle passage of their triangular voyage, to be exchanged for crammed cargoes of human shame and misery. Black ivory. Black gold.

By contrast, the fine-clad merchants, many of them dealing, as Charles Angus one day would, in slavery, parading in their pomp and pride, and dignity-robed professional men, safe and comfortably insulated behind the bastions of the Athenæum, the exclusive gentleman's club, hard by St Peter's, in Church Street. The clean-limned, beautifully-architected houses of the prosperous, made gracious the town's rapidly expanding hinterland. The country poked green fingers in close above Shaw's Brow, where, no distance at all away, lay Everton.

Glenn Chandler lyrically describes the scene:

> In those days Everton was a pretty village across rolling countryside where many of the wealthier merchants had their grand mansions, and where they kept their carriages in which they rode into Liverpool each day to do business. Once a barren sandstone ridge, it now flourished with tiers of well-kept gardens full of blossom and cascading greenery. … on summer mornings, with

the scent of hay and honeysuckle in the air [it] must have
been … idyllic.

In this vibrant new and challenging town, Angus made a lowly start, well
pleased at securing a position in a druggist's counting-house. Who should
have guessed that this young man, tall, dark, curly-haired, tending towards
stoutness, was to become the epicentre of a terrible life and death mystery
that would puzzle the Liverpool citizenry down the years, and seems certain
to remain unsolved over the centuries. A mystery concerning which, at my
insistent instigation, my good friend Glenn Chandler, the creator of *Taggart*,
television's celebrated Glaswegian detective, carried out a masterly
investigation of his own, which resulted in his writing an outstanding book
about the case, *Burning Poison*.*

Time has washed away the records of Angus' first ten years in Liverpool,
leaving only hints and whispers. Certain it is that as he sat like a coiled
spring on the druggist's counting-house stool, it grew a progressively less
comfortable perch.

There is evidence that this fringe-medical occupation stimulated Angus'
interest in medicine and medicines. He appears to have taken the trouble to
acquaint himself thoroughly with the contents of standard works on the
subject, until he eventually reached the stage where he felt confident to
prescribe and dispense for patients, and even to instruct young persons how
to be doctors, and secure positions for them on Africa-bound ships.

At some point, as the century moved towards its close, Angus contrived
a start as a general merchant in a small way of business. Before too long, he
had his own counting-house, then went into mercantile partnership with a
fellow ascendant Scot, Robert Copland, and the pair set up trading premises
in Mersey Street, just off Canning Place. The partnership was dissolved in
1799.

The next milestone in Angus' life was his marriage into money. He was
thirty-three. His bride was Maria McQuistin, the 13-year-old daughter of
Thomas McQuistin, a wealthy coffee plantation owner and livestock
breeder, lately retired from Jamaica, and settled into a fine house, 2 Trinity
Place, off St Anne Street, in a very good professional class neighbourhood.
The couple were married on 5 March 1800, at St Nicholas', the Mariners'
Church.

Angus' new father-in-law was in his eighties, and made it plain that he
wished Angus to take over his affairs and conduct his business for him, both
in Liverpool and Jamaica. It was in this way that Angus became profitably
involved in the slave-trade, and the owner of two slave-ships.

A slight storm cloud blew up on the Angus horizon. Thomas McQuistin
had decided to make a new will and sent a note round to his solicitor,

* *Burning Poison: The Murder That Rocked Georgian Liverpool. Glenn Chandler. (Lea Valley Press, 2000).*

Richard Statham, demanding the return of all his papers, and stating that he no longer wished him to act for him. As Statham rightly guessed, it was Angus, now living at Trinity Place, who was behind his dismissal. Mr McQuistin's revised will left the bulk of his estate to Angus, who must have intuited that Statham, a former executor, would have been strongly opposed to this. The resultant ill-feeling between Statham and Angus was to prove of subsequent significance.

Four weeks after signing the new will, Thomas McQuistin died. Angus was now a man of wealth and station. The seal was set upon his social acceptability by an invitation to join the Athenæum. In 1801 Maria bore him a daughter, Jane, and the following year a second daughter, Maria.

But now the first zephyr of an ill-wind began to blow. Angus lost two of his slave-trading ships, and as many cargoes, and things were going disastrously wrong with the Jamaican property, not a penny from which had thus far found its way home to the steadily diminishing coffers at Trinity Place.

In June 1804, Maria gave birth to a third child, a son, Thomas. She was still barely 18, and after all this child-bearing her health seemed to be failing. To ease the strain upon her, Angus decided to employ a governess who would take care of the children, and invited Maria's half-sister, Margaret Burns, to come to Trinity Place as governess-cum-housekeeper. For all these thoughtful provisions, poor Maria did not survive long. She died, on 25 June 1805, of tuberculosis.

Let it be said at once, and unequivocally, that Margaret Burns was in no wise attractive, either as to physical appearance or psychological temperament. It was no fault of hers, but she was pale and sallow of complexion, small and broad-chested of build, and a martyr to dropsy, her deliverance from the lethal effects of which, she ascribed to infusions of powdered Peruvian bark in wine, administered to her by the medically skilled Angus. Her temperament, in that it was 'pawky', which is to say 'mean-hearted', was very much akin to that of her half-brother-in-law. Indeed, taking into the reckoning their shared penuriousness and mutual delight in the practice of parsimony, there were those who would have said that Charles and Margaret were made for each other!

It will come as small surprise then that not a great deal of time had passed before Miss Burns found her way into Mr Angus' bed. And not a great deal more time passed before – at the beginning of March 1808 – it was observed that Miss Burns was getting larger. Could it perhaps be that Margaret was *enceinte*? This was to be a pivotal question.

There are some surrounding circumstances of which we need to take cognisance. About the middle of February 1808, Angus paid a visit to John Steele at the druggists' shop, Steele & Oakes, in South Castle Street, and asked him if he could let him have a quantity of Oil of Savin. Steele, who knew Angus quite well, was not worried about selling it to him, despite its being a potentially powerful poison. Its medicinal uses were in the treatment of chlorosis, the so-called green disease, an iron deficiency commonly found among adolescent girls, and in cases of menstrual absences or deficiencies. It is also an abortifacient, producing tetanic uterine convulsions. Administered in improper dosage, its characteristic symptoms are excruciating pain, accompanied by vomiting and diarrhoea, and climaxing in death. Steele would recall Angus' dismay at being told that *Oleum Sabine* cost five shillings per ounce. Pawky as ever, he settled for two drachms, that is a quarter of a fluid ounce, saying that that would probably answer his purpose. He did not, however, expatiate as to what that purpose might be.

A couple of weeks later, Angus betook himself to the shop of Thomas Richardson, cutler and surgical instrument maker. Saying that he wished for it to be sharpened, he produced a ten-inch-long tube with a three-edged point to it. It was an instrument designed for the purpose of causing a miscarriage. On hearing that the sharpening would cost him ninepence, Angus, true to form, grumbled and growled before grudgingly paying up. He told Richardson that he would be using the instrument to pierce his children's ears.

With oil and perforator in the forefront of our minds, we come to the crucial days, the veritable Ides of March. At a quarter past nine on the morning of Wednesday 23 March, when the maid, Betty Nickson, came into the parlour at Trinity Place to serve breakfast, she saw at once that Margaret Burns was very ill. She lay down on the sofa, complaining of severe bowel pains and extreme thirst. She then began to vomit. The vomit was very black in colour. All that day she remained supine upon the sofa.

At eleven o'clock the following morning, Angus suggested that they should send for the family doctor.

"You need not," he assured the ailing woman, "be afraid of the expense."

But no doctor came, either that day or the next.

Friday, however, seemed to bring miraculous recovery. Miss Burns took some warm beer, which she kept down; later, a bowlful of gruel, which she also kept down; and later still, at about ten o'clock, she fancied some white wine. There was none in the house. Betty Nickson traipsed off to Mr Winstanley's, the wine merchant in Henry Street, near Duke Street, fully three-quarters of a mile away, right across the town, to buy a couple of bottles.

It would be coming up to a quarter past eleven by the time Betty got back from her long trek. The tableau that greeted her eyes when she pushed back the parlour door on her return was to haunt her for the rest of her life. It was a bizarre, horrific scene. Margaret Burns was 'cowered in a lump in a corner of the room, her elbows on her knees, and her face pressed against the wall.' She was dead. And there, in his easy-chair, a quilt pulled over him, was

Charles Angus – fast asleep.

It was at the Liverpool coroner's behest that, at two o'clock on Sunday afternoon, the doctors plied their autopsy knives. The corpse lay in the upstairs bedroom immediately above the parlour, where, on that Friday afternoon, it had been carried.

A story was being bruited around that Miss Burns had been with child. The medical men, five of them, peered into the dead woman's uterus. Yes, they all agreed. She had recently given birth to a nearly full-term child. But where was the child? No one had seen sight nor heard sound of it. How had it, dead or alive, been disposed of? And of what had its unfortunate mother died? Neither of these questions was ever to be satisfactorily answered.

The doctors found inflammation in the small intestine, on the edge of the liver and on part of the curvature of the stomach. In the latter there was also a hole, which, they suspected, could well have been caused by some sort of corrosive poison.

An inquest was held at the new Liverpool Exchange, in Castle Street. And who should turn out to be clerk to the coroner and solicitor to the corporation, but Angus' old enemy, Richard Statham. Another menacing shadow was cast by Mrs Sarah Lawson, Angus' sportive next-door neighbour, whose cupidinous advances it may well be that he had resent-triggeringly rejected. She was dedicating herself to a vengeful scouring of the town for former servants in Angus' employ, to testify to his sexual relationship with Miss Burns.

The Reverend John Vause, incumbent of fashionable Christ Church, in nearby Hunter Street, was adamant that he had encountered Angus at the Athenæum early on the Friday morning – the newsroom there opened at 7am, and Angus would often go there before breakfast to read the day's news – and walked back with him to Trinity Place. This was in direct contradiction to the statements of the servants, who said that the master had not left the house that Friday. The prosecution theory was that if Miss Burns had given birth to a child on the morning of her death, Angus had got rid of it on his way to the club.

Charles Angus was arrested and deposited in the Tower, the Borough Gaol, in Water Street. His house was searched from top to bottom for the body of a child and any poisonous substances. A vast array of bottles was found – one was marked 'Jacob's Water' and another 'Poison Water'. Both were submitted to Dr John Bostock, physician to the Liverpool Dispensary, for analysis. He found that the bottle labelled 'Poison Water' contained corrosive sublimate of mercury, saturated with a strong solution of arsenic.

Angus was committed to Lancaster Castle for trial at the Assizes.

It seemed a long, long time from April to September, waiting in Lancaster Castle Gaol to be brought up to the dock, but at last, at eight o'clock on the morning of Friday 2 September 1808, he was led up the flight of steep steps from the cells and through the trap-door into the court.

A prosecution witness of very great importance was a retired timber merchant, Peter Charnley, who, testifying to a conversation that had taken place twelve or thirteen years before, said that Angus had then shown him a silver, tube-like instrument. A slide ran up the centre, and it had a three-edged dart at its point. He had been told by Angus that by introducing it through the womb, and letting the air in, a miscarriage could be brought about.

The doctors then stepped up with their evidence. They were sure that Miss Burns had given birth. They admitted that no corrosive sublimate of mercury had been found in the dead woman's stomach. Dr Bostock, however, authoritatively asserted that the corrosive sublimate might be taken into the stomach in a state of solution, that following violent symptoms of vomiting and purging and the drinking copiously of diluted liquors, death might take place, and yet the most minute examination of the stomach and its contents might fail to detect the slightest trace of the corrosive sublimate of mercury. He, too, had examined Miss Burns' uterus. He had found it large enough to contain a quart of fluid, whereas an unimpregnated uterus had scarcely any cavity and was barely larger than a pear or a fig.

Mr James Topping, leading for the defence, asked Dr Bostock if he was aware of the perfectly innocent domestic use of a mixture of corrosive sublimate and arsenic as a bug destroyer, frequently employed for washing furniture. Angus had himself so used it, and he had requested the medical men to inspect the drawers in his house, when they would see a consequent whiteness about them. Angus pointed out that the 'Poison Water' in his possession was expressly labelled as such, and said that he had obtained the mixture in order to destroy moths which, seven years ago, were injuring his blankets, woollens and valuable carpets.

Referring, in the statement which he read to the Court, to the surgical instrument, Angus said:

> It was never intended for any purpose relative to women. As I had studied Bell on the venereal disease, and had cured many venereal cases, it was in these instances that I applied it. The instrument was much longer, and as thin as a knitting-needle, and this probe was neither more nor less than to be introduced into men's urethras, in cases of stricture or warts.

'It was around midnight,' goes Glenn Chandler's evocative description of the scene, 'and the oil lamps of the Crown Court in the mediæval castle cast their eerie glow …' On to the stage stepped the last witness, Dr Carson.

So far as his medical brethren in Liverpool were concerned, James Carson was something of a maverick. Accustomed to taking up an opposition stance, the view which he chose to take in this case was, predictably, the reverse of that subscribed to by all the other medicos. The hole in Margaret Burns' stomach, he declared, had occurred *after* her death. He backed this diametric opinion by the provision of the details of three cases reported by the great surgeon, John Hunter, in which such holes had been found post mortem. He did not, however, concur with Hunter in thinking that the holes had been produced by the action of the gastric juice. His startlingly idiosyncratic view was that water in the stomach at a temperature of 90 degrees, mixing with the common salt taken in food, could cause the stomach to dissolve!

As regards the alleged pregnancy, he put forward the even more bizarre diagnosis that the appearance of the womb was due to a 'dropsy of the hydatids'. In plain language: hydatids are largish vesicles or bladders containing either the larvae of a genus of tapeworms – *Echinococcus* – or sometimes simply sterile, fluid-filled cysts, which may develop as tumours or cysts in nearly all mammals. What Carson was hazarding was that Margaret Burns had 'given birth' to a huge mass of tapeworm cysts, which had grown pediculate in her uterus. An ingenious, but distinctly eccentric, notion.

The judge, Mr Justice Chambre, summed up with scrupulous accuracy and even-handed fairness. The jury, without leaving their box, found Angus not guilty.

The acquitted man's return to Liverpool was something less than a triumph. Stares, whispers, and hostility followed him. They confirmed his decision to show the town a clean pair of heels. In November 1808, he resigned his membership of the Athenæum, and took coach for Scotland.

After he had gone, the Liverpool medics, piqued by what they regarded as Carson's audacity, got hold of the controversial uterus, still preserved in spirits, and took a close-focus look at the ovaries. To their delight and vindication, they discovered in one of them a *corpus luteum*; that is a yellow mass formed by a follicle which has matured and discharged an egg. If the egg has been impregnated, the *corpus luteum* grows and lasts for several months. If impregnation has not taken place, the *corpus luteum* degenerates and shrinks.

Charles Angus died at Turnberry Lodge, Turnberry, on the Ayrshire coast, on 21 May 1820, at the age of 53. He is buried in Kirkoswald churchyard.

In Liverpool, he has left no trace. The merciless waters of time have washed everything away. All that beautiful and gracious part of the town to which the young Charles Angus aspired, and eventually succeeded, has vanished into the limbo of lost things. The mansions of St Anne Street have long since crumbled, their once-lovely gardens have been crushed out of life beneath grey paving-stones. Number 2 Trinity Place survived – if you can call it that – as the Mohamed Sultan Lodging-House right on until the days of the Second World War. But for the rest, all that we are left with is old, old ghosts, hovering for just as long as there are memories to hold them, about the bleakly altered landscape of hinterland Everton, where once the lovingly cultivated roses and the wild thyme blew.

The Great Greyhound Gambler

It was a somewhat anxious and undeniably careworn Mr Gustave Bennett, who, arriving in Liverpool from Paris, booked himself into the Adelphi Hotel.

Gustave Bennett was not, in fact, his real name. Indubitably a cosmopolitan, he was known in France as Monsieur André Chandon. In New York, he was Lester Travers. This strange, multi-nominate man had emerged alive from the terrible crucible of the First World War. That, he congratulated himself, remembering the catastrophic slaughter of the trenches, was an achievement. But now he wanted more than mere survival. He wanted to Live – with a capital 'L' – and that meant having capital – money.

All around him he saw the Brave New World prosperity. The flourishing Stock Exchanges, the burgeoning Bourses. The rich getting richer. Desperately, he wanted a profitable slice of the action, the super-cream gateaux.

Things were not, however, going well. Attempts were being frustrated. Carefully laid plans were crumpling. Really determined efforts to borrow money in Paris had failed outright. It had even proved impossible to exploit his beautiful brochure there.

He knew not a soul in Liverpool, and that all-important capital of his was down to precisely 12 shillings, which, even in those days of pounds, shillings and pence purchasing power, was woefully inadequate. Fortunately, though, he still had what every successful rogue needs, a good wardrobe of smart clothes that lends to him the appearance of prosperity.

He had been sitting, suitably clad of course, in a corner of a popular Parisian cocktail bar when the Divine inspiration had flashed like a Damascan revelation into his mind. Why hadn't he thought of it before? Greyhound racing … yes, *greyhound* racing … that was the answer.

A, comparatively speaking, new sport, a novelty, it was getting enormous publicity because of the huge profits that were said to be being garnered in by its promoters. There were, he knew, people who looked with sanctimonious horror upon horse-racing, but who, deluding themselves, viewed investing in greyhound tracks – that was what they called themselves, investors, not gamblers – as perfectly, respectably permissible. They would be his quarry. The set-up, dummy hares.

He – gambling or investing? – sank almost all that remained in his terminally threatened bank account in the printing of 500 copies of a magnificently produced pamphlet, written and designed with considerable panache by himself.

High-lighted on the cover, was a seductive artistic reproduction of a noble greyhound in the even nobler act of winning a race. Inside, were impressive photographs: of a vast greyhound stadium; of a grandstand crowded with the élite of Paris; of the finest, most up-to-date club-house in the world. And backing all this up, action pictures of exciting races in progress, of smart starting-traps, and generously-smiling bookmakers.

Awaking refreshed in his comfortable Adelphi bedroom on his first morning in Liverpool, he was encouraged to find in his morning paper, flicked through over a good, substantial breakfast, by beneficent coincidence, an article recommending the sterling virtues of greyhound companies as an investment.

Carefully washed, shaved, powdered, and neatly coiffured and caparisoned, Gustave Bennett set out from the hotel to find a lawyer. Allowing chance to guide his footsteps, he settled upon the office of an elderly solicitor quartered in the shopping centre of the city.

Once, after a formal handshake, safely ensconced in the lawyer's inner sanctum, he plunged straight into the business that had brought him there.

"I will not waste your time, sir," he said, producing from his pocket a copy of the brochure. "You can either accept or refuse my proposition. I assume you are a man of means. If you are not, I will not trouble you further."

That, he believed was the kind of talk that would command a serious hearing. Bennett was playing for high stakes. He was not asking for hundreds, but thousands of pounds.

"I want capital to develop the largest and finest greyhound stadium in the world. At present the profits are only about fifty per cent, but experts agree with me that they can be increased sixfold. Now I am prepared to accept sums of not less than two thousand pounds from responsible persons. Anything under that will be useless, and I don't want mere gamblers."

It was a cheeky, forceful opening gambit. The playing of it took nerve.

"I've never gambled in my life," said the solicitor. Nevertheless, he stretched out his hand for the proffered brochure.

In saying that he had never gambled, the solicitor believed that he spoke no less than the truth. Admittedly, it was his almost daily habit to telephone his broker and permit himself a modest flutter in options, but that was business, he did not regard it as gambling.

As the lawyer looked at the pamphlet's persuasive pictures, noting the grandeur of the stands, the very obvious affluence of the patrons, who had been carefully selected for photographing, the voice of the tempter droned silk-smoothly on.

"There's three hundred per cent for those who come in now, and perfect security. The stadium is within seven miles of Paris, and the value of the ground alone exceeds the entire capital. But I want another grandstand and more land. At our last meeting we had to turn away 10,000 people for lack of accommodation. There was a regular riot and it cost me a large sum to square the police."

It worked to Mr Bennett's clear advantage that the lawyer whom he had chosen happened to be one of those who believed himself to be sharp, shrewd and swindle-proof. He was, moreover, one of those who, with virtually nothing to confirm it, believe themselves to be gifted psychologists and sound judges of the natures of their fellow-men. He thought that Bennett looked and talked like an honest man. The fact that he talked big money was in his favour. Surely, if he had been a crook he would have been keen to get his hands on even small sums of money.

But it was the magnificently presented and cunningly contrived brochure that really wooed and won the lawyer over, made him seriously contemplate investing.

Then, after a longish silence: "I'll come into this, Mr Bennett. I have a cousin who's making a fortune in London out of greyhound tracks and he's a shrewd investor."

"It's a pity London is being overloaded with tracks," commented Bennett. "I'd have started one if there'd been room. Lucky I didn't, for it turned my attention to Paris, where we're pioneers, with everything in our favour."

At the end of a mere half-hour, Bennett was out again on the Liverpool street – with a cheque for £2000 in his pocket.

He popped in next to see a bank manager. Another round of convincing sales talk; another enthusiastic showing of his brochure; another £1000 to his credit.

Mr Bennett's *tour de force*, launched with such success in Liverpool, ended three weeks later in London with its promoter personally the richer by more than £20,000. And after an enjoyable spell among the flesh-pots of the metropolis, he was off on tour again.

He went, via Paris, where, after changing it into francs, he stashed away the major part of his ill-gotten gains. Then, under the name of Lester Travers, he set sail for America. He took with him £10,000 worth of Irish sweepstake tickets. In obeisance to that well known Yankee philosophic dictum, 'Never give a sucker an even break', he sold these colleen-and-Erse-plastered forgeries, whose counterfoils would never see the inside of the Dublin drum, and sailed back, richer still and richer, to Paris.

He was as surprised as he was delighted to find that not a single complaint had been raised to the Parisian *gendarmerie* by the English shareholders in the bogus greyhound stadium. Having gone, as it were, to the dogs successfully, he decided to transfer his allegiance now to the gee-gees. Another well known underworld maxim was that 'Fools follow horses'. So, in eager quest of a profitable selection of those fools, reverting to the name of Gustave Bennett, our anti-hero set about devising an 'infallible system', one which guaranteed unlimited winnings to anyone who would entrust to him the relatively speaking small investment of necessary stake money.

As every wise man knows, circumstance has a cruel way of turning the tables, and Mr Gustave Bennett was about to become the biter bit. He fell in with a French stockbroker, a man with political leanings and a famous name, who offered to put his *bon ami Anglais* on to good things on the Bourse. Before leaving for Ostend – Belgian betting men were about to be favoured with a chance to follow Bennett's infallible (so far as he was concerned!) system – he delivered into the multiplicatory hands of his French stockbroker the £25,000 cache gleaned from his greyhound and sweepstake 'investors', believing as devoutly and deludedly as any of his own dupes that by the time he got back from Belgium his new friend would have trebled it.

Bennett had barely begun his garnering among the trusting ones of Ostend, when, perusing beyond the blaring headlines announcing: 'Another French Political Scandal. Arrest of Prominent Financier', he read, with sick and turning stomach, the name of his so well-disposed friend.

Furious, distracted, filled with self-disgust at his own naïvety, Bennett sped back to Paris, only to find, as he well knew that he would find, that he had been well and truly plucked. Filled with righteous indignation, he spouted wild, pot-calling-kettle talk of prosecuting his fallen false friend. Which spouting promptly ceased when he heard, with some alarm, that Scotland Yard had approached the Chief of Police in Paris for information about the greyhound stadium.

Discretion triumphing over dolour, he swiftly entrained for Berlin. The expedition, though expedient, was not a success. Germany was at the time rent with rumour of revolution. Poverty scented the air. There were few pickings to be had, for those foolish enough to be taken with his patter were too poor to take advantage of its mendacious promises, or be taken advantage of. He did, driven by the necessity to find the money for board and lodging, try his hand at a small swindle. But, worried, over-anxious, he made a hash of it, was detected, arrested, and packed off to prison.

Released, he returned to Paris a broken man. His confidence had drained away. Within weeks, he became seriously ill. Suffering from double pneumonia, he was removed from his squalid lodgings and taken to hospital, where he died.

Little or nothing could be found out about his origin or antecedents. No one could even be sure of his nationality. The man of many names had proven entitlement to none. They buried him in a pauper's grave, and indexed him under the bland and very English name of Smith.

A PAIR OF LIVERPOLITAN JADES

Two extraordinary Liverpool ladies. Well … that's strictly a courtesy title. Women, con women, to be more precise. One is the Princess Soltykoff. The other is Frederica de Furneaux, also known as Lord Arthur Clinton.

Let us take them, as I am sure they would have wished, in order of social preferment.

Royalty first. Sad to relate, the Princess was not! She was the daughter of an industrious joiner, plain James McKillen, and the far from royal household which, on 1 December 1873, bore her, was in Upper Mason Street, albeit situate in the regal domain of the late troglodytic King of Edge Hill, Joseph Williamson.

We discover her standing, at the age of 32, in the dock of the Old Bailey, charged, under the name of Lady Muriel Paget, with the defrauding of shops and stores in the West End of London.

It was alleged against her that she had first struck by obtaining a miniature of the Marquess of Anglesey, her cousin she had said, from Esme Collings, of Bond Street. This stroke she had followed up by targeting Debenham's and other well-known London stores, giving to them such fine-sounding addresses as Winwick Hall, Haydock, Lancashire, actually a lunatic asylum; her residence in Arundel Square, which turned out to be a boarding-house near Pentonville Prison, North London; an impressive address at Portslade, in Sussex, where she had been a probationary nurse; and that well-known retreat for aspiring turn-of-the-century swindlers, the Metropole Hotel, in Brighton.

She was described by the *Morning Leader's* reporter at the Central Criminal Court, who was obviously half in love with her, as:

> … entertainingly beautiful … rich complexion, medium height, commanding presence, mass of beautiful brown hair, elegantly dressed and full of Southern fire. Her mouth is the work of an actress, and her manner – even in moments of excitement – is quite the manner of old nobility.

Looking every inch a tragedy queen, swathed in a long red 'wrapper', reaching from neck to ankles, draped in an ostentation of luxurious furs – although the court was suffocatingly hot – and even the hat which she was so fashionably wearing alleged to have been obtained by fraud, she stated coolly, calmly, and most firmly, that she was the one and only Lady Paget.

After a sister had given evidence of the accused's lowly birth, into the witness-box went the lady herself, producing a large family Bible which she made great play of kissing.

Asked her name, she replied: "Nina Olga Trew-Prebble."

Counsel was inquiring of her where she was born, when the judge, His Honour James Alexander Rentoul, interrupted: "Surely that is hearsay."

She told the Court that she had been educated at Liverpool College and Windsor College, at the expense of Major the Honourable Alfred Paget.

It was at this point in her evidence that the court usher suddenly took it upon himself to decide that she was a Mohammedan and had, therefore, taken the oath incorrectly. To administer the oath properly it would be necessary for her to take off her boots, place one hand on the Koran, and the other on her forehead. Would she mind taking off her boots?

"We'll look the other way," volunteered George Elliott, Counsel for the Prosecution.

"I don't mind," said the Princess.

Which was just as well, for no one did look the other way! And the Koran, when produced, was an absolutely elephantine tome, which, as one commentator put it, "looked like a selection from *One Hundred Best Books*!"

The proper swearing having been duly executed, it was a chequered history indeed that the Princess unfolded before the Court. She deponed that in 1892 she had changed her name to Slolterfoht. Who, she was asked, was he? A boy who had made lucky investments for her, she said. The name change had been purely talismanic.

In her earlier days she had, she claimed, tried to study medicine. She had also, at one time, run a bakery in Everton. It was after that that she went on the stage, which she left to marry Prince Alexis Soltykoff. They had tried to marry in Scotland, but had not remained in residence there for the required period. Instead, they had married in St Petersburg. Most unfortunately, she was unable to produce her marriage papers as she had given them into the safekeeping of a woman whom she had met in a convent – and had never seen either her, or them, again. She left Prince Soltykoff behind in St Petersburg and returned to England "under the guardianship of an old gentleman".

She had subsequently learned that Alexis had died in a Russian prison, and, using the name Solterfoht, she had married a man named Prebble. He had been "at the 'Varsity", and was studying medicine at Guy's Hospital, but funds ran out, and he had run off into the Army.

"So you are Mrs Prebble?"

"No, I – I think I am Princess Soltykoff."

The prosecution said that it believed that Mr Prebble was a serving corporal; in the Army. Whether or not he had enlisted simply to escape from the clutches of the Princess was a mute point.

A few years later she had undergone another change of name. By this time

Lord Anglesey was, she said, making her an allowance. In 1895, she had become stranded in Paris, and when no money was forthcoming, she took, as she believed was her right, the name Paget.

She went on to admit to the Court that she had taken to drink after the death of her sixth child. The previous five had all passed away in the course of the preceding eighteen months.

How much was she drinking? A quotidian two bottles of vodka, plus stout. Worse still, she was taking also morphia and opium pills.

Summing up, the judge, obviously subscribing to the lamentably widespread contemporary delusion that the working classes could not have intelligent children, but nonetheless patently captivated by the pretty prisoner, described her as: "a person of undoubted ability, particularly so when it is considered that she is the daughter of a joiner."

The jury took half an hour to come back with a verdict of guilty.

Then came the customary pre-sentencing question: "Anything known?"

And the Princess' nemesis, in the shape of Detective Inspector Drew, stepped up to tell the Court that the prisoner had left home in 1893, when she was 19, after her mother had made "a certain accusation". Mother was right. The Princess-to-be had given birth to Annette Tarbett McKillen, on 10 April 1894, in Liverpool. It was then that she had obtained a position as a probationary nurse down in Portslade, and had apparently proved to be a good one.

What the judge especially wanted to know, was the truth regarding her marriage to Prince Soltykoff. The prince's father had vehemently denied any such union.

"Could it not," asked Judge Rentoul, "have been a secret marriage? Where is Prince Soltykoff now?"

"Dead," was the answer.

So the marital tangle was never satisfactorily, which is to say decisively, unravelled.

"Any previous?"

"Fifteen months at Suffolk Assizes for fraud in August 1902."

The judge wondered if police supervision would help.

"No," said Drew, emphatically. "It would not work."

Her counsel then launched into a lengthy speech in mitigation, along the lines that his client had got into trouble in a social sense at an early age, and that everything followed from that.

But the Princess would not have it.

"That is not true," she proclaimed loudly.

Rentoul thought that the offence merited five years' imprisonment, but sentenced her instead to eighteen months with hard labour.

"She will probably be doing the same thing over again," he added.

But there does not seem to be a record of any further misdemeanours by her. Perhaps His Honour was wrong. It would be nice to think so.

Our second delectable miscreant is, criminally speaking, bisexual, female in primary persona; secondarily facultatively male. *Her* name, almost certainly assumed, was Frederica de Furneaux. *His* name, definitely assumed, was Lord Arthur Clifton.

I came to know of the existence of this enigmatic duality through a book which dealt with the life of another strange character bearing the contrastingly commonplace cognomen of Joe Smith. But there was little commonplace about him. He was born, the book does not say when, but from internal evidence I would hazard some time in the 1870s, in Liverpool, at the Tam o' Shanter Hotel, owned and managed by his father.

As a young man, Joseph Edward Smith, to give him his full style and title, was, in a way which is not really made clear, associated in some capacity – possibly that of an enthusiastic and practically active unofficial agent or informer – with, it is claimed, both the Liverpool police and Scotland Yard.

This probably came about because his father had cordial relations with the Liverpool force, whose headquarters was close by his hotel, which became the scene of all the police department's banquets and other festivities. It was here, also, that many of the detective officers who came down from Scotland Yard investigating important cases were brought by their Liverpool brethren for a friendly noggin or two. Help from the local knowledge of Smith the elder was not infrequently sought, and the Tam o' Shanter became, in effect, a sort of unofficial annexe.

It is not surprising that growing up in such an atmosphere young Joe became fascinated by the snatches of the stories he heard the detectives retailing to his father, and, seduced by the thrill of police work, was ultimately, and increasingly, using his eyes, ears and feet to help his heroes. What is surprising is that, as the 'Boy Detective', he is said to have given the police 'valuable aid in building up their case against Mrs Maybrick'.

He subsequently emigrated to America, held the rank of captain in the US Army Reserve Corps, which he had earned by his prowess at tricking and trapping enemy spies in World War One, and thereafter spent thirty years as assistant manager and chief house detective at the famous and fashionable Waldorf-Astoria Hotel, in New York City.

It is Joe Smith, who, before his departure from our shores, is credited with with the running to earth of Signora Frederica de Furneaux. A wealthy South American widow, she lived quietly, but in considerable luxury, with her maid in a fashionable Liverpool street. The reserve with which she surrounded herself was perfectly understandable, as was the fact that she made no friends among her neighbours, this being accounted for by the circumstance that she was unable to speak more than a few words of English.

The Signora stood about 5 feet 10 inches tall. She had raven-black hair and very beautiful black eyes. She played the part as perfectly as she dressed for it. No one would ever have guessed that her luxuriant black tresses were a wig, beneath which her hair was smartly bobbed.

Neither would they have recognised her in the dim figure of the man who would slip out of the rear entrance of her residence under the cover of darkness, make 'his' way to Lime Street Station and catch a night train for London, where she, a brilliant male impersonator, was warmly welcomed in the highest circles of society as the handsome and eminently eligible Lord Arthur Clinton. In her rôle as His Lordship, Frederica maintained a suitably splendid apartment in an exclusive part of the city.

The bogus Lord Arthur was the possessor of two superlative skills. He had the small hands and light touch of a woman, and could remove jewels from necks, arms and corsages so deftly that often their disappearance would not even be noticed until several hours had elapsed. Diamond-studded pocket watches, gold cigarette cases, well-filled wallets and cheque books could be similarly lifted undetected from male pockets.

His Lordship's second and complementary skill was an aptitude for forgery. The stolen blank cheques would be filled in for very substantial sums, duly signed, and subsequently cashed.

In many cases it was at first supposed by the unsuspecting victim that the valuables had simply been lost. But when, after the most rigorous searchings they were never found, and the tally of losses began to mount, the losers gradually came round to the belief that in England's smartest society an even smarter thief was operating.

A clever conversationalist, a talented musician, a fascinating Lothario, who, with flashing dark eyes and faultless aristocratic manners, made indiscriminate amorous advances to, and caused rankling rivalries and jealousies among, the high-born ladies, Lord Arthur would be the very last person to attract suspicion. Moreover, his campaign had been planned and executed with consummate proficiency. Never did he make the smallest dishonest move until his acceptance and position among the aristocracy, minor royalty even, amidst whom he moved, had been established *sans doute.*

He never committed more than one robbery at one party. When a fellow-guest hysterically announced that she had been robbed, Clinton was always the first to offer to submit to a search. He was safe in doing so, for in those apartments with which he was most familiar and in which he was most at home, he had ferreted out secret hiding-places into which he would pop the spoil, and recover it just before leaving.

The robberies, intermittent but seemingly never-ending, had been going on for more than a year, and the value of the loot was running into many thousands of pounds, before a finger – a very, very ginger finger – was hesitantly pointed in what proved to be the right direction.

Scotland Yard had had some of its crack detectives working on the case for months. And they were getting nowhere. So it was, we are told, that finally one of the Chief Inspectors, who had known Joe Smith as the 'Boy Detective' in Liverpool, asked him to take a hand in the faltering investigation.

Studying the facts of the case calmly and coldly, Joe considered that the likelihood was that so artistic and socially well-placed – according to the circles in which he moved – a thief, would be disinclined to have any transactions with a common fence. It was, he decided, far more probable that he would make use of a pawnshop for the disposal of the stolen property. That he would resort to a London pawnshop, all of which were under constant observation, struck him as unlikely. But what about Liverpool?

At this point we are, I feel, asked to make a great act of faith. We are asked to accept that, against very heavily stacked odds, Joe's pure guess was to prove spot-on.

The tale that we are told states that after weeks of patient watching, Joe found some of the missing jewels in a Liverpool pawnshop. Questioning the proprietor, he learned that they had been pledged by a tall young woman, with black hair and dark eyes. Expensively dressed, she had all the appearance of being a lady, and explained her resort to the pledging of her jewellery by a recitation of a sad and very plausible story. She had given the name of Mrs George Robinson, and an address, at which, when Joe went there in search of Mrs Robinson, there was nobody answering her description, and no one knew anything of her.

This is said to have given young Smith his first clue that the thief might be a woman posing as a man. Or it could, of course, equally well be that the jewels were being pawned by the thief's wife or girlfriend.

'But,' says the book, 'without being able to explain why, he [Smith] inclined toward the male impersonator idea. That was one of his uncanny hunches.'

So, another seeming *non sequitur*, 'he set himself to watch the night trains from Liverpool to London.' After a long wait, he was rewarded by the sudden manifestation on the Lime Street Station platform of a tall, rather slender and effeminate-looking young man, who corresponded closely to the mental picture that he had formed of the person he was after.

Losing no time, Joe scrambled aboard the train and went with his suspect to London. There, he followed him to an apartment in a high-class neighbourhood, made certain inquiries which confirmed that the young man moved in those exclusive circles in which the robberies were being committed, and in due course trailed him back to his Liverpool home, where he discovered that the supposed 'he' really was a 'she'.

Thereafter, Frederica in Liverpool and Lord Arthur in London were put under ceaseless close surveillance. Other robberies took place and detectives in Liverpool followed Frederica when she pawned her loot. She was observed, too, cashing forged cheques. The game was up.

Her arrest and trial in 1882 are said to have caused an immense sensation, and Joe Smith was one of the chief witnesses for the prosecution.

Frederica de Furneaux was sent to prison for twenty years.

A cautionary note. I have not had the opportunity to cross-check and confirm the details of this story in the way that I usually do. There are certain aspects of it which somewhat tax my credulity, but the source from which I obtained it seems to be a respectable one, and so I present it in just slightly tongue-in-cheek good faith. It should not prove too difficult for any reader who feels so moved to seek out a confirmation for himself.

HISTORIC
ECHOES

The Night the Scuffers Went on Strike

It wild-fired from mouth to ear … the vital intelligence … "Dem scuffers is owt. D'ere on strike!" The worm had turned. The good old 'Dixon of Dock Green', he of the dependable, slow, measured tread on the beat, and the reassuring "Goodnight all", as he disappeared into the darkness to make sure that decent folk could sleep safely and soundly in their beds, was up in arms.

The First World War – the Great War of 1914-1918 – was over. The grand slaughter nine months ended. England was to be, said Lloyd George, a fit country for heroes to live in. Not in Liverpool, where mile upon mile of back-to-back, not-so-slowly-rotting, rat-infested, slumland houses, with their foul-smelling earth closets, breeding in summer hosts of disease-carrying flies, still stood; a festering legacy from Good Queen Victoria's Golden Days. And for many of their struggling, under-privileged tenantry, striving to scrape a living from Liverpool's world-famously prosperous docks, a foreman's frown could mean empty stomachs for the unlucky recipient's breadline wife and hungry children.

At least the scuffers – Scouse for policemen – had a job, bread on the table, scouse in the pot, but, in the Liverpool of 1919, in the words of WS Gilbert's Savoy Opera, *The Pirates of Penzance*, 'a policeman's lot is not a happy one'. The chairman of the Liverpool Watch Committee was an Alderman Maxwell, a dictatorial and deservedly much-detested man, who commanded no respect from the force. Neither was Liverpool's Head Constable (as the title then was), Francis Caldwell, MVO, by any means a front-runner in the popularity stakes. He was remote. A deputiser. "Never saw him but once – and that was when he presented a cup to the Bowling Club," testified one Liverpool constable.

The vast majority of his men had never seen him at all! But the rare few of the rank and file who were to experience a closer acquaintance with him in the course of the riots, discovered him to be 'a perfect gentleman', and a brave one, who displayed considerable courage and a remarkable capacity to lead and understand his men during the worst of the brutal fighting in Scotland Road.

Conditions were undeniably bad. There was a lot of bullying. Sergeants of the force behaved like mediæval barons, inspectors like despotic princes, superintendents ruled their divisions by terror rather than by leadership. Such was the atmosphere of petty distinction between the ranks, that, as one honest PC phrased it: "It was difficult, if not impossible, for top and bottom of the structure to say as much as 'Good morning' to each other."

Moreover, the men were nursing a grievance about the non-payment of back monies owed to them, for the Watch Committee had failed to pay compensation in respect of rest days forfeited at the beginning of the war, which back-dated allowance the members of practically all other police forces had since been duly paid.

Worse still, in spite of an award in 1918, Liverpool police pay continued to be way below what could be earned by a labourer in the docks. A shortage of constables in the force was the direct consequence of the Watch Committee's stinginess, and the result was that the men had to work on alternate rest days, thus getting only one day off in two weeks. To add to their troubles, they were also badly housed.

But the principal cause of nationwide dissatisfaction among the country's police forces was that, despite Lloyd George's previous half-hinted half-promise that he might do so, the Government had subsequently refused to recognise the National Union of Police and Prison Officers.

It was a wrong-headed decision by the authorities which was to bring in its wake strange consequences – a battleship and two destroyers racing down from Scapa Flow to drop anchor off the Pier Head ... tanks clattering noisily over the tramlines and rumbling across St George's Plateau ... soldiers with fixed bayonets appearing menacingly in the city streets ... wild mobs running crazily out of control, smashing, pillaging, burning ... and not a policeman in sight.

Those who remembered that August Bank Holiday of 1919, when these things came to pass, remembered it as the 'weekend from hell'. One man lay dead in the mortuary. More than 300 men and women were sentenced for violence, burning and looting, acres of the central city were laid to waste, and the Liverpool City Police Force was literally decimated.

It was in July 1919, that the Police Bill was published. This made membership of any trade union, including the National Union of Police and Prison Officers, an automatic disqualification for a police appointment, and members of NUPPO were given a month to resign. Instead of a union, a Police Federation was officially proposed. Only serving policemen would be able to belong to it, and it was to be completely independent of trade unions and politics.

The effect of this Bill was to outlaw the NUPPO, and at noon, on Wednesday 30 July 1919, the union executive set up an emergency meeting, at which it would have to decide either to wind up its affairs, or – in defiance of the Bill, which made it an offence punishable by two years' imprisonment – call a strike.

Constables Holliday and Smithwick were the two militant Liverpool delegates despatched to London to attend that meeting, at which, when the question of a strike was mooted, they stated unequivocally that, in the event of its being called, the Union could count on the total support of Merseyside.

The signal that set the fury that was to explode in the heart of the city ablaze, arrived in Liverpool in the form of a telegram from Jack H Hayes, a former Metropolitan Police sergeant who had risen to become General Secretary of the NUPPO. 'Strike declared. Over the top. Best of luck.' Immediately the call-out plan moved into smooth action, with the prompt hiring and deployment of taxicabs, liberally plastered with the placarded message: 'Police Strike Tonight.'

At 10pm Union officers began touring the streets in the taxis, blowing police whistles to locate constables out on the beat to inform them of the state of play. Pickets were posted at every police station. By 2am a noisy crowd of strikers had surrounded Police Headquarters at Dale Street. They were watched from his office window by Head Constable Caldwell and Alderman Maxwell.

The glad tidings that the scuffers were opting out sounded like music in the ears of a certain segment of the population of Liverpool – the poor, the needy, the downtrodden. The papers called them 'the mob'. There had, over the years, been sporadic ebullitions of mob violence. The wearing of the orange and the green, the espousal of the Pope, or King Billy, venerable old loves and hatreds living and dying hard, had led to more than a few cracked heads and gutters flowing with blood.

But what was in the wind now was different, utterly different. If the current threat of a total absence of police from the streets were to be translated into actual fact, it would give this grievously disadvantaged section of the community its opportunity for a strike of a different kind; the chance to strike back in its own way for all the horrors that poverty had inflicted upon their innocence. The empty bellies. The bare feet. The thinly, inadequately, clad bodies. The unnecessary deaths.

Dreadful to relate, it was in those days no uncommon sight to see starving children hanging about the gates of the great, riches-spinning enterprises – Bibby's and Tate & Lyle's factories – hoping that the men coming off shift and heading homewards just might have a sandwich left in their lunch boxes and some pity left in their hearts.

Things were indeed looking serious, and thoroughly worrying for the authorities. The warning was circulated to all police stations:

> Every member of the force who does not return to work immediately, or parade at his divisional office at 8pm, on this first day of August, will be dismissed.

You couldn't have it much clearer than that. No room for manoeuvre or excuse of ambiguity there.

The first day of August 1919, dawned bright and clear on Merseyside. Head Constable Caldwell, a tall, trim man, standing just short of six feet, just coming up to his 60th birthday, carrying not an inch of surplus fat on his slender, straight-backed frame, having been advised on the Thursday afternoon that the Union leaders in Liverpool were making ready for a strike, had spent the night at Police Headquarters, in Hatton Garden. It had passed quietly. But now there came the sudden sounds of blowing whistles and shouted slogans. The striking policemen had surrounded the adjacent Central Fire Station, and were trying to pull the firemen out in their support. They had no success and so joined the pickets already massed in Dale Street.

That afternoon the report came through that the Birkenhead branch of the NUPPO had met. There had been some 106 men present. The resolution was put that they should come out in support of their Liverpool and London brethren. The voting result was 64 to 42 in favour. This was not the two-thirds majority required by the branch rules.

When, however, the night shift arrived to parade at Branden Street police station, they found around a couple of hundred Liverpool strikers, who had come over on the ferry, waiting outside to greet them – and stiffen their backbones with intimidatory cheers and jeers. By the end of the night, 60 Birkenhead constables had come out on strike. Ultimately, 114 of the town's 225 policemen joined the strike, leaving Birkenhead open to the untender mercies of the resentful mob.

It did not take the good citizens long to get to work. One of the largest of the local pawnbrokers' shops was situated in Price Street. Made bitterly familiar to all by brutal economic necessity, it was, not surprisingly, a prime target. It, and the boot store next door, were stripped bare in half the time it would a swarm of locusts to clear a field of wheat.

But it was on the Liverpool side of the river that, on the Saturday night, the real mayhem occurred. As the hot summer's day turned slowly into night, the thin reserves of the remaining loyal police were quietly drafted off to what were thought to be the most likely trouble spots. Little groups were strategically placed on street corners in intentional full view of the inhabitants and of the public-houses. Elsewhere, close to the most vulnerable shops and temptatious warehouses, small garrisons of Specials took up their positions.

The defence teams of the law waited. So did the women of the slum houses. Clutching their shawls around them as the wind from the river turned the evening chilly, they waited for their menfolk to come back from the pubs. And the hordes of rag-doll-like children went on playing obliviously in the rapidly chilling streets. There was an ominous air of unity of intent pervading the whole area, which the watching police were quick to appreciate.

A prodromal. Diagnostic. A highly illegal, strictly forbidden, pitch and toss school was being openly, unashamedly, and cheerfully conducted within full sight of, and mere yards from, a local Liverpool 'nick'.

What have been logged as the very first incidents in what was to develop into a full-scale riot, were the stonings of the late-night tramcars by roaming gangs. Windows were smashed and alarmed passengers forced out on to the street. Passing carriages and cars had also been stopped – and destroyed.

From 7pm onwards there had been ominous signs in the Great Homer Street area. Groups of out-of-workers, shawlies, and a scattering of ragged children, far larger than usual, had been gathering outside the public-houses.

An hour later, the groups, augmented by drunken emergents from the pubs to form a consolidated crowd, set off on the move, like an untidy column of Browning's Hamelin Town rats, following their pie-eyed, high-piping pipers to Sandon Dock. Presently, mixed with the high-scale, raucous babel of the mob, came a duller, more rhythmic, sound, as of the thudding of axes on timber, or the thump of the descending guillotine blade, a sort of French Revolutionary shrill-dull counterpoint!

They were trying to batter down the dock gates. The attack was repulsed by the timeous arrival of a phalanx of police officers and police recruits.

There was trouble back in Great Homer Street itself. Sturla's, the big department store there, the Aladdin's cave of unaffordable luxuries, whose name was a Merseyside byword, had been set upon with a jealous vengeance. Everything, but *everything*, that was transportable had been transported; everything that was non-transportable had been wantonly destroyed. The shop's carpeting, along with the window frames, had simply vanished. The showcases, light fittings, mirrors, and dummies, had all been reduced to rubble. By the time of the vestigial police's somewhat tardy arrival, all that remained was a sea of broken glass and a desert of pulverised detritus.

The battle front switched to Scotland Road. It was a youth, never traced, never named, who set the serious rioting off by hurling a brick through the plate-glass window of Latarche's Family Jewellers' shop there. At the sound of shattering glass, people, reacting to it like packs of dogs to a Pavlovian reflex, came tumbling out of the pubs and houses, racing through the side alleys to join in the main road mob action.

The looting was soon in full swing. Silverware, watches and rings were grabbed by the gang who had staged the initial break-in. Men who had smashed their way into other shops were tossing the booty out to those who waited in the street. Women and children, pushing handcarts and battered prams, were wheeling the goodies away as fast as their wheels would spin. Tiny children could be seen struggling manfully with great, swamping sacks full of purloined groceries.

While all this was going on, the beleaguered police authorities were not idle. Volunteer citizens were being sworn in and issued with armbands, whistles, and truncheons and assistance from the military had been requested.

Violence broke out next in London Road. Apart from sweet shops and toy shops, a very special target there for the children was the Mo-Jo Chewing-

Gum factory, which was to them as the whisky warehouses were to their fathers, and the clothes shops to their mothers. Grown brazen, the rioters actually switched on the lights of the shops that they were pillaging.

As the rioting gained momentum, farce and drama, human kindness and human brutality, manifested themselves hand in hand. There were sundry unforgettable vignettes.

The man on crutches hobbling down London Road with a pair of boots in each hand, and several more suspended from his neck.

The inordinately fat-seeming old shawlie, found upon closer investigation to be wearing eight purloined pairs of corsets over her dress.

The women cheering and blowing kisses as each gift – blouses, hats, stockings, dresses, bales of cloth – were passed out to them through the shattered windows.

The impromptu mannequin parades provided by those who were either lacking in acquisitive instincts or too drunk to be bothered to indulge them, preferring to provide light entertainment by parading the pavements swathed in furs and ablaze with the sparkling of cheap jewellery.

The tiny lock-up greengrocer's shop, with the three planks which had constituted its pathetic counter, left mercilessly trashed.

The beaming looter shouting in high glee to a policeman in plain clothes whom he mistook for a brother thief:

"I've got a cash box. What've you got?"

"A baton," replied the PC, bringing it crashing down on his head.

And from over the water, the heart-warming story of the little sweet shop at the corner of Old Bidston Road and Roe Street, run by a Mrs Hughes, who had endeared herself to the children of the poverty-stricken neighbourhood by her generosity in the matter of sweeties, and to the older youths whom she would allow to have their packets of five Woodbines on credit, because they were short of the necessary tuppence. When the looting started up in Price Street, the older boys mounted guard outside her shop, and the mob, seeing the lads prepared to defend her, laughed and went good naturedly on their way leaving her shop intact, where every other was wrecked. A wonderful lesson in casting one's (sweet) breads upon the water!

Determined to show the flag, the authorities despatched a city magistrate there in an armoured car, a machine gun projecting menacingly from its turret. Extremely nervous, flanked by soldiers with fixed bayonets, he clambered up, a megaphone in his hand, to face the hostile, screaming mob. Rapidly, he read the Riot Act, commanding all present to disperse in the name of the king. Rapidly, he clambered down. Then, rapidly, under a shower of bricks and brickbats, duty done, made a grateful! escape.

His exit was followed by the entrance upon the scene of a squad of soldiers. They formed a khaki barrier across the road. Steel-helmeted, in battle order, the light from the street lamps glittering upon their wicked-pointed bayonets, the soldiers, looking intimidatingly businesslike and lethal, steadily advanced. That did it. One look was enough. Without further ado, the mob scattered, about turned – and ran.

It was unreasonable to think that a mere handful of troops could clear a street the length of London Road, with all the myriad streets leading off from either side of it, for more than a span of minutes. But those rioters who doubled back, emerging from the cover of the side streets in the wake of the advancing soldiery, expecting to carry on looting unharried, were in for a nasty shock.

Following on the boot heels of the troops, several lorries arrived to debouch their cargoes of the hated 'Jacks', burly CID detectives, trusty truncheons in hand, plus support bands of lusty young 'Specials', freshly recruited from the sporting and athletic clubs and business houses of Liverpool. Brandishing truncheons and pick handles, issued to the Specials as there were not enough truncheons to go round, these stalwarts waded into the ranks of bewildered looters, weapons of correction punitively flailing, cracking skulls and fracturing limbs.

The battle was short and bloody. *The Times* described London Road as 'The Ypres of Liverpool'. But the police sustained only two casualties, one of which was a 'home goal'. The plight of Detective Sergeant Levitt, tussling valiantly with half a dozen rioters, was observed by one of the soldiers. Anxious to rescue him, he stepped in, dealt a swingeing blow from a misdirected rifle butt … and felled Levitt.

The majority of the prisoners taken that night were carted off to Rose Hill police station. So was most of the abandoned property found on the streets. The place looked like a miniature Paddy's Market!

The night's activities were over. The now empty road shone with a glittering frost of fragments of broken glass. Its pavements were strewn with the abandoned débris of attack, the thrown bottles and stones, the staves of wood, the wrenched off doors and torn out window frames, the widespread litter of abandoned booty. As they, the late combatants, police, soldiers and bandits, limped back to their various lairs, each knew in his aching bones that this was not the peace. Only an armistice.

At first light on Sunday morning, 3 April, a sorry shambles was revealed. The church bells rang out over a scene of devastation such as Merseyside had never known before, but was to come to know all too well twenty years on, in the days of Hitler's holocaust, the Great May Blitz.

The shopkeepers were out with their brooms sweeping up the broken glass, gathering up what remnants of their stock remained, and practising mend and make do-it-yourself on such portions of their premises as seemed to prove amenable to their restorative efforts. The place was filled with the unaccustomed Sabbath sound of universal hammering, betokening the boarding up of doors and the ugly open gashes of broken windows.

Across the town, traffic was light, the pavements empty. Those rioters who were not already tucked safely up in cells, were sleeping-in. The exhausted police were snoring, too. Only the armed sentries, posted to mount guard over vulnerable premises, were keeping un-forty-winking vigil. There was, moving amid the stark landscape of the ruins, a fair sprinkling of visitants from the suburbs, come to see if things were actually as bad as rumour had reported them.

Down at the Pier Head, bills advertising bank holiday sailings to the Isle of Man had 'Cancelled' pasted across them.

By midday, the regulars had started to drift in, and the pubs were once again packed and buzzing with their normal dinner-time trade. The air in the bars was thick with boasting. The likely lads, the leading lights of last night's entertainment, were out boozing in force, and loudly recounting their piratical adventures. The city had been theirs for the taking, hadn't it? Still was. Drink flowed. Tongues loosened. As the beer in the glasses went down, the Dutch courage level went up. Why wait until darkness for a second go? They didn't need the protection of night. The scuffers were out, weren't they? Liverpool was wide open.

Loudest-mouthed among the loud, was one Cuthbert Thomas Howlett. Known to the police. A great exponent of a personally modified version of the Smilesian doctrine of self-help. A petty crook. A small-time thief. Big now with drink, bloated by last night's takings, no sooner had "Time!" been called, than he hied himself and a gang of already half-drunk cronies off to Vauxhall Road, where they opened up O'Brien's Bottling Store, before cracking Burke's Bonded Warehouse, in Love Lane, and setting its whisky flowing.

Suddenly, the ransackers saw, through the spiritous vapours, the disturbing vision of two lorry loads of soldiers materialise. Howlett, tooled up with a wicked claw hammer, drunk and fighting mad, started aiming killer blows at the nearest soldiers. It was at this juncture that the troops began firing their rifles into the air. A stray .303 from the Lee-Enfield of Lance Corporal Seymour, 3rd Battalion, Sherwood Foresters, hit Howlett.

The party was over now. "Time!" had been finally called.

The silenced crowd watched as he was carried away to the Northern Hospital, where, 12 hours later, he died. He was the sole fatal casualty of the entire April uprising.

The town was swept by the rumour – just possibly bruited abroad by the authorities bent on the recovery of stolen property – that thousands more troops were on their way to carry out a house-to-house search, that Martial Law was in force, and that anyone who was discovered to have been looting was liable to be shot. The result was that the jiggers behind the rows of houses were suddenly found to be jam-packed, the gutters overflowing, with foodstuffs, clothing, shoes, carpets, mattresses, and even brand-new suites of furniture – discarded booty.

Sunday evening was reported as 'oppressive, unhealthily sticky', and it was said that: 'The half-hearted breeze from the Mersey had collapsed in the city's dust.'

When darkness fell, battle was again joined. To the north, Scotland Road had begun to boil. To the east, London Road was already boiling. And that Sunday night's fighting was to surpass anything that had gone before.

The soldiers wasted no time. The instant the stone-throwing and the looting started up again in London Road, they went into action with their rifle butts, clearing a way, sparing no quarter. Men and women fell like ninepins. The military was stoutly supported by a solid line of police officers, who had marched up from Dale Street, and who used their truncheons with subduing ferocity.

Meanwhile, with every available police body up in London Road dealing with the fresh outbreak of trouble, the mob down in Scotland Road was enjoying an unsupervised orgy of destructive revelry.

Labour Exchange premises were very special targets of mob fury, where every effort was made to settle old grudges by the destruction of all the records – but particularly their own!

Crane's music shop had been attacked. The roadway was strewn with musical instruments of all kinds. Piano stools and pianos had been dragged out to be wantonly reduced to splintered timber and twisted metal. When the forces of law and order arrived, having regrouped after their gory victory in London Road, a Hogarthian scene met their eyes. A single grand piano had been preserved intact. It stood by the kerbside. A seated figure was punching out on it the latest ragtime hits, and in the darkness, coloured red along the edges by the reflected light of crazily-lit bonfires, a host of drunken figures flitted and pranced, while other Hieronymus Bosch-style men and women beat time with mugs, bottles and fists, egging the dancing dervishes and the demon pianist on.

Now came the rain, to save the day. It rained … and rained … and rained… The lancing spears of the continuous downpour helping to quench the smouldering embers of the mutinous fire, and chasing the drenched mutineers off home to bed. It ended up a washout, literally. It was after 3am.

Sunday night brought its quota of vignettes.

A group of children sitting on the kerb outside a ravaged shoe shop, breaking open cases of shoes, frowning with concentration as they try to match the shoes to their feet.

The suddenly terror-stricken faces of a gang of looters who, having broken through the door of a jeweller's shop, are confronted by the woman proprietor, who has appeared at the top of the stairs and is blasting away at them with a revolver.

The frustrated mob whirling and dancing around the bonfire blaze they had made of stacked items, looted from a furniture store that they had set alight, in their anger at finding them too heavy to carry away.

A post-Sunday-night vignette is that of the rioter who, a few days later, appeared in court charged with stealing jewelry from a looted shop. He asked for bail on the grounds that he had a bayonet wound in his back. Enquired Mr Stuart Deacon, the stipendiary magistrate:

"You mean you're a wounded ex-soldier?"

"No, your honour, I was wounded in London Road."

Another prisoner, vehemently aggrieved, pleaded not guilty.

"How can I have stolen a pair of shoes," he demanded, "when they were both left feet?"

The legal nicety was obviously lost on Mr Deacon, who sent him down for three months.

Bank holiday Monday. Came the dawn. Dismal with drizzle, in typical bank holiday weather fashion. Things were quiet, but at the Corn Exchange, Head Constable Caldwell, addressing a meeting of worried businessmen, was stressing the need to remain alert for days ahead. Liverpool had become a war zone in peacetime. He did, however, also underline how unexpectedly well the authorities had done in managing to keep the trouble confined to one particular part of the city. There could be no denying that it had certainly been in many respects a close shave. In streets that were only a penny tram ride from home, it had needed just one angry finger on a trigger, one bayonet thrust an inch too deeply, and the powder keg city could have exploded.

Liverpool had, indeed, looked out beyond its boundaries in its hour of need. Help had been sought, and supplied. The military had despatched reinforcements – garrisons of the Sherwood Foresters, the Notts and Derby Regiment, the Leicesters, the Royal Welch Fusiliers and a force of Hussars from York, whose cavalry horses, unused to the stone setts of the Liverpool streets had been unable to cope with them, and the city's mounted police had had to lend the troops their habituated steeds. Rough and ready billets for the incoming troops had been found in such unlikely locations as St George's Hall and the Rotunda Theatre, up Scotland Road.

A bonus was the provision by the Army of four tanks. Rattling noisily over the tramlines and rumbling majestically up the steep slope of William Brown Street, with its impressive dressing of fine public buildings, solid monuments to Liverpool's fully justified civic pride, to St George's Plateau, where they came to rest on their massive haunches, hulls bristling with hardware, they were a sight to refurbish confidence in the bosoms of restive city men, whose clerks had remained in their offices and counting-houses throughout the emergency, sleeping with loaded guns beside their pillows.

In the Mersey, the two destroyers – *Venemous* and *Whitley* – which had arrived in the early hours, were riding the river alongside the landing-stage, and later in the morning the vast grey silhouette of the battleship *Valiant* was to emerge from the rain haze, nose her way up, and drop anchor in mid-stream.

Tuesday (5th) and Wednesday (6th) saw the odd skirmish, but to all intents and purposes the riot was over.

More than 300 prisoners had been sentenced. One man lay dead in the mortuary. Liverpool City Council was faced with an eventual bill of £122,000 for riot damages alone, to say nothing of costs incurred by the military and naval assistance. Every last one of the policemen who had struck in violation of their oath of fealty had been dismissed from the force.

When something is written superlatively, it is not only pointless, but also stupid, to attempt to rewrite or paraphrase it. That is why I propose to quote in full a passage from AV Sellwood's *Police Strike – 1919*.

> In Liverpool's Rose Hill police station, as in practically every other police station in the city's thirty-three mile circumference, a shapeless mound of discarded dark blue uniforms and helmets was growing larger every hour. Several of the cast-off tunics carried the bright splash of medal ribbons above their left breast pockets: Long Service; Good Conduct; Personal Gallantry. There were other ribbons, too, on the breasts of the uniforms, mementoes of times when the men, so recently dismissed as 'mutineers', had been hailed as heroes for services performed in scarlet and khaki in the Empire's cause. In the War in the Sudan, the War in South Africa, the War in Europe, only recently concluded, Liverpool policemen had extended the horizon of their beats to the Himalayan passes and the veldt of the Transvaal. But now, like the careers and livelihood of those who had proudly worn them, tunics and ribbons lay ingloriously in the dust.

So that was it. For the younger men it was a bitter blow, but not a knockout one. After a few months they would find other jobs in other spheres. But many of the veterans of the force had received their final dismissal. Older men, after a long and harsh career, pathetically in sight of the hard-won reward of a comfortably provided for retirement that would never now be theirs; ageing men, many of whom would never work again. Even though they had, it might be said, brought it upon themselves, it was a cruel prospect, a great Liverpool sadness, that so many who had given so much were, because of a few blind hours of folly, destined to end their days in an unrelenting winter of discontent.

The Anatomy Museum in Paradise Street

In Liverpool's Victorian heyday, the city boasted an attraction which, from the time of its establishment in the 1850s, enjoyed considerable popularity. It was the Liverpool Museum of Anatomy, housed, aptly and happily optimistically, since it dealt with grave issues of life and death, in Paradise Street.

In attenuated form, and in another location, this gruesome exhibition of the ills to which frail human flesh is heir, was, as we shall see, to linger on to instruct and inspire a gentleman of the name of Peter Sutcliffe, aka the Yorkshire Ripper, Victorian Jack's lineal descendant, in the refinements of the dissecting knifeman's art of the unpicking at the seams of his female fellow-mortals.

To begin, as Dylan Thomas was wont to say, at the beginning ...

There was born in Halifax, in the year 1816, a young Yorkshireman named Joseph Thornton Woodhead. Having reached that point in his childhood at which in those halcyon days he was considered ripe to be put out to work, he was bound apprentice to a cabinet-maker. Some years thereafter, discovering himself to be of a roving disposition, and discovering also the opportunity to indulge that disposition, the lad set off for Dresden, which is where he found instruction and ultimate proficiency in the difficult art of wax modelling.

This new-found talent he set to excellent use in the making of anatomical models of the sort for which the museums and anatomical galleries of the Continent were justly famous.

Before he had reached the age of 26, he had returned home to Halifax, bringing with him a goodly harvest of his ceraceous creations, married a fine Yorkshire lass, and fathered a daughter, Margaret.

He and his little family subsequently crossed over to America, where they made a reasonable living with a travelling exhibition of anatomical wax models and drawings.

All seems to have gone well until, in 1850, the Woodheads reached New York, whence they were driven out by an angry puritan element of the citizenry, who misconstrued their display of warnings against, and the consequences of, sexual slapdashery, as wanton obscenity. Obliged to decamp posthaste, the demoralised Woodheads fled, via Dublin, to Liverpool.

When they got off the boat at Liverpool, Joseph hired a four-wheeler hackney to transport him, his family, and his waxen treasures into the centre of the town. It was as they were rounding the corner into Lime Street, that a most unfortunate accident occurred. Such was the weight within, that the floor of the carriage suddenly gave way, depositing some 750 models of organs of the human body, in health and disease, in the roadway.

With the fabled luck of the pox doctor's clerk, Woodhead, when he had succeeded in extricating himself and his loved ones from the shambles, espied, standing just across the street from the disaster spot, beckoningly vacant, what he conceived to be the very building for which he had been looking. Scooping up his scattered and repugnant artefacts, there it was that he settled himself in, and set up the first Liverpool Museum of Anatomy, transferring it to 29 Paradise Street, in the heart of Sailortown, some years later.

After the death of Joseph Woodhead, the museum continued under the auspices of his son-in-law, who survived until 1932. It then passed into the custodianship of a Mr Henry A Holmes. In 1937, the museum finally closed its doors, much to the relief of the Liverpool City Fathers, who in their petty way had always regarded it as an embarrassment to their fair town.

The exhibits were then purchased *en masse* by Louis Tussaud, and put on show, curtained off, on the upper floor of his waxworks exhibition on the seafront at Blackpool.

I myself remember it well, having paid regular visits to the place as a boy, and, indeed, in my medical student days. Beside the seaside, the Museum of Anatomy was, I recall, treated with a tremendous sort of pseudo-reverence, allied to a stealthy prurience. The goggle-eyed holidaymakers who drifted furtively in were strictly segregated as to gender. Adults only were admitted to the far side of the curtain tantalisingly masking the entrance to the anatomical gallery, in alternating males only, and females only, sessions, each lasting about ten minutes, and its termination signified by the ringing of a bell. All this hocus-pocus was, of course, cunningly contrived to accentuate the mystery and exclusivity of that which lay guarded and hidden behind the curtain, which only a proffered extra sixpence could rent.

With its 'Upwards of 750 Models and Diagrams Procured at the Anatomical Galleries of Paris, Florence and Munich', the Museum of Anatomy's original, and continuing, purpose was cautionary; to warn the, principally working-class, visitor, as it had warned the seafaring men of the port of Liverpool in the old days, against the evils of sexual profligacy, and to display to him – and her – the grammar and 'sin tax' of anti-social diseases.

It was designed to disabuse the self-abuser, illustrating with a loose-lipped, crazy-eyed, waxen head of an aged, degenerated, habitual onanist, the wages of solitary vice; and to put a curb upon the libertine by presenting to him – or, again, her – realistic models of the corporal cost of non-solitary peccancy.

In the area of normalcy, there was the wall of torsos – female, headless, limbless – scooped open, inferior ventrally, to expose the fœtus in the 'Nine

Stages of Pregnancy'.

It must be admitted that as the dancing-dust-moted sunbeams struck in through the frosted glass, there was an overall freakish ethos of two-headed dogs, six-legged lambs, Siamese-twin cats and like *lusus naturæ*. The ultimate teratoid was the life-sized effigy of Thomas Lane, a young man of Sherborne, in Dorset, who died and was found, *post mortem*, to have developed within him the fœtus of a child of six or seven months' growth.

'This model,' a notice pridefully informed, 'is Protected by Act of Parliament.'

Another well-remembered life-sized model was that of a young woman of Victorian days, laid out fully clothed in her coffin. A Gothic-scripted label related that she had died as a result of the pernicious fashion fad of tight-lacing, said to be the cause of chlorosis.

Not far away, always a source of great fascination to visitors, was the full-length Florentine model of Louise Lateau, the young Belgian Roman Catholic girl who exhibited the extraordinary phenomena of ecstatic fits or trances accompanied by the stigmata, which is to say the marks of the wounds displayed on the body of the crucified Christ. Blood would flow, it is said, from the holes in her hands and feet, from her left side, between the fifth and sixth ribs, where the Roman soldier's spear penetrated, and a sweat of blood appeared on her head, where Christ had worn his crown of thorns.

I would never have believed that there could have survived two such wondrous anatomical *reliquiæ diluvianæ*, but Gordon Burn in his most excellent study of the case of Peter Sutcliffe, *Somebody's Husband, Somebody's Son*, describes Sutcliffe's gloating pilgrimages to savour sadistically the anatomical horrors on view in a waxworks at Morecambe. What was once the old Whitehall Theatre, on the seafront at the west end of the town, had been converted in 1956 into the waxworks premises of Mr George Nicholson, late of Tussaud's, Blackpool. And here was to be found, albeit a substantially diminished, but still satisfactorily horrific, version of the Liverpool Museum of Anatomy.

Around the mid-1970s, Sutcliffe was employed driving wagons to and from Wales and Scotland, regularly passing along the M6, and Morecambe was barely more than a ten minutes' turn-off from the motorway at Lancaster. It would have been the easiest thing in the world for him to enjoy a recreational interlude at Nicholson's Waxworks, skipping, eager with anticipation, up the steep wooden staircase, and along the waxen dummy-cluttered upper gallery to where the sign warning that the sights beyond were not suitable to be beheld by anyone under the age of 16, extended its delicious promise.

Burns' brilliant evocation of what he believes to have been the Yorkshire Ripper's anatomical Mecca does sound uncommonly like my Blackpudlian Nirvana:

Two rather small, dimly lighted and musty chambers ... Time, however has eroded definition and basted the developing fœtuses and the glistening ropes of internal organs to a uniform ox-blood colour. ... Their antiquity is highlighted by the paleness of the simulated flesh and the freshness of the butcher's muslin which provides a 'bed' for the bodies and is neatly tucked and trimmed to just above the bare breasts and just below the pubic area.

But it seemed passing strange that something so unquestionably unique as the collection that had formed the Paradise Street Museum of Anatomy, and that had then been indubitably transferred to Blackpool, could also be on show in Morecambe.

According to Gordon Burn, Mr Nicholson acquired his anatomical exhibits in the 1970s, 'from a friend and associate of many years, recently bowed out of the world of wax'. Was that unnamed friend perhaps Louis Tussaud?

A possible resolution of the locus perplexment emerges from a piece contributed by a Mr Des McKenna, of Liverpool, to the June 1997 issue of the *Ripperologist*, a journal devoted to the study of Jack the Ripper.

McKenna writes:

In 1951 I worked in what had once been a workhouse in Liverpool: the old Kirkdale Homes. Its name had been changed to Westminster House and its purpose to that of an infirmary for the aged, confused and dying. The division in which I worked was devoted to the acutely chronic senile dementia sufferers and the GPs (those suffering from General Paralysis of the insane – the third and last stage of syphilis). Sometimes the nurses would mention the old Museum of Anatomy, which was the first mention I heard of this place. A place displaying waxworks of diseased genitalia ... and other disgusting sights.

Sometime later when I had finished working in that ghastly hospital, I was working as a traveller for a confectionery manufacturer, and having some spare time when I was in Blackpool I wandered into Louis Tussaud's waxworks. I went into their Museum of Anatomy, and remembering what had been told to me by the older nurses at the Kirkdale Homes, I wondered if this had any kinship with the now defunct Liverpool Museum of Anatomy.

Mr McKenna resolved to find out what he could about the museum, and by diligent research, uncovered the whole story of Joseph Thornton Woodhead and the foundation and history of the collection. He is able to tell us that:

> A man named Nicholson bought [the collection] from Tussaud, took [it] to Morecambe, and opened up an exhibition there. Once again the town was appalled at this disgusting exhibition and wanted it closed and he had to hide the artefacts behind an amusement arcade. I last saw some of them about ten years ago but now they are gone.
> I spent the winter of 1982-3 wondering if this dreadful thing, and the man that created it, could have been even more obscene than it appears to have been, and could that ancient whisper that I heard all those years ago have connected Jack the Ripper to Liverpool? Could it just possibly be that someone to do with the Museum of Anatomy could have been Jack?

I do not really think so, but it is a nice conceit that, nearly a hundred years earlier than Sutcliffe, the veritable Jack may at least have made his club-footed way to Liverpool and stood among the transfixed sailors in the obscure building in Paradise Street staring at the lurid images of dirt and disease. And, filled with loathing for the prostitutes and loose-living women who, as he saw it, were responsible for the wreaking of such terrible fleshly havoc, returned to London to embark upon his saturnalia of destruction, exposing the private parts of public women of the streets, and mutilating them in a way which gives a whole new meaning to the term 'body language'.

THE WASHINGTON BELLE

Considerably more than once upon a long-ago time, making a periodic episcopal visit to my old see, I would put up at my good friend Jim Montgomery's venerable hostelry, the Washington Hotel, which had stood for nigh on a hundred years in Lime Street, on the spot where that spanking new young upstart, the St George's Hotel, now raises its regimented glass eyes to the Liverpool sky.

Among the ghosts – living and dead – who haunted the mahogany and frosted glass bar of the old Washington, was that of a buxom Irish colleen by the name of Kitty Flynn. At 15 years of age, turning her even then shapely back upon the Dublin poverty into which by the inscrutable workings of the will of her Catholic God she had been born, Catherine Louisa Flynn, to accord her the dignity and style of her full and proper title, had taken the steamer across the sea to Liverpool, bearing her on the first stage of her ambitious determination to court her chosen trinity – fame, fortune and respectability.

The auspices, in the form of her thick blonde hair, bright-gleaming, merry eye, and enticing display of dimples, were unquestionably good. And, sure enough, by the time she was 17, grown pleasingly plump and eye-catchingly vivacious, she was a universal favourite, presiding coquettishly over the bar at the Washington.

It was in January 1870, that opportunity came swaggering through the hotel door in the guise of two wealthy American businessmen who promptly took the two best rooms in the place, which, they announced, they would be occupying indefinitely, as they planned a no expenses spared, open-ended business trip to the Old World.

The sharp as a tack Kitty, assaying appreciatively their height of fashion best broadcloth frock-coats, silk cravats, pearl tie-pins, gold watch chains, finest beavers, dandiacal silver-topped canes, and indiscreet encrustation of high carat diamonds, swiftly made up her mind that these two Yankee swells – Mr Henry J Raymond, merchant banker, and Mr Charles H Wells, Texan businessman – sent by a repentant Almighty, were just what she had been looking for; if not precisely knights in shining armour, at least alien gentlemen with money to burn, which would do just as well, thank you. What Kitty did not know was that these two superlatively smooth operators were in reality a pair of top-flight international professional criminals – real names, Adam Worth and Charles W Bullard.

Adam, born Werth or Wirth, at some unrecorded location in Eastern Germany in 1844, had been just five years old when his German Jewish parents emigrated to the United States. The family went to live in the town of Cambridge, Massachusetts, where his father set up shop as a tailor. Like a duckling to water, Adam Worth took to crime at an early age. By 1870, he had a tally of criminous triumphs behind him – bank robberies, safe-breaking and the like – that were fully to justify the title of 'The Napoleon of Crime', later bestowed upon him by Robert Anderson, Assistant Commissioner (Crime), at Scotland Yard. While, in similar tribute, on his native side of the 'duck pond', the head of the great American private detective agency, Pinkerton's, dubbed him, with grudging admiration, 'the outstanding criminal of the Victorian Age'. And Conan Doyle immortalised him, under the guise of Professor James Moriarty, the grand master of a criminal organisation that controlled much of Britain's underworld and extended its influence to the Continent, and the one man of whom Sherlock Holmes could never get the better.

Worth's close friend and partner in crime, Charles W Bullard, was of a very different vintage. Hailing from an old and wealthy New York family, he had drifted, a real-life Raffles, into brigandry after his record high-speed dissipation of the fortune left to him by his father. The contrast between the two men was marked. Where Worth was slight – 5ft 7in tall and never weighing more than 9st 4lbs – with a sad, almost melancholy, face, large luminous eyes, thick black hair, luxuriant sideburns and bushy eyebrows, and undeniably on the plain side, Bullard, tall, with a thin, rather aloof, aristocratic face, thick curly hair and sideburns, was a decidedly handsome man. He was, moreover, well educated, speaking French and Italian fluently. Whereas Worth, although highly intelligent, versatile and inventive, had had precious little schooling. Another card up Bullard's elegant sleeve was the fact that he was an exceedingly accomplished musician. Indeed, his underworld reputation for virtuosity on the 'old Joanna' was such that he was universally known as Charley 'Piano' Bullard.

In larcenous partnership, the pair had, in 1869, descended upon Boston, focusing covetous eyes on the contents of the vault of the Boylston Bank. Bullard, having rented the next door premises, they promptly set to cautious work cutting a hole in the side wall. On Saturday 20 November, they broke through, and proceeded to remove cash and securities to the tune of $450,000 from the rifled vault. It was with this plunder plumping up their wallets that the successful bank robbers, fleeing, at Bullard's suggestion, from America to Europe, had arrived under false names in Liverpool.

Both were fascinated by Kitty. Both sought sedulously to capture her affection. Both bore her away to expensive candlelit dinners innumerable. There followed a month or so of serious besiegement by these two so diverse suitors. Worth was almost teetotal. Bullard was drink orientated, and tended to lugubriosity. While Adam tried to impress Kitty with his probity and the prospect of his being a more solid matrimonial investment, Charley relied on charm and light-hearted pianoforte serenading. It was Bullard, calling himself Charles Henry Wells, who carried off the prize. His unrelenting day and night courtship, with its unflagging additional provision of – as well as a succession of superb late suppers – flowers and rides in a trap did the trick.

The wedding took place on 22 February 1870, at St Francis Xavier's Church, Everton. Henry J Raymond, a worthy loser, was Wells' best man. The reception was held at the Washington Hotel, in a room filled with flowers and overflowing with guests. The guests danced and drank champagne until the early hours. Legend has it that the city's famous fishmongers, with their large bare feet and foghorn voices, stood outside and bellowed their congratulations to Kitty, who was one of their favourites.

Worth was surprisingly unbitter about his defeat in the matrimonial stakes. As it turned out, he had every reason for equanimity, for Kitty, with admirable generosity of spirit, seems to have been perfectly happy to divide her favours between them. She always reserved for Adam a place in her heart – and her bed. An unconventional arrangement, but it apparently worked out, unmarred by any jealousies. That Bullard accepted this situation may in part be accounted for by the circumstance that, unbeknown to Kitty, he already had a wife and two children alive and well in America.

Feast consumed, speeches made, toasts drunk, the wedding festivities having reached their bibulous apogee, Mr and Mrs Charles H Wells were, to a tumultuous send off of cheerings, congratulations and confetti, driven away in a splendid coach and four to spend a short honeymoon – their *viaggio di nozze*, as the romantic Italians call it – in Paris.

Left behind, bored and alone and missing Kitty, Worth improved the shining hour by meticulously planning and faultlessly executing a successful robbery of a large pawnbroker's shop, which netted him an estimated £25,000's worth of jewellery, and caused a considerable sensation in Liverpool. Clasping his booty close to his bosom, he then bade a triumphal farewell to the city and embarked, via London, for Paris. There, he found Charles and Kitty comfortably ensconced in a luxurious house across the street from the apartments occupied by the *ci-devant* Queen Isabella of Spain, whose daily outings in her magnificent carriage, drawn by four white-plumed horses, was a sight that never failed to fascinate Kitty.

A variant account of the life of Adam Worth has Charley and Kitty returning to Liverpool after their Parisian honeymoon and remaining there until the end of 1870, when the trio packed up their belongings, checked out of the Washington Hotel, and, after dawdling in London and southern England, awaiting the outcome of the Franco-Prussian War and the cessation of the bloody events that were being enacted during the siege of Paris, eventually crossed the Channel at the end of June 1871.

Both accounts agree, however, that, in 1871, Bullard and Worth invested the proceeds of previous crimes in the purchase of a large building at 2 rue Scribe. This was to become the American Bar. The place was sumptuously fitted out at a cost of around $75,000. Enormous wall mirrors, gigantic crystal chandeliers, impressive oil-paintings, rich mahogany furniture, and the most expensive glassware, were imported. Also imported were bartenders from the United States, expert mixers of exotic cocktails and other American drinks, which were at that time unknown in Europe. The restaurant catering arrangements were put into the hands of a superb and vastly expensive master chef.

On the first floor was established what was in effect a club-room for both resident and visiting Americans; a place where they could relax in comfort, reading the latest editions of American newspapers and current issues of magazines, which were regularly provided, and where there was a series of pigeon-holes from which visitors and expatriots could pick up their mail.

The upper floor had been transformed into a fully equipped, top quality, illegal, gaming den, complete with specially engaged American croupiers and baccarat experts. It was to become famous as the place where you could find the finest game of faro in all Europe.

The totality represented what was the first American night club to be opened in Paris. And Kitty, outstandingly beautiful, dressed always in the height of fashion, an exceptionally good conversationalist gifted in the mouth with the Irish gab, but her give-away Irish brogue now miraculously evaporated, and possessed of a wonderfully engaging manner, was the ideal hostess – and, gorgeous in silk and ringlets, was for many, the main attraction.

Worth also bought a yacht, which, with Kitty breaking a bottle of vintage champagne against its bows, was named in her honour the *Shamrock*. Its image is preserved in an old woodcut showing it as a large vessel with one stack, steaming gallantly along, pennants stiff in the wind. Furnished with the usual Worthian lavishness, it boasted, as well as a bar and well-appointed dining-room, a gaming room that lacked no gambling facility. *Shamrock* was serviced by a captain and crew of 24, and Worth took his piratical band of international villains and their ladies on cruises which provided opportunities for the reconnoitring of banks, jewellery exchanges, business premises, and other likely heist targets in each port of call. The 110-foot vessel was subsequently sold to Lord Lonsdale.

Ashore for three years, Kitty revelled in a Parisian life that was a round of champagne parties, balls, and regular spells of *de luxe* foreign travellings. The American Bar prospered mightily, until the *gendarmerie*, despite a previous canny buying-off by Bullard and Worth, were forced, coming under combined pressure emanating from Inspector John Shore, of Scotland Yard, and William Pinkerton, to close the premises down. Bullard, the nominal owner, was arrested and charged with maintaining a gambling house. He skipped bail and headed back to London. Worth and Kitty were left to salvage what they could. She packed up as many of the Bar's expensive appurtenances – chandeliers, oil-paintings, brass fittings, mirrors and so forth – as she could, and then she and Worth sailed for England, and joined her husband.

The year was 1875, and it was now, in pursuit of his persistent dream of becoming 'a worthy gentleman of London', that Adam Worth took West Lodge, a large mansion, standing well back out of view of the too curious in its own grounds at the western corner of Clapham Common, where Kitty and Charley joined him. The sad truth is that Bullard was no longer the dapper, dashing, happy-go-lucky figure for whom Kitty had fallen in the old Washington Hotel days. Now, he would vanish for long periods, losing himself in the purlieus of London's seamiest and most vicious quarters. From these sorties he would return hung-over, filled with morbid guilt and remorse. Morose and depressed, he would sit for hours on end at the piano playing, not the cheery tunes with which he used to charm Kitty, but dreary, dirge-like cacophonies.

To compound the unacceptability of his degenerative metamorphosis, Kitty had learned of his pre-existing marriage and children. She was furious. As the religiously maniacal placard-carriers in the streets colourfully phrase it, so far as her marriage was concerned, the end was nigh. She upped and left Charley and England. Taking with her her two daughters – Lucy Adeline, who had been born in October 1870, and Catherine Louise, born in 1877 – both of whom were almost certainly the fruit of Worth's loins, she boarded ship for New York.

She also took across the Atlantic with her a hefty cargo of the aforesaid costly appurtenances, which she had prudently rescued from the wreckage of the American Bar. These she sold. And to top up her coffers, she pawned several consignments of the expensive jewellery lavished upon her over the years by the continuingly infatuated Worth. The resultant monies made it possible for her to despatch the girls to expensive schools and, calling herself the widow Flynn, to open a boarding-house for fashionable gentlemen.

Worth begged her to return to London and marry him. She declined. She remained very fond of him all her life, and he, to the end of his days, went on wistfully loving the winsome colleen of the Washington Hotel.

Meanwhile, Bullard, who had also returned to his native land, was becoming progressively more and more dissipated. The speed with which for years the musical felon had been heading off the rails and going downhill seems to have been accelerating dramatically. A reckless alcoholic, he fell into the hands of the police, and finally wound up in the Concord, Massachusetts, State Penitentiary, having been retrospectively tried and sentenced to twenty years for his part in the Boylston Bank robbery of 1869.

On 13 (Lucky for some) September 1878, he succeeded in escaping from prison in Concord, and fled, via New York, to Toronto. There, he was reduced to petty pilfering, and, tragically, the man who once upon a time was said to have pianist's fingers so sensitive that he could open a combination safe with his hands alone, now stricken with the shakes made so clumsy a fist of trying to shoplift a watch chain in a jewellery store, that he was arrested and given five years. He was serving his time in the Canadian Penitentiary at Kingston when, in the winter of 1880, he received the news that Kitty had divorced him.

Released, Bullard teamed up with a villain named Max Shinburn, the self-styled Baron Schindle. They planned to raid the Provincial Bank, at Verviers, in Belgium, but were caught at the 'casing' stage. Tried at Liège, Bullard was, on 21 February 1884, sentenced to twelve years' hard labour. In 1892, eight years into his sentence, poor, life-battered Charley Bullard died. At the end, there was, in the crumpled figure with straggling beard and staring eyes caged in Liège gaol, pitifully little remaining of the bright, charming, ivories-tinkling young swell, who, twenty-two years before, had triumphantly carried off the laughing Kitty.

For Mrs Kate Flynn the weather glass was rising. Her boarding-house (cum-bordello, according to some), was ticking over extremely profitably, and a new man, this time a *real* millionaire, was being borne on wings of chance into her ambit.

History fails to record precisely where it was that Juan Pedro Terry, darkly handsome, with startling blue eyes inherited from his Irish father, bearded like the pard, or a conquistador of old, heir to one of Cuba's largest sugar fortunes, first sauntered elegantly into the 28-year-old Kitty's life. But the mutual attraction was immediate. She seized him from beneath the twitching nostrils of the many high-bridge-nosed society matrons who had set their lorgnettes on this prize for their daughters.

They were married in the spring of 1881. The service was a civil one performed by Judge Morgan – some say Judge Parker – at Jefferson Market Court, in New York. Juan moved his bride into luxurious apartments in Stuyvesant House, Manhattan. The marriage was an exceedingly happy one, and Kitty was absolutely distraught when, suddenly and inexplicably, on 17 October 1886, while on a trip to Menton, Juan Pedro died, leaving her seven months pregnant. He left her also a wealthy woman. The gangster's moll had been transmogrified into one of the richest women in New York high society. In these later years she insisted, with all the passionate conviction of truth-speaking that characterises Irish lying, that she had never realised that her husband and his close friend were notorious criminals. Two months after Juan's death, Kitty gave birth to his daughter, Juanita Teresa, in Paris.

Juan left a fortune of $6,000,000. Kitty received $1,200,000. The rest was to be invested in securities from which she would derive the income until Juanita came of age. The 21-year-old girl would then inherit it all.

As soon as she felt that the baby was old enough to travel, Kitty headed back to New York with Juanita. She settled into a mansion at 102 West 74th Street, where she lived in considerable splendour. In the course of the six years of life left to her, Mrs Kitty Louise Flynn Bullard Terry was to establish herself as a gracious Grande Dame, a noted and notable pillar of New York Society, a sought-after guest at the city's social functions, a byword for her charitable works and gifts to charity.

Kitty died of Bright's disease on 13 March 1894, in her New York home. She was forty-one. But in the words of the New York Herald, 'She had lived enough history to make most women old before their youth', and yet she had remained eternally young.

She was laid to rest in the Terry family mausoleum, in Green-Wood Cemetery, Brooklyn, the most exclusive graveyard in New York, with its fine prospect across the harbour to the Manhattan skyline.

Kitty, the girl who had 'chaffed with seamen in Liverpool', married a bank robber, and 'danced with shysters and crooks in Paris', the girl from the Dublin slums, had, in the end, achieved all those things to which she had aspired. She would, with all the down-to-the-grave's edge snobbery of the Irish, have been delighted by her final quarters in this highfalutin' New World dormitory of the distinguished dead, which included among those who slumbered near her there, Henry J Raymond, founder of the *New York Times*, whose good name Adam Worth had stolen, and her reception into eternity with full earthly panoply.

When her will was examined, it transpired that all she had left of personal money was $5,000. She had managed to spend more than $1,000,000 in less than eight years. She died almost as poor as when she started out.

Adam Worth, loving her to the bitter end, survived her by eight years, dying on 2 January 1902, in his apartment in Regent's Park, as the early winter darkness closed over the London that he also loved.

THE LIVERPOOL DYNAMITARDS

I never knew the roarin' bhoy, Brendan Behan, but I used to drink with his brother, Dominic, in the Irish pub in the Edgware Road. Brendan was to achieve wide distinction as a playwright before staggering to a Dylan Thomasesque end, drowning in drink at the age of 41, in 1964.

Always himself the 'quare fella', Brendan had stepped off the Dublin boat at the Pier Head, in 1939, a sixteen-and-a-half-year-old with his 'conjuring box' of tricks, his private bombing set, intent upon following in the footsteps of the historic dynamiteers, who, for decades, had been coming across the sea from Ireland, terrorists determined to blast the auld enemy into submission, to force the Strangers to get out and leave Ireland for the Irish.

It was never the custom of the genuine dynamitards to bring the 'stuff' over with them in their baggage. The explosive material would be supplied in England, and the bombs assembled there.

To the Liverpool detectives who arrested him, young Behan boasted:

> I have been sent over to take the places of Chris Connelly, Nicky Lynch, and the others who have been arrested. I was to reorganise further operations in Liverpool. I intended to put bombs in big stores, Lewis and Hughes, I think they call it. I was making up some to put in letter-boxes tonight. I would have put one in Cammell Laird's shipyard if I had the chance.

It was moonshine, all moonshine. The Irish mouth running away with him. But it still landed him in Walton Gaol. And on Ash Wednesday, 8 February 1940, up at Liverpool Assizes in front of Mr Justice Hallett, he was sentenced to spend the next three years as a Borstal boy.

The Irish Trouble had been going on long before Behan's brief appearance on the scene. It was, in fact, exactly 59 years before that the first Dynamitards had menaced Liverpool. That was in 1881, and, interestingly enough, the very year that Patrick Ford, the notorious Fenian editor of the *Irish News*, published in New York, had chosen to make public the history of his 'Skirmishing Fund', which had been initiated in 1875. Its object was to underwrite fiscally the project of laying the big cities of England in ashes. The first Secretary to the fund was the equally notorious Fenian, Jeremiah O'Donovan Rossa. The Irish-American Dynamite War on Victorian Britain was to become a very serious and costly affair.

In 1881 there was living in Liverpool, a 27-year-old man calling himself Robert William Barton. His real name was James McGrath, and he had been born in Glasgow, of Irish parents. He had also lived in Dundee for some time, and had found work as a steward on a ship plying between Scotland and London. He subsequently emigrated to America, where he lived at first in New Orleans, and then moved on to New York. He is believed to have come under the influence there of O'Donovan Rossa, joined the team of bombers known as Rossa's Skirmishers, and received instructions to mount a series of attacks in the north of England.

McGrath had duly arrived in Liverpool. Acting on orders, he contacted James McKevitt, at 11 Naylor Street, off Vauxhall Road. McKevitt, 32 years old, born in Warrenpoint, County Down, had worked at the Liverpool Docks since 1870. A regular recipient of Rossa's *United Irishman* newspaper, still freely circulating in England, if not in Ireland itself, he was a 'sleeper'. Posing as a cattle dealer, McGrath moved in on 15 April, to share lodgings with McKevitt.

The target selected for their first terrorist joint-operation was Liverpool's main police station, in Dale Street. Considering itself, with every reason, to be, as the main port of entry from America at that time, the most vulnerable city in the kingdom, Liverpool was keeping its public buildings under close surveillance. Already, in the January of 1881, Manchester's Salford Barracks, and then, in March, the Mansion House, in London, had been attacked by Irish bombers.

As McGrath and McKevitt well knew, no building in the city would be better guarded than the Dale Street bridewell, and this they saw as a challenge. After carrying out a series of careful observations, they decided that their best chance lay in planting their explosive device in the vestibule inside the doorway of the police section house, attached to the main building, but situated just round the corner in Hatton Garden. This was the place where a large number of young constables resided.

Their chosen instrument of destruction was a 16-inch-long piece of iron pipe, three inches in diameter, filled with explosive, with each end firmly plugged, and through a hole drilled in one of which a fuse had been inserted, and set in tar.

The pair arrived in Hatton Garden just before midnight on 16 May 1881. They found the doorway deserted, the patrol responsible for its security being away covering another part of its beat. They lit the twisted fuse, positioned the bomb, and swiftly retreated. There was a loud explosion. It shook the building and shattered windows, but, because the gunpowder had been loosely poured in instead of being tamped down hard, the result was not as dire as the hate-motivated bombers had hoped. The bomb exploded in the lobby, but did not disintegrate: only the end of the device was blown off, causing limited damage. No one was killed or injured, and the effect of the explosion was confined to the entrance portion of the house.

A disappointed McGrath and McKevitt set to work at once planning a second, and more ambitious, onslaught. This time the target was to be the Town Hall. One of the first things that they did was to change lodgings. They moved to a house in the Kensington district. That would have been around 1 June. Then they set to work preparing their bomb.

For a start, they got hold of two large sections of cast-iron piping, five eighths of an inch in diameter. Water or gas mains had recently been renewed in the neighbourhood, and the discarded pieces of pipe had been left lying around for the taking. They filled the interior cavity of one of the bits of pipe with slabs of dynamite, then plugged it with two-inch sections of deal. The job was completed by the insertion of a detonator cartridge and a fuse through one of the plugged ends of the pipe. The device, extremely heavy, was packed into a large seaman's bag, which was tied up, leaving only the fuse exposed, and stowed away ready for action.

At 4am on 10 June 1881, John Ross, a cab driver looking for a fare, spotted two men as he was driving up Water Street. Thinking, because of the large canvas bag they were carrying, that they were sailors, he turned his horse along Exchange Street, drew up, and asked them if they wanted a cab. They said that they did not, so, disappointed, he drove off to the cab stand in Castle Street, opposite the Town Hall.

Shortly after 4am that same Friday morning, walking his beat, Police Constable George Read of the Liverpool Force, 26 years old and a native of County Wexford, saw, as he came up Castle Street towards the Town Hall, two dark figures on the steps of the building. One of them was stooping down to a bag which was lying on the step beside him. Read watched as the man lit a match. Remembering what had happened at Hatton Garden a little over three weeks before, Constable Read's suspicions were strongly roused, and he immediately ran towards the pair.

As soon as they saw him, leaving the mysterious bag where it was, they took to their heels, bolting off at top speed, running like hares across the Exchange Flags. Read, who was a big, stoutish man, gave chase as best he could, but was soon left well behind. He had, however, the presence of mind to keep blowing his whistle as he ran. He was pelting and puffing across Chapel Street when he spotted PC Creighton lumbering quietly along his beat, shouted out to him a brief and breathless situation report, and told him, "Go back to the Town Hall, it's being set on fire. I saw them strike the match and heard the fuse." Creighton, a former Royal Irish Constabulary officer, darted off with a will.

Read ran on. Coming into Oldhall Street, he saw PC Carey plodding towards him. The fleeing fugitives also saw Carey, and, realising that they were caught between the two policemen, plunged down a side street. Unluckily for them, it proved to be a cul-de-sac.

It was Carey who, literally, collared McKevitt, pulling him out from where he was hiding beneath a cart. McKevitt drew a gun on him. Nothing daunted, Carey, the son of Irish parents and a young and active man, closed with McKevitt, and seized the hand holding the revolver. McKevitt, suddenly jerking his hand free, and managed to throw the revolver over the low wall of an adjoining coal-yard. He continued to struggle, making violent efforts to escape, but was at last overpowered by the athletic Casey, and handed over by him to another constable who had just appeared on the scene.

Of McGrath there was no sign. Arming himself with McKevitt's revolver, all six chambers of which were loaded, and which had been picked up from where it had been thrown in the coal-yard by a carter, who had brought it to him, Casey embarked upon a close quartering of the neighbourhood. Eventually, after an unsuccessful search of all the adjoining coal-yards and interlacing thoroughfares, he came to the bottom of a street, another cul-de-sac, that ended in a stone wall topped with a vicious row of iron spikes. The canal ran below it. There was a narrow ledge, perhaps eight inches wide, between the water and the wall. And out on the water there, Casey saw an empty coal barge moored.

That was where Casey found McGrath crouched, a large piece torn from the seat of his trousers by his hasty passage over the spiked wall, and dripping after his precipitation from the wall-top into the water. Catching hold of him by the collar of his coat, he pointed McKevitt's revolver at him.

"I'll make no resistance. I'm half-drowned. I've had a narrow escape of my life," said McGrath.

He had, he told Casey, only just managed to reach and climb on to the barge.

Asked if he was armed, he replied that he had a revolver in his pocket. Casey then made him precede him at gun point, along the ledge by the canal, through the adjacent coal-yard, and out into the street. He was then taken off to the Central police station, in Dale Street, to which McKevitt had already been conveyed.

McGrath at first gave his name as Barton, but later, although refusing to give any further information, admitted to his real name. When he was searched, two bronze medals were found in his pockets. The larger one commemorated the Fenian Brotherhood, and carried on its obverse in large letters, the inscription, 'Ireland and America', with the date 1866, and a hand-in-hand emblem. On the reverse was a ship, surmounted by the word 'Irish', and below it, the word 'Republic', and with the letter 'F' on the left side, and 'B' on the right. The smaller medal was a '(Daniel) O'Connell medal', which bore the inscriptions, 'Ireland for the Irish', 'The Irish for Ireland', and 'Repeal Year, 1843'. He had also a notebook containing Fenian addresses and information.

One of the two men was found to be carrying a Roman Catholic prayer book, in addition to dynamite detonators. Both of them were carted off under armed guard to Walton Gaol.

Meanwhile, Police Constable Creighton, accompanied by Constables McBirnie and Sinclair, who had joined up with him, had arrived at the Town Hall, and, following PC Read's directions, had their eyes peeled for the bag on the Town Hall steps. They could hardly miss it. There it was, with smoke curling out of its mouth. At first they thought it was a seaman's bag which had caught fire. It was when they started to handle it, felt its weight, and the hard, bulky unknown object inside it, that they began to suspect real danger.

It was too heavy for one man to lift, but they manhandled it between them off the steps and on to the pavement. Having managed to fling it a further three or four yards distant, McBirnie started to try to unfasten the string round its neck. Creighton shouted out to him to be careful, and to come away from the thing as it was very likely dangerous. He did so, and all three of them moved a few yards off – just in time.

Suddenly, there was a tremendous explosion – an ex-artilleryman described it as like that of a 32-pounder cannon – and pieces of glass, iron, lead-piping, stone, and heaven knows what else, fell all around in a great shower. But the constables' swift action had saved the main body of Liverpool's Town Hall, which had only had its windows shattered. The railings outside had been fairly badly damaged, and the spikes of many of them had been completely blown off.

The Phoenix Fire Office, which stood over on the other side of the street, had fared less well. Its windows, too, had been blown out, but its walls were quite extensively damaged, having been heavily dented by being struck by large pieces of flying iron. The cornice of the Fire Office was also severely defaced.

A number of fragments of heavy iron piping were scattered about the street. A piece of carpet and part of an old dress were also picked up.

Rumours were rife that their escape from Walton Gaol was being organised by Mc Grath and McKevitt's Fenian brethren, and that it was planned to take place on the Sunday morning. The area around the prison always attracted large gangs of men playing pitch-and-toss, and indulging in various other questionable amusements, on Sunday mornings. But the police put a stop to the planned cock fight that had been going to take place that Sunday morning of 12 June. There is said to have been some concern expressed, too, about the large number of Irish navvies – employed at that time in the construction of the Walton tramway – who were hanging menacingly around. In the event, nothing happened.

Chief Inspector 'Dolly' Williamson, head of the Special (Irish) Branch at Scotland Yard, arrived on 15 June, to see what he could learn from the Liverpool experience. His hope was that he would be able to connect McGrath with the men, Coleman and Mooney, who had carried out the Mansion House attack in London. He failed to do so.

The two men responsible for the attempted bombing of the Town Hall were tried at the ensuing Liverpool Assizes. McGrath, against whom further evidence had been obtained, was additionally charged with causing the explosion at the Hatton Garden police section house. Witnesses for the prosecution included the woman in whose house he had lodged, the joiner who made the deal plugs used in the bomb for him, and an informant, who accused him also of complicity in Fenian outrages in London and elsewhere. It was further asserted, but was impossible of proof, that he was connected with O'Donovan Rossa and the Irish-American conspiracy.

The jury found both men guilty, and in passing sentence the judge observed:

> There is a distinction between your offences, and I desire to give effect to it. You, McGrath, have been found guilty of two offences; you, McKevitt, of one. The sentence that I pass on you, McGrath, is penal servitude for the rest of your life, and that you, McKevitt, be kept in penal servitude for fifteen years.

Liverpool's next brush with the Dynamitards was in June 1882, when the police received information that a man who was passing under the name of Timothy Featherstone, and describing himself as a newspaper correspondent, would be arriving from Philadelphia, and taking up lodgings at 43 Regent Street, off Great Howard Street. It was known that his real name was Edmund O'Brien Kennedy, and that he was connected with the Irish-American revolutionary conspiracy.

On arrival, Featherstone was accordingly placed under close observation, which meant that all his movements were shadowed. It was duly noted that from time to time he would take trips to Glasgow, to Dublin and to Cork.

On 9 December 1882, when in Glasgow, he had, giving the name of Daniel O'Herlihy, purchased from J Montague & Company, a carboy of the strongest form of nitric acid, which he arranged to have sent off to Cork, addressed to him under that assumed name.

Two further despatches from Glasgow to O'Herlihy in Cork took place. On 14 February 1883, another carboy of nitric acid went off, and on 19 February, carboys of sulphuric acid. On their arrival at Cork railway station, the carboys were all collected by one Denis Deasy, a railway porter, and delivered to the premises, at 10 Great George's Street, of the real Daniel O'Herlihy, who was by trade a stationer and newsagent, and a maker of ink.

A telegram from Mr (later Sir) Edward George Jenkinson, head of the Irish operation of the Secret Service, received at the end of February by Captain (afterwards Sir) William Nott-Bower, Head Constable of Liverpool, advised him to keep Patsy Flanagan, a railway signalman at St Helen's Junction, under surveillance.

Midway through March 1883, another telegram from Jenkinson brought the intelligence that bombs, manufactured in Cork, would shortly be brought to Liverpool by Denis Deasy. He would be arriving aboard the City of Cork Steamer Packet Company's vessel, *Upupa*, and would bring with him a large deal box. This would very probably contain explosives, which it was thought were to be used to blow up the Town Hall in St Helens. Nott-Bower was told that Deasy was to be searched carefully for a letter of introduction to someone near Liverpool, most likely Patsy Flanagan.

The *Upupa* docked at Prince's Landing Stage at about 7pm on 28 March 1883. It was met by Detective Inspector George Marsh, together with several other Liverpool detectives, and two Royal Irish Constabulary detectives, names of Canning and Curran. Ten minutes after the gangway had been run out, a thickset young man of about 25 came ashore, and engaged the services of a porter named Shannon. A few minutes later, they disembarked and, with the porter carrying a heavy wooden box, made their way towards the Waterloo Dock Gate.

As they were about to leave the dock, Marsh stepped into their path.

"What have you in this box?" he asked Deasy.

"Cattle food," was the reply.

Marsh then escorted Deasy along to the police hut, called a cab, and bore him off to the police station in Dale Street, where Nott-Bower, hastily summoned from a dinner-party, was waiting to supervise his questioning.

Deasy claimed that he had been employed by a commercial traveller named Murphy to deliver a box of cattle spice to Liverpool for him. He was then searched and the key to the wooden box and two documents were found on him.

The first was a reminder:

> Pat Flanagan at Mr Brennan's, 24 Covert Road, Sutton.
> Go to St Helens Junction. Stay at 43 Regent Street,
> Liverpool. Go to Lime Street Station.

The second document was a letter of introduction written in the same hand as the first. It indicated that Deasy had not met Flanagan before. It began 'Dear Pat', and went on to recommend the bearer, Denis Deasy, as:

> *... the young man I asked you to find employment for. He is a*
> *good fellow and will mind his business wherever placed.*

It was signed 'Edmund'. At the top of the letter a shamrock had been drawn, with the number 31 below it. The detectives interpreted this to signify that St Helens Town Hall was to be bombed on 31 March.

Both these documents were recognised to be in Featherstone's handwriting.

Deasy had also in his possession a pocket-book wherein was written an entry detailing the use of nitric acid.

When the box of cattle food was opened, it was found to contain two large tin canisters stitched up in canvas and filled with lignine dynamite – a highly dangerous explosive and one never used for any legitimate purpose – a packet of chlorate of potash, a packet of pounded sugar, a quantity of red orpiment, a lump of realgar bearing the label 'Lesters' Cork', two bottles of concentrated sulphuric acid ('oil of vitriol'), all the ingredients necessary for making fuses, and three brass taps so constructed as to ensure an interval of 20 minutes between the lighting of a fuse and the explosion of a bomb.

Royal Irish Constabulary Detectives Johnston and Canning meanwhile made their way to St Helens to arrest Flanagan. He turned out to be a railway signalman. He was, in fact, on duty when the detectives arrived, and they proceeded to his signal-box to arrest him. He was taken back to his lodging in Sutton, where they thoroughly searched him and his room.

In a large tin trunk, which Flanagan admitted to be his, they found, among the clothes which it contained, a small locked bag. Flanagan protested against their opening this, saying that there was nothing in it except "some private little matters". They insisted on forcing it, however, and inside were a false beard, a revolver with five chambers loaded, a box of 40 cartridges, a tin canister filled with a mixture of chlorate of potash and powdered sugar, a bottle of concentrated sulphuric acid, together with a number of other ingredients for the making of fuses and the causing of explosions.

Flanagan, who under questioning had insisted that the powder in the canister was tooth powder and the liquid in the bottle was medicine for a liver complaint, was then conveyed to Liverpool to join Deasy in Walton Gaol.

As soon as it was known that Deasy had landed at Liverpool, the Cork police had gone ahead with the arrests of Featherstone and O'Herlihy, and they were shipped over to join Deasy and Flanagan in Walton. The London police, hearing of the arrests made in Liverpool and Cork, decided to arrest a man named Dalton, real name John O'Connor, who was known to be closely connected with Irish-American revolutionary circles. They ran him to ground on 5 April, in an American reading-room in the Strand, and he was duly despatched to Walton Gaol.

At Liverpool Assizes, on 2 August 1883, Deasy, Flanagan, Featherstone, O'Herlihy and Dalton, were arraigned before Mr Justice Stephen on the principal charges of treason, felony, conspiracy to murder, and being in possession of explosives with felonious intent.

Having listened to the evidence, the learned judge concluded that there was insufficient evidence being offered against O'Herlihy, and accordingly directed the jury to find a verdict of not guilty. But he summed up strongly against Featherstone, Deasy, Flanagan and Dalton, and after an hour and a quarter's retiral, the jury came back with a guilty verdict against all four.

Addressing them before sentence, the judge told them:

> It would be impossible to imagine a graver offence, and those who take part in such enterprises must expect the heaviest punishment when convicted.

He then proceeded to sentence each of them to penal servitude for the term of their natural lives.

So ended this early phase of a war that continues to this day – a sporadic theft of life and desecration of property, a poor foundation, I would feel, upon which to raise a new regime. But there you are.

LITERARY
ECHOES

NATIVE QUILL-BEARERS

Beryl Bainbridge

It seems all of a million years ago, in another part of the wood, that I was fox-trotting around the municipal gardens beside St George's Hall, with not the faintest inkling that the pretty raven-haired girl in my arms was to become one of our finest English novelists.

Picking up the London *Evening Standard*, back in November 1991, I was surprised by delight at finding, in the column that she was then writing for the paper, that she, too, remembered pleasurably our terpsichorean interlude of getting on for forty years before; although, she admitted, her memory of the occasion was a shade hazy. I think, perhaps, that the liquid refreshment of which we had both that night liberally partaken, may account for the slight misting.

In the years since, Dame (as she now is) Beryl Bainbridge's dancing feet have twinkled her up to a highly respected place on the literary ladder, and Liverpool, whose distinguished daughter she is, has good reason to feel pride in her.

Turning up the facts in order to write this appreciation, I could not help but be struck by the uncanny confluence of our lives.

We were both born in Mossley Hill, within minutes' pram-push of each other: she, on 21 November 1934 – making her precisely ten years younger than me – in Menlove Avenue; me, just round the corner in Queen's Drive.

We both, subsequently, lived within minutes' walk of each other in feisty Liverpool 8: she, at 12 Huskisson Street; me, just round the corner at 7 Percy Street.

We both lived the first decades of our lives through the same hours measured on the face of the Liver Clock, breathed the same river-tanged air, and shared the same sights and sounds of *our* Liverpool – since vanished, or, as Beryl has more exactly and succinctly put it: 'Someone's murdered Liverpool – and got away with it.'

We both used to go to The Nook, the Chinese public-house in Nelson Street, presided over by Mrs Eileen Jones, the Irish Queen of Chinatown, a magnificent, full-sailing, *Fighting Téméraire*, who wore hats like massive fruit-bowls, or an up-spaded segment of parterre, of full-blooming, old-fashioned English rose-garden, and who, wearing aseptic, surgeon's-like, long white gloves when serving behind the bar, would always greet me with the patently sage observation, "Your health's everything, dear!"

Beryl did her courting in the snug at the back. So did I.

We both explored St James' Cemetery, the marble forest in the hollow at the cathedral's foot, with its tall, circular temple tomb of William Huskisson, MP (who managed to get himself knocked down and killed by the world's first train, Stephenson's *Rocket*), its catacombs and chalybeate spring.

We were both familiar with the man in Williamson Square, who made his living by having boulders broken on his chest with a sledge-hammer. And we both knew Brown's Café, also in Williamson Square, where you could buy great, big, thick sandwiches, and knock back cups of mahogany-brown, sweet, invigorating tea.

We shopped at Henderson's, long gone, where her Auntie Margo served behind the material counter, and at Cooper's, wreathed with the fragrance of roasting coffee beans; we were old acquaintances of Blackler's parrot, humped in its gilded cage; we regularly explored the pet market, in the narrow little back street behind the Playhouse, with its irresistible, cuddly, in-need-of-a-good-worming, puppies; we ate the occasional meal at the Bear's Paw, visited the Rialto to dance or go to the pictures.

We rode the *Royals* – *Iris* and *Daffodil* – going over the water to Wallasey, Seacombe and New Brighton. We rode, too, the Overhead Railway, she, as a child in pixie hood and rabbit-fur gloves, holding her father's hand, me, as a child, but also on the last night of its life, when I made the final journey, reporting for the BBC the sad closing of the 'Dockers' Umbrella'.

We both left Liverpool in the Fifties; she, in 1954, me, in 1957, both to live in London.

Beryl's father, Richard Bainbridge, was born in 1899. His father, had been born in Hunter Street, off Scotland Road, was a cooper by trade, and worked in a brewery. He had married a girl called Ellen Kidd, who could neither read nor write.

The Bainbridge family hailed from Flookburgh, in the Lake District, whither they had come down from Scotland. Liverpool-born Richard had done well for himself, having become a flourishing Merseyside businessman, until, like so many others, he was wiped out by the stock market crash of 1929.

By the time Beryl was born, five years of struggle in a systematically descending scale of jobs – in shipping, cotton, property, and bottoming out as a commercial traveller – had transformed the bright and bustlingly confident young Socialist, whom his wife-to-be, Winifred, had met on the top deck of a tram heading along Lord Street for Everton Brow, into a dour and deeply disappointed, 35-year-old man.

The family had moved from Mossley Hill to Formby, where Beryl grew up in the village beside the Lancashire shore and sandhills. The idea that he, who had been wont to boast that he had imported the first safety-matches to Berlin, was ending up as a failure, made him a difficult husband. He and Winnie bickered fiercely; were continually at daggers drawn. He was subject to fearful rages.

"Mum kept quiet and looked white-faced,"says Beryl.

Her father did the shouting.

"He had a terrible temper, which could last for months. He'd sit in his room for weeks. We took his food up and left it outside the door …"

This was surely something more than mere 'temper'. We seem to be looking at the unmistakable symptoms of clinical depression.

In the calm between such storms, Beryl's father would read Dickens to her, and used to tell her stories. He would also take her on walkabouts with him: to the business quarter of town, showing her the different places in which he had worked in his heyday, and the spots where he had concluded significant business deals; to the Pier Head, where he liked to play a game called 'Departures', putting Beryl on a ferry-boat to New Brighton, and waving her off as if she were departing for America on an Atlantic liner.

Beryl has admitted that, when she was little, she hated her father. But, happily, she came to know and understand him by the time she was 16, which was about four years before he died. Her mother, who came from a slightly higher grade of the middle class than her husband – her father was the owner of a prosperous paint firm – was suspiciously secretive and would never talk about her family. She had become progressively more and more embittered, because she hated the unglamorous Formby life that she was forced to lead, and her spouse's residual ill-humour did not tend to make things any easier to bear. No, it was not a happy household.

People have been very ready to suggest that Beryl and her brother had a dreadful childhood, but Beryl herself does not think so.

"They were," she says, "good parents. I loved them and think about them always."

Certainly, her mother, whose upbringing had included a finishing-school in Belgium, where she learned French and had lessons on the piano, encouraged the young Beryl to write. Indeed, by the age of 12 she had completed her first full-length book, *Filthy Lucre*, which she describes today as 'a crib from *Treasure Island* and Dickens'.

It was her mother, too, who, answering a BBC Manchester advertisement for child actors, gave her her first experience of acting, and while still at school – Merchant Taylor's, Crosby – she was heard regularly taking part in the radio programme, *Children's Hour*.

> I couldn't have written for publication when my parents were alive because [her first books] were about childhood, and would have hurt them.

It was not until 1976 that, in *A Quiet Life*, she allowed herself to evoke the oddities of her 'conflict-ridden, but united family'. At school she displayed a vigorous aggression, which earned her the nickname of 'Basher Bainbridge'.

She loved a fight and had a penchant for beating-up the boys. She was expelled at 14, when her mother, having found a mildly rude limerick in her pocket, delivered it into the hands of the headmistress. It was about this time, too, that 'Naughty Beryl' did, she confesses, a spot of pinching from Woolworth's; but she was terrified that God was watching!

Aged 15, in 1949, after a short period of study at the Come-Ripman Ballet School, at Tring, she managed, because her father was on nodding terms with the Lord Mayor, to get into the Liverpool Playhouse, joining the company as an assistant stage-manager and occasional actor in the rôle of character juvenile.

Their requirements of her were as multifarious as their expectations. She would be told to sit in the prompt corner with the book. She would be instructed to understudy. She would be sent to fetch and carry sandwiches from Brown's Café, on the opposite side of Williamson Square, and distribute them to peckish actors and actresses. She was also expected to help with the costumes and props.

She would, she remembers, sit in the prop-room, huddled over the smoking fire, gossiping for hours on end, listening to actors' tales of the road. And at night, the cups and glasses washed, the props stowed away, she would hare off up Stanley Street and Moorfields, 'past the joke shop with the rubber masks grinning behind the glass, past the chemist's shop with its whirling spray stuck like a red-hot poker in the window', to Exchange Station, to catch the last train home to Formby.

She left the Playhouse, and with her possessions – her Sunday frock, ration book, and a photograph of Rasputin – in a carrier bag from Lewis', and little more than 30 shillings in her mac pocket, set off for London.

Early on, there was a stint as usherette at a Tottenham Court Road cinema, and when she lost the job there she had to travel every Friday from her Hampstead digs by trolley-car to Islington, where she collected her weekly 15 shillings dole hand-out, and enjoyed her only breakfast of the week – fried bread, egg, sausage and tomato.

Later, finding more suitable employment, she embarked upon a spell of touring, with temporary engagements with several provincial repertory companies. This period of her teenage movements through a panorama of assorted bed-sits, and her insider view of the provincial theatre of the early Fifties, is recorded in her 1989 novel, *An Awfully Big Adventure*.

It was in the course of her wandering minstrel life, that, in Dundee, in 1953, aged 19, Beryl became a Roman Catholic. The conversion was short-lived. She lapsed in 1954. That was the year of her marriage.

She had, while at the Playhouse, fallen irrecoverably in love with a tall, thin, bearded Liverpool artist, Austin Davies, who was at that time engaged in the painting of scenery at the theatre. They married and settled into 12 Huskisson Street. She had two children by him, a son and a daughter, Aaron and Jo-Jo. The Davies left Liverpool and moved to the house in Camden Town, North London, where, nearly half a century later, Beryl still lives.

Sadly, the marriage was not a success. Beryl, desperately upset, threw Austin out when she discovered that he was having an affair. They divorced in 1959. She was just 25. She had stopped work after giving birth to the children.

"As a mother, I wouldn't work," she says, "however little money one had. It's sad for women that they want this career business. A man used to know what he was supposed to do – earn money and pay the bills."

Emotionally free, Beryl fell in love with a writer named Alan Sharp. By him she had a daughter, Rudi. It was somewhat disconcerting, though, to find that it had slipped Alan's memory to mention that he had had two previous wives, and, currently, another woman pregnant by him. Mr Sharp put in a dutiful appearance for Rudi's birth, said that he was just going to his car to collect a book … and disappeared like a pantomime demon in a cloud of evil-smelling exhaust smoke. He has not been seen since. His daughter has, as Rudi Davies, become an actress. All this is commemorated in *Sweet William* (1975).

There have, over the years, been other lovers – 'mostly happily married' – but Beryl has never remarried.

She explains:

> I probably wouldn't have wanted to write any more books. It's a very second-hand occupation. If you're happy, you don't need to shut yourself off. I started with a dysfunctional family, and I've repeated another set of mistakes. It's not deliberate, but it goes on and on. You can't win.

Extremely sympathetically, Austin Davies, now remarried, insisted on treating Rudi as his own daughter. But things began to go financially wrong for him. He had done well out of the property boom of the Sixties, but it ended, and Davies only just saved his bacon by going off to New Zealand. Beryl signed a document releasing him from the necessity of supporting her. She was lucky to find a mortgage broker who said that she had – although she actually *hadn't* – enough income to take on the mortgage on her home.

It was then that she found herself on her own, isolated, with three young children, badly off, and intensely lonely.

She has since admitted:

> If I'd known as much as I know now, I wouldn't have divorced. You'd be more sensible, realise how hard it is. All this business of being angry because a man is

unfaithful … you'd think, "Just a minute. That's what men are like. They're sexual beings, whereas women are into children, so it's important to have a breadwinner."

She had to have a number stabs at breadwinning herself. She worked in a North London factory, sticking labels on bottles of wine – out of which experience she conjured up *The Bottle Factory Outing* (1974).

In 1965 she made a brief return to acting, appearing in Episode 7 of *Coronation Street* as Ken Barlow's girlfriend, holding up a banner in his kitchen and shouting "Ban the Bomb". She took a clerkly job at the publishers, Duckworth's … and that changed everything.

The company's chairman and managing director's wife, Anna Haycraft, otherwise Alice Thomas Ellis, the novelist, née Anna Margaret Lindholm, had been born in Liverpool, and, by one of those curious coincidences which make life suddenly so piquant, it transpired that her grandfather was the Mr Lindholm who had previously been the landlord of The Nook, and shot himself in an upper room there, and her parents had been members of the Church of Humanity, in Upper Parliament Street.*

These links in no wise hindered the very friendly relations which sprang up between Beryl and Anna and her husband, Colin Haycraft. Beryl joined the list of Duckworth authors and, more specifically, the 'Duckworth gang'

> … a group of women writers bringing a touch of the macabre to their brief novels of domestic life.

In 1972, Duckworth brought out *Harriet Said …* , which had been rejected by previous publishers, one of whom stigmatised its characters as 'repulsive beyond belief', and one scene as 'too indecent and unpleasant for even these lax days'.

There followed, in 1973, *The Dressmaker*, based on her Auntie Margo, who received her customers in the front parlour of 19 Bingley Road, Anfield, where she lived with her sister, Beryl's Auntie Nellie.

Liverpool figured again in *Young Adolf* (1978), which deals with Adolf Hitler's supposed visit to his half-brother, Alois Hitler, who had set up house in Upper Stanhope Street with his Irish bride, Bridget Dowling, in 1912. Their son, William Patrick Hitler, was born there.

In 1984, Beryl pointed an elegant toe well into my criminous field, recounting, in *Watson's Apology*, what the late William Roughead would have called the attaching tale of the Reverend John Selby Watson, the Stockwell clergyman who became the unlikely-seeming focus of a notorious Victorian uxoricide.

She has, since then, taken various other historic events as the centrepieces

---

* See my Liverpool Roundabout (1957) and Liverpool Ghosts and Ghouls (1986).

around which to weave her fictional or factional magic. In 1991, *The Birthday Boys*, dealt with Captain Scott and his disastrous Antarctic expedition. *Every Man for Himself* (1996), the story of the sinking of the Titanic. *Master Georgie* (1998), the centripetal presence of a novel set in the isinglass of the Crimean War. And *According to Queeney* (2001), enhaloing Dr Johnson and Mrs Thrale.

For each of her novels, it is the author's custom to paint a series of pictures, depicting scenes and characters relating to the story. These works of art have never been seen. They are kept stored away from human gaze somewhere in the cluttered house in Camden Town, where access through the narrow entrance passageway is seriously impeded by the formidable bulk of Eric, the life-sized, stuffed Water Buffalo.

In the last thirty-five years, Beryl Bainbridge has written some 21 books. She has been awarded the Whitbread Prize and the *Guardian* Fiction Prize, and been short listed for the Booker prize six times. Her writing regime – and we all have them – is, in her own words, 'Five months on a 15-year-old computer, sitting at a school desk, breaking off only to watch soaps.' And, she told Andrew Duncan of *Radio Times*, "I don't eat much because food slows you down. You have to be tense to concentrate."

Dame Beryl Bainbridge, novelist, artist, playwright, daughter of Liverpool and grandmother to seven grandchildren, you have brought literary lustre to the city of our birth, and it is a matter of abiding satisfaction to me that once in the long-ago, our lives and paths crossed.

James Hanley

I was living in chambers at 4 Doughty Street, in London, when, in 1959, I first met James Hanley. His son, Liam, a journalist and talented amateur artist – who, incidentally, painted the picture for the dust-jacket of Dr Geoffrey Smerdon and my biography of the Liverpool poet of the Nineties, Richard Le Gallienne* – lived in the chambers across the landing, where James and his wife, Timmy, were regular visitors.

I remember James as a small, shy, quietly-padding-about figure, softly-spoken, diffident, yet eyebrow-raisingly quizzical and whimsically humorous, not at all, in fact, as you would have expected the author of such violence and cruelty on paper to be.

I had, in fact, known all about James Hanley long before I actually met him. My father had an unexpurgated copy of his banned book, *Boy*. Published in 1931, it was the scarifying, loosely autobiographical, story of a cabin-boy's first and tragic sea voyage in the Merchant Service. It dealt with the, in those days, taboo subjects of homosexuality and syphilis, and ended grimly with the abused boy's murder aboard ship. The book was seized by

---

* *The Quest of the Golden Boy: The Life and Letters of Richard Le Gallienne. Unicorn Press (Martin Secker), 1960.*

police in Britain because it was allegedly obscene. It was eventually available in an expurgated edition in this country, and was published in full in Paris.

Although he was actually Irish, born in Dublin, on 3 September 1901, the son and grandson of working-class Irish seamen, Hanley – the name was originally spelt Hanly – grew up in Liverpool, which is said to be the capital of Ireland, anyway.

His parents, Edward H and Bridget (*née* Roche) Hanley, were poor, and his was an unhappy backstreet boyhood. He left board-school, tenuously educated, at 13, and went to sea. It was an escape from a static to a floating slum.

He was still at sea when the First World War broke out in 1914, and his experiences on troopships were to brand an ineradicable scar on his memory; a scar that remained long after the seafarer's tattoos had faded. He jumped ship at New Brunswick, and, although still in his early teens, managed to enlist in the Canadian Expeditionary Force, seeing service with them in the trenches on the battlefields of France and on transports at the Dardanelles and in the Mediterranean.

At the war's end, he returned to the sea, working as a deck-hand and as a stoker, travelling the world, until, surfeited, he decided to leave the Merchant Navy. In 1924 (the year of my birth), at the age of 23, he quit the sea for good, and became a land-lubber. Returning to Liverpool, he held a considerable variety of jobs, uncongenial and menial – dock labourer, butcher, cook, clerk, postman and railway porter at Bootle station – before succeeding in breaking into local journalism, contributing freelance pieces to the *Liverpool Echo*.

As some men are driven to drink by adversity, Hanley was driven to print. During this period of his life, he undertook a rigorous programme of self-education, reading widely and deeply, and becoming skilled in, among other subjects, music. He had, in fact, had a passion for music from boyhood, and it was to remain with him all his life: his chief recreation. He taught himself to play the piano, which he did most adequately, although, sadly, his hands were too stiff from years of hard manual labour for him ever to become anything more than an enthusiastic amateur of the keyboard.

His first book, 500 copies of which were printed privately, was *The German Prisoner* (1930). It was the horrifyingly brutal and explicit story of the sexual torture and eventual murder of a German soldier at the hands of two British privates, who, in a sort of *deus ex machina* ending, are killed by a shell. Richard Aldington, a literary lion of the time, wrote an Introduction to the slender volume. A second work, again privately printed – 200 copies – appeared in 1930, *A Passion Before Death*.

His first commercially issued novel, *Drift*, appeared in 1930, too. It had been offered to 19 publishers. He was paid the miserable sum of £5 for all rights. It was followed during the next decade by an immense consolidating output of a further 23 books, and a simultaneous torrent of opinionated journalism.

Before Hanley found his dominating theme – the conflict between man and that disturbing revealer of human nature, the sea – he had first to write certain bitternesses out of his system. Like Somerset Maugham, he could not rest until he had externalised the burden of torments and unhappy recollections which nagged for an outlet. Maugham disembarrassed himself of them in *Of Human Bondage*. Hanley set down in such works as *Drift, Men in Darkness* (1931) and *Resurrexit Dominus* (1934), the ugliness, brutality, and frustration of his youth in Liverpool, the traumatic disillusionment of his wartime experiences, his guilt-edged spiritual disgust with the Roman Catholic Church into which he had been baptised, and his troubled resentment of the restrictive class structure which had imprisoned him.

All these were written while he was deeply influenced by Russian politics, literature, and music, and emotionally committed to the ideals of the British Independent Labour Party, and they were a powerful indictment of bread-line Britain of the inter-war years, written with a pen dipped, like that of Dostoevsky, in his own nerves.

It was not until 1938, with the publication of *Hollow Sea*, that the emotional conflict fouling up his artistic sensibility was expunged, and the early propagandist element subsided. As late as 1958, when the fifth and final volume, *An End and a Beginning*, of his powerful saga (1935-58) of a Dublin working-class family, residing in a fictional Liverpool, the Furys, again quasi-autobiographical, was published, there still lingers a muffled echo of the drum beats of revolt that deafened him in the 'thirties.

But like all angry young men, Hanley grew up. Purged of the obsessive necessity to ventilate social and environmental injustices, he turned, in what may be identified as his second phase, to the sea.

It was the baseness of men, their twistings and turnings under stress that intrigued him. 'I am much more interested in how low a man can sink than in how high he can reach'. An odd claim at first sight, but the point is this: over and above all else, Hanley was fascinated by character, and believed that, for good or ill, adversity is the greater moulder. He says, with Baudelaire, *'Je sais que la douleur est la nobelesse unique.'*

Unlike many other writers, Hanley maintained that he created the majority of his characters: they were not consciously modelled on any person he had known. Artistically, he regarded the development of his characters as far more important than the initial working out of a plot. Indeed, it was the autonomous response of character to devised events which supplied the direction of the movement. In other words, it was they who created the action. They were never the mere puppets of circumstance. This free-choosing decisiveness of his personæ is tacitly acknowledged by their creator in his choice of titles. Several of the books bear simply the name of the primary character – *Stoker Haslett, Captain Bottell, Quartermaster Clausen, Stoker Bush, Emily Levine.*

The Closed Harbour (1952), one of his most admired novels, provides a useful example of how this technique works in practice. One hot summer afternoon in 1951, Hanley was sitting listlessly in the garden of his cottage at Llanfechain, Montgomeryshire. Suddenly he felt the urge to start a new book. Without an idea in his head, he went upstairs to his workroom. On his desk lay a pile of white paper, the sun shining on it. He sat looking at it in the heat, then began to picture something dark moving across its gleaming white surface. He picked up his pen and started to write about the dark figure of Captain Marius, the skipper who had lost his ticket, walking in his black sailor's cap and reefing jacket up a white-hot afternoon street in Marseilles. Hanley had been introduced to his character. From that point onwards it was simply a matter of recording how Marius manipulated his crisis.

Hanley wrote fast and rarely needed to revise. The novels were painstakingly scribed in longhand, some in large ledgers of the kind that you might see in any office, others in exercise books. A considerable number of his neatly written manuscripts are now preserved in the Picton Library.

His work method was a curious mixture of discipline and spontaneity. In the cottage where he and his wife had lived since 1943, his day would begin at 6am, when he brewed himself a pot of tea. Breakfast was at eight, and then, at nine o'clock, he would go upstairs to his workroom – a simple, plainly-furnished room, with a bed, chairs, some books and a desk. It had two windows; one looking out on the garden, the other looking across the railway line, and up the valley to the wider world. An apt touch of symbolism, remembering his days as a porter. But he had his desk facing the wall, for he preferred to have no diversions. Between nine and noon he wrote. Then, before lunch, an hour's walk. The afternoon would be spent in reading and perhaps having a nap. Tea at four. Another walk. Then, upstairs to write until supper-time. Sometimes he would go upstairs to work again until 9pm, or give way to the temptation of his main relaxation, an evening of Bach, Beethoven, or Mozart at the piano. He would watch television, but it was the radio that ruled the house. He used to retire to bed at about 11.30pm, perhaps to read, more often to write, sometimes until two or three in the morning.

Although he had read extensively, Hanley told me that he believed that he had been influenced by European rather than by a purely native literature. Writers like Tolstoy, Dostoevsky, Turgenev, Balzac and Cervantes had been his exempla. On the other hand, he was the first to admit a non-stylistic debt to Arnold Bennett, EM Forster and Richard Aldington, all of whom gave him a great deal of advice and personal encouragement.

The works of Henry Green and Anthony Powell afforded him great pleasure, but, he told me:

> Most of my reading nowadays is poetry. My bedside
> book is Gerard Manley Hopkins. I am an ardent admirer

of George Barker and enjoy TS Eliot, Edwin Muir and RS Thomas. The novels of Hardy and George Eliot move me profoundly.

Surprisingly, perhaps, perhaps not, he disliked Conrad, who "saw the ship from the officers' deck". This chimes with his statement that:

> The more insignificant a person is in this whirlpool of industrialised and civilised society, the more important he is for me.

He rejected out of hand any comparison with Conrad:

> Sea life enabled me to unlearn all that I had learned and thought of Conrad, the romantic writer of sea stories.

Essentially a storyteller, there are times when he is unexpectedly difficult. His prose is sinewy rather than ornate, a taut structure of bone and muscle. It seldom coruscates: equally, it is rarely banal. Sometimes the blunt clarity of the writing invites comparison with Melville. In other places it has all the complexity of Durrell at his most wilfully obscure. The total is a bewildering amalgam; now an unvarnished, but always skilfully polished, piece of plain narrative, now a sudden esoteric liquefaction, a full-spating stream of consciousness; now a stab of sly Dickensian observation; and yet somehow contriving an overall homogeneity unmistakably hall-marked 'Hanley'.

In his early and middle years of authorship, Hanley's main concern was to explore:

> I preferred walking in deserts to jungles. I was making a path for myself and had a lot to get out of the way. I liked to feel a challenge, to work on what seemed the impossible, alone, after the lights had gone out and the doors had closed. I took the end of a story as my point of departure.

He has found, and laid bare, imperfect man, then carefully swaddled him in the garments of compassion.

Certainly, there are no more splendid evocations of the sea-going life anywhere than in the sequence of highly individual log-books in which the author has charted his voyages of discovery into troubled waters, where men splash and thresh, and often drown.

Hanley has always been highly praised by critics and fellow-writers, among them William Faulkner, EM Forster, Henry Green and TE Lawrence.

He was regularly compared with Joseph Conrad and Dostoevsky, but his work never seemed to catch on with the general reading public. He was never brought out in paperback, and throughout the 1970s and 1980s, most of his novels were unavailable.

To a great extent, Hanley had only himself to blame for his lack of popular acclaim. So many of his novels and stories have been informed by an uncompromising realism and antipathetic morbidness, reflecting the face of life as he had known it too faithfully for comfort. Unappealing, too, are his consistently depressing themes of appalling existences among the working-class, outcasts and seamen (of whom he was the singer of the endlessly repeated song, a sad sea shanty), as well as the grim, often despairing, tone of his writing. His style has been described as a mixture of raw realism and Melville-like visionary poetry.

I remember a discussion I had at Cambridge with FR Leavis, and he subsequently wrote to me in December 1963:

> Of course I recall James Hanley as a fact, but haven't a convinced enough memory to be able to say anything to the point. It's very possible, as you say, for a considerable writer to get no proper recognition when he appears, and then to be allowed to lapse into oblivion. I myself have never been free enough from urgent immediate pressures, preoccupations and distractions for it to be possible for me to believe that I have missed nothing I ought to have registered appreciatively and remembered critically. The impression I retain of Hanley is just one of documentary first-handness – anyone's impression, that is all. I'm too beset with deadlines, correspondence and military obligations to think of looking him up and refreshing my memories – revising, possibly, my first implicit judgment. This much, at any rate, can be said: the present is the time when a study of Hanley might count on receiving some attention. You are right about the disconcertingness of the way in which talent can suffer sustained neglect. So can great genius: both James and Conrad suffered something like life-long neglect.

Hanley has, in fact, since been cited in *The Concise Cambridge History of English Literature* as one of the half-dozen novelists most likely to provide classics for a future generation.

During the 1960s, on a retainer from the BBC, Hanley turned for ten years to the writing of plays for television and radio. One of his novels, *Say Nothing* (1962), a psycho-pathological study of three despairing residents in a drab boarding-house in a working-class street in Liverpool, first came into existence as a play. Thematically, *Say Nothing* was a brilliant portrayal of abstract states of mind, a new departure for Hanley, which added an innovative dimension to what had always been his paramount strength – a unique capacity to dissect, explicate and communicate emotion.

In the 'seventies, he returned to the novel for four final works. They showed absolutely no flagging of his powers.

After living in London in the 1930s, Hanley spent thirty years in a cottage in Wales. His wife died in 1980. He had been long and happily married. He lived out his final years back in London, living in a council flat off the Highgate Road, near his son, daughter-in-law and grandchild. He died on 11 November 1985, aged 84.

Nicholas Monsarrat

It was on one of his annual visits to London from his latter-day home in Gozo, in Malta, that, in the mid-1970s, I had what proved to be a last chat at Claridges Hotel, where he always stayed, with Nicholas Monsarrat.

Nicholas had achieved enormous celebrity and immense fortune with his bestselling novel, *The Cruel Sea*, published in August 1951, which was based on his war years in the Royal Navy, serving on Atlantic convoys. Monsarrat, the wartime sailor, saw the sea as cruel – unlike Hanley, the peacetime merchant seaman, who wrote: 'The sea is not cruel. It is simply indifferent. It is men who are cruel.'

My family had known the Monsarrats since the early years of the last century. Nicholas' elder sister, Molly, having been at Huyton College with my mother (Helen Margaret Barrington or Zuegheer-Herrmann, who, incidentally, was said to have been the finest wicket-keeper that the college had ever had!) before she went on to Cheltenham Ladies' College.

Nicholas was born at 11 Rodney Street, in Liverpool, on 22 March 1910. His father, Keith W Monsarrat, FRCS, was an exceedingly prominent and successful consulting surgeon, Dean of the Faculty of Medicine at Liverpool University, and lecturer in operative surgery at the Northern Hospital. His mother came from a family of Victorian consequence; that of Sir John Turney, of Nottingham, who dealt in leather, had been Lord Mayor of that city, and dwelt in considerable magnificence at Gedling House. This, the couple's fourth child, was christened Nicholas John Turney, at St Luke's, which used to be known as 'the doctors' church, at the bottom of Leece Street, which was subsequently reduced by the bombs of the Liverpool May Blitz of 1941, to the burnt-out shell that still stands, a fire-blackened memorial to itself.

Although he was fourteen years older than myself, and technically an Edwardian, Edward VII not dying until 6 May 1910, whereas I, born on

22 October 1924, am solidly a Georgian, the Liverpool of his childhood was, in many respects, much the same as that of mine.

He remembered views from the pram that I, too, remembered. The solid slog along the Boulevard to Prince's Park – past the Greek Church, only a little less magnificent than St Isaac's at St Petersburg and St Sophia's at Constantinople; past the high, ritualistic, Anglo-Catholic Church of St Margaret, and the Synagogue; in through those wonderfully ornate sun-ray gates at the entrance to the park; down past the hallowed spot where Judy the donkey, 'The Children's Friend', whom Nicholas and I both knew and loved to stroke, used to stand, and where stands now her little gravestone, commemorating her death on 12 August 1926, after twenty-one years' sterling service, delighting the children, and pulling a roller in the park; and on to the lake, beyond which, at 1 Windermere Terrace, my uncle, Schofield Cannington's enormous house reared up beside what was known in those days as Cannington's Gate.

When he was about six years old, Nicholas was sent to St Christopher's School for Boys, in Linnet Lane, a matriarchal establishment ruled over by two sisters, co-owners and principals, Miss Smith and Miss Nellie, strange figures to modern eyes, wearing small, black bonnets, and both dressed invariably in deepest purple. They ruled severely, each with a slim ebony ruler, carried at all times, and plied with unseemly vigour to the palms of wrongdoers' hands.

This was, of course, the time of the Great War, and although there was, in stark contrast to what would happen in the days of the Second World War, 'no suffering or slaughter in Liverpool, no thunder of guns along Rodney Street,' the war was bringing about inevitable changes.

Nicholas' father's armchair stood forlornly empty. Its occupant was absent, a major in the Royal Army Medical Corps, at first in France, and then in a strange-sounding place called Salonika, trying to repair with the surgeon's steel, the ravages wrought by the enemy's rougher metal on the enormous throng of terribly wounded soldiers.

New and alien words and phrases were stealthily trespassing into even the language of the nursery – the Dardanelles, the U-Boats, which had sunk the *Lusitania*, Zeppelins, which dropped bombs and murdered innocent people in their beds, a terrible gun called Big Bertha, and the Kaiser, the most wicked man in the whole world.

But there were also other things of those days … lost and vanished things … sad ghosts of the Liverpool streets. There was the Muffin Man, tray-on-head, the echoes of his bell fading away, ting-a-ling-ting, in the winter afternoon's gathering dusk. There was the lone, crumpled-seeming figure blowing patriotic airs, sounding somehow hopeless and fathomlessly sad, on a cornet, reaching out with his shabby cap for the too few down-tossed pennies. There were the melancholy strains of a barrel-organ, tinny and a bit off-key, its handle turned by a swarthy Italian, a sad-faced, leashed little monkey, dressed up in miniature breeches, scarlet bolero, and tasselled fez, perched on top, holding out with an air of hopelessness a tin cup to passers-by, and when rewarded with a coin, the little fellow, brightening up, would hand out in return a small piece of yellow paper with a lucky motto inscribed on it. More rarely, happily, a dancing bear on a chain, a huge, shaggy, docile, and obviously brutally bullied beast – a spectacle to tug at the heart strings of anyone who ever had a heart – a peaked cap, vaguely Russian, crammed on its unhappy head, would execute a sort of shambling, hopping movement, probably as much to keep itself warm as anything else. "The bear was much taller than the man who led it," Nicholas recalled. "Its claws fairly rattled on the pavement, and you could see its teeth from across the street."

Vivid shades of the grey streets, as lost and remote as the tricorn-hatted and brocade-coated men who, three centuries ago, walked the city pavements in the days of good Queen Anne.

And always, lined up, waiting, at the corner of Rodney Street, the young Monsarrat would see hansom cabs, breathing, in 1916, an air of the Victorian days of top-hatted and bewhiskered men and their dainty crinolined womenfolk. The best that my memory can serve up is the recollection of Liverpool's last horse cabby, Old George, who used to sit with his horse-drawn cab plying for hire outside the Sefton Drive gate of Princes Park Mansions.

The war ended. In 1921, the Monsarrats moved their home to a big, rambling, old-fashioned house, surrounded by a large garden, with greenhouses and an orchard, called Melbreck, at Allerton, which was then in the heart of the country.

Going into town became a positive expedition. It began with a long walk, past Steele's Dairy Farm next door, past the rectory where lurked the formidable Canon Gibson-Smith, past the Convalescent Home with its wounded soldiers in their bright hospital blues, white shirts and red ties, past Allerton Church, and into the village, where the tram-car for Liverpool started. The journey took about 50 minutes, covered some seven miles, and cost twopence.

Passengers were decanted outside Lewis', opposite the Adelphi Hotel, where the young Nicholas would attend for his weekly dancing class, held in the small ballroom. The pick of the shops included George Henry Lee's, – "where we were fitted for shoes by an X-ray machine which showed the actual wiggling bones of the feet and toes", the Bon Marché – "where sales-invoices and money were propelled by a fascinating system of overhead wires", Philip, Son & Nephew, the bookshop and stationers, MacSymons, the big fishmongers, and Cooper's, the fine provisioners at the bottom of Lord Street.

And there was Bold Street, the Bond Street of Liverpool, with its "chic, luxurious, expensive … gorgeous dress-shops, and furriers and jewellers and leather specialists", and Clay & Abraham's, the chemist's, with its huge red and green flagons, the emblems of their trade.

All this was splendid for the prosperous, but, let it be soberly remembered, and not without shame, that, in 1921, poverty's children still ran barefoot on the harsh Liverpool cobblestones. 'Street Arabs' *Punch* christened them, with misplaced pawky humour. 'Gutter-snipes' was what Nicholas' mother called them.

One saw the children of the poor, "said to be dying of 'galloping consumption', taking the meagre sun in the outside cages of the Children's Royal Infirmary."

One saw the streets filled with beggars, both men and women. There was a blind match-seller whose regular station was at the foot of Bold Street, "a gaunt old man who said 'Thank you kindly!' when the penny rattled into his tin cup, but who looked astonished if he felt you taking a box of matches off his tray."One saw limbless ex-servicemen in wheelchairs, propelling themselves painfully slowly along the gutters of the well-heeled's shopping streets. There were old soldiers in faded khaki overcoats hung with medals tootling jauntily on cornets and thumping drums, into whose eyes one dared not look as they chirruped with make-believe cheeriness, "Spare a copper for the Old Contemptibles!"

But a boy could not be expected to dwell on these things; they could very easily be banished from his mind. Did he not have serious worries of his own? For it was in 1921, too, that the eleven-year-old Nicholas was sent to his first boarding-school, The Leas, at Hoylake, over the water in Cheshire. He did not like it. He liked even less his second boarding-school, Winchester College, later describing his time there as "A season in hell".

The one consolation was that there were always the holidays to look forward to, and Liverpool was a good place in those days to which to return.

There was the cinema, or 'kinema' as Mrs Monsarrat insisted upon calling it – "Do not say 'cinema'. It sounds common. The word is 'kinema'. It starts with 'K' , because it is Greek." The two principal 'kinemas' were the Scala and the Futurist, both in Lime Street. There was the theatre, and visits by the D'Oyly Carte company with Gilbert and Sullivan. Stars of the musical firmament who came to the city in 1921, included Myra Hess, Sir Henry Wood, Heifetz, Tetrazzini, Pavlova, Chaliapin and Pablo Casals.

In the summer, there were holidays to Trearddur Bay, a seaside village, near Holyhead, where he learned to love the sea and sail; Christmas brought the excitement of the pantomime – *Robinson Crusoe, Jack and the Beanstalk, The Babes in the Wood, Dick Whittington, Mother Goose*, and, that year, *Aladdin*, at the Olympia – and such stars as Jack Buchanan, Cicely Courtneidge, Dorothy Ward, Leslie Henson, Gertie Gitana, Naughton and Gold and Wee Georgie Wood.

Thus it was, with these alternating spells of horror and delight, home splendours and school miseries, that boyhood melted away, and the gratefully delivered youth was despatched to Trinity College, Cambridge, where he scraped a BA, Law.

He came down from Cambridge to spend a summer's dalliance in Liverpool, where the family had moved from Melbreck to an equally fine house, Holmfield, at 10 Holmfield Road, Aigburth – loafing by the river watching the huge Cunarders sailing off to America, afternoon teas at the Adelphi, evenings at the Rialto ballroom – before being despatched again, this time to his uncle Thornton Simpson's office (Messrs Acton, Marriott & Simpson, Solicitors) in Market Square, Nottingham, as an articled clerk.

The legal way of life he hated, too. It was not long before he quit, setting off to London with a portable typewriter in his hand, £40 in his pocket, and the determination in his breast to become an author. The struggle began. He was reduced to sleeping on the Embankment and in St Martin's-in-the-Fields' crypt.

He was eventually rescued from the doldrums by his pen. Half a dozen books between 1934 and 1948, and, in 1951, the publication of *The Cruel Sea*. There was no looking back.

He married, in 1939, Eileen Rowland. She bore him a son. The marriage was dissolved in 1952. He married again that same year, Philippa Crosby. She bore him two sons. The marriage was dissolved in 1961. His final marriage was to Ann Griffiths, in 1961.

Over the years he lived successively in Johannesburg, a flat in Ottawa, on an island in the St Lawrence River, in the Channel Islands – where, according to his wife, he used to write at night, between 10pm and 3am, and sleep in the afternoon – and, for the last period of his life, on the Mediterranean island of Gozo.

He arrived back in England towards the beginning of August 1979, suffering from terminal cancer. He was admitted to the King Edward VII Hospital, in London, for treatment. He had been there for over a week, the last two days in a coma, when, in the early hours of 8 August 1979, his ship put out on its final voyage. His third wife, Ann, was at his bedside when the 69-year-old master mariner quietly slipped his moorings.

Signal: HMS *Monsarrat* will enter harbour.

In Search of Liverpool

Throughout the 1920s and '30s, there issued forth, from the publishers Methuen & Co, what was to become an extremely popular, best-selling sequence of travel books, the *In Search of ...* series, covering England, Ireland, Scotland and Wales.

Their author, H (for Henry) V (for Vollam) Morton, was a Lancashire lad, who first saw the light of day on 25 July 1892, at Ashton-under-Lyne. Both his parents were writers. His father, Joseph V Morton, born in India, was at the time, second in command of a local paper. His mother, Margaret Constance Mclean Ewart, was a Scot, boasting descent from Charles Ewart of the Royal Scots Greys. He captured a French Standard at the Battle of Waterloo, in recognition of which brave deed his statue stands on the rock below Edinburgh Castle.

Shortly after Henry's birth, his father was appointed Editor-in-Chief of the Birmingham based Pearson's group of newspapers, and specifically editor of the *Birmingham Mail*, and the family moved south to that city.

Leaving King Edward's School, where he had been a pupil from 1906-1908, young Morton, decided, in defiance of his parents' wishes and advice, to eschew the university and enter instead the precarious universe of journalism. He was just 17 when he got his first job on the staff of the *Birmingham Gazette and Express*. His flare for descriptive writing showed early, and in 1912, at the age of 20, he was made the paper's assistant editor.

It was not long, though, before, seduced by the glamour of what Sir Philip Gibbs called the 'Street of Adventure' – Fleet Street – he was off to London. There he worked at first on the staff of the *Empire Magazine*, before moving on to the *Evening Standard* and the *Daily Mail*.

Then, in 1914, he went to war, enlisting as a private. After passing through the Cavalry School at Netheravon, on Salisbury Plain, he received his commission in the Warwickshire Yeomanry. Briefly ill, he was sent into hospital at Colchester. While convalescing, he occupied himself by studying the Roman history of the town, acquiring an interest in British archaeology and ancient history which was balanced by his fascination as a boy with Egyptology, about which he had read in the many books in his father's library.

He had also, as a boy, developed a marked distaste for foreign travel, which, considering the supremely successful travel writer that he was to become, seems odd. This is how it happened. When he was in his early teens he was given £10 to go off on a trip on his own to the Rhineland. He had got as far as Wiesbaen when he found to his horror that he had spent all his money, and, in a state of considerable anxiety, he had to tramp to the coast in order to make it home. After that unpleasant experience he believed that he had finished with travelling for ever.

He came through his army service unscathed, and at the war's end returned to Fleet Street as a special writer for the *Evening Standard*, subsequently moving on to the *Daily Express*, where he became one of 'Lord Beaverbrook's young men'.

A colleague, SPB Mais, recalled Morton as:

> … a thin, tall, quiet man with a deathly-pale face and jet-black hair … he was sent out on all the biggest stories and invariably came back with the least fuss and the best results. He was entirely devoid of arrogance, haste or bluster, or of the attributes we are apt to associate with star reporters.

His success in reporting, in 1923, Howard Carter's discovery of the tomb of Tutankhamun, led to his being given the chance to write a series of vignettes about London life for the *Daily Express*. These were later reprinted in book form as *The Heart of London* (1925), *The Spell of London* (1926), and *The Nights of London* (1926). For good measure, he also produced in 1926, *A London Year* and, *The Methuen Little Guide to London*.

While on a newspaper assignment in 1923, Morton fell seriously ill in Jerusalem. At his lowest ebb, he was filled with an overwhelming home-sickness for England, and made a vow that if he was destined to recover, he would return home in search of England. And that is exactly what he did.

Happily, he made a complete recovery, returned to England, and, true to his word, set off from London driving a bull-nosed Morris to explore and record over the years his wanderings throughout the British Isles.

It was in 1927 that he arrived, notebook in hand, in search of Liverpool. On the day of his coming a gale from America was battering old Sailortown, 'beautiful women were being blown up Lord Street', and the pair of Liver birds were clinging on like grim death to their green dome perches as the wind swept wildly past, failing, however, to ruffle a single metallic feather.

He found it easy, he said, to fall in love with Liverpool, an 'elusive, moody city, so full of variety, beauty; so full of warm vitality.'

The Pier Head attracted him especially – 'A magnet. All roads lead you there; it is the end of all tramway journeys.' He watched the red funnels slide smoothly over the galvanised roofs of the landing-stages, above the gleam and movement of the grey water. His worst rage, his deepest mood of self-pity, his most painful sense of injustice, would all, he said:

> … fly downwind at sight of those ships' funnels and the Liverpool chimneys rising side by side against the sky.

The Anglican Cathedral struck him as unquestionably the grandest thing in the city, 'the greatest piece of church-building since the early Middle Ages'. He saw the 'gigantic red sandstone temple' as Liverpool's splendid contribution to the historic monuments of England, and predicted that if, in the uncertainties of a thousand years, the docks were to fall silent, the cranes to rust and rot on their iron perches, men from every corner of the globe would still make pilgrimage to Liverpool to see and wonder at her unique twentieth century ecclesiastical creation.

Morton thought to have discovered the voice of Liverpool in the sound of the Great Dock Road; the clatter of hooves blending with the rasp and rumble of ironbound wheels bumping over cobbles, to the cadenza of carters' clicking tongues, their geeings and whoaings, and chorus crack of whips.

But the journalist in him is quick to spot the *other* side of the Great Dock Road. He sees where, in the sharp-biting, grey dawn's wind, a hushed crowd of perhaps five hundred men stand waiting. Waiting and hoping. Beyond the massive dock gates, the ships are awakening to a smell of frying bacon and strong brewed coffee. The five hundred go on standing – cold, silent, and breakfastless, each one of them praying to be of the chosen. It is the foreman who makes the choice, decides, in effect, in which slumland hovels the stomachs of wives and children shall that day be filled. Sixty-odd men are selected. They are today's casuals. The ones whose backs and arms and shoulders will reinforce the regular pool of strength that lifts the boxes and totes the bales wherein is packed the Port of Liverpool's prosperity. The four-hundred-odd, the passed-over, the day's rejected of the all-powerful foreman, melt sorrowfully away. Perhaps there will be something for them tomorrow. Perhaps, for them, tomorrow never comes.

Appropriately, it was a Liverpool cotton man who took Morton along to see the Cotton Exchange. His first impression, standing outside, gazing up at the beautiful confection of Doric, Ionic, Renaissance, and so forth, admixed in dignified grace and proportion, was of calm, of perfect harmony, of supreme sanity. It did not last long. Up a stairway, through a door, out to a colonnade of dark, polished granite pillars, and he thought himself to be a safely embowered observer of the zany life lived in a luxurious lunatic asylum.

Down below on the floor of the Exchange, men, a good hundred of them, some bareheaded, some wearing hats, assembled about the perimeter of a circular rail set up in the centre of the great hall, were all babbling, shouting and gesticulating at one another as in a frenzy. In fact, they were buying cotton – cotton which, crazily enough, did not yet even exist. What was being sold were Cotton Futures. It was a sort of gamble, really, on upcoming crops. The commercial mechanics of it all were a little difficult for the novice of the Cotton Ring to fathom.

'I walked out,' wrote Morton, 'still puzzled, but vaguely glad to know that the price of a cotton vest was fixed for April next year!'

His last port of call that visit was to the largest tobacco warehouse on earth, a place jam-packed with millions of bales of St Nicotine's weed of every known variety.

His guide led him up to floor after floor:

> ... each a gloomy, dark, evenly-temperatured, malt-smelling prairie, stacked with hogsheads ... This warehouse contains tobacco which our infant sons will smoke; cigars with which our unborn grandchildren will comfort their declining years.

Finally, he was shown the vast furnace with a high chimney-stack 'rather like a giant's briar'. They call it the King's Pipe. Into it every year go hundreds of pounds' worth of pipe tobacco, cigarettes and cigars, on which, for one reason or another, no one will pay the duty.

> Whenever a dense aromatic smoke issues from the chimney-stack the dockers outside, the loungers round the 'Green Man' and the proppers-up of walls, sniff the air sadly and say: "King's havin' a smoke today." They sniff and sigh. What a waste of good stuff! Plug, probably! Twist, perhaps! What a waste.

When his guide was not looking, Morton stole half a Virginia leaf. He excused himself:

> I did it in the interests of knowledge. This was the kind of tobacco that Sir Walter Raleigh smoked, right from the plantation.

His subsequent verdict:

> It only remains for me to say that if Sir Walter Raleigh brought home from Virginia the kind of leaf tobacco which I stole and smoked in my pipe with some historical emotion, he must have made hundreds of enemies.

Morton added the gigantic tobacco store to Liverpool's other record achievements:

A cathedral which is twice as big as Westminster Abbey. The largest spot cotton market. The largest electrically-driven clock. The largest organ in the world. The first overhead electric railway. The first under-river tunnel. The first enclosed dock.

So great was the impression made on him by the city of Liverpool that he wrote:

I fled from Liverpool, as men occasionally fly from affection. The city is too full of things worth writing about for any man who is supposed to be making a motor-car tour.

At the time of his visit to Liverpool – a Liverpool which has, I may say, in the main long since vanished – HV Morton was 35. Another 51 years of life remained to him. He had already published, in 1927, *In Search of England*, and in 1928 he brought out *The Land of the Vikings* and *The Call of England*, In 1929 came *In Search of Scotland*, followed by *In Search of Ireland* (1930).

He joined the *Daily Herald* in 1931 as its star writer, and published *Blue Days at Sea* (1932), which contained, as well as new work, reprinted pieces from the *Daily Express*, the *Sunday Express* and the *Herald*.

It was in 1932, too, that *In Search of Wales* came out. It was reviewed by Lloyd George, who said of it that it was "The best travel book on Wales I have ever read". Doubtless, that comment played a part in the decision to crown Morton as a Bard at Wrexham in August 1933.

A series of articles which he wrote in which, with the aim of touching and bestirring the country's conscience, he highlighted the terrible plight of the unemployed, was republished in 1933 as a pamphlet under the title, *What I Saw in the Slums*. And 1933 also saw a final volume added to his British travel series, *In Scotland Again*.

Morton's industry was quite extraordinary. His method, a friend said, was simple. He assumed that he was not the hundredth person to write about a subject, but the first.

Between 1934 and 1938, he produced three books on the Middle East. These were the result of an irresistible offer made to him by the publishers Rich and Cowan – an, at that time, unheard of advance of £10,000, plus a royalty of 33 per cent on all sales above 150,000. The first was *In the Steps of the Master* (1934), in which he followed the journeyings of Christ through Palestine, Syria and Transjordan, sold more than half a million copies in the 1930s. Next came *In the Steps of St Paul* (1936), traversing the route of the greatest missionary journey ever made, which sold more than 100,000 copies in the month of publication, and, thirdly, *Through the Lands of the Bible* (1938), reporting his own travels from the Euphrates to the Nile.

A Guide to London (1937), and *Ghosts of London* (1939), bring us up to the outbreak of the Second World War. In the next couple of years three more of his books appeared – *Women of the Bible* (1940), *H.V. Morton's London* (1940) and *Middle East* (1941).

In August 1941, Morton received an intriguing request from Brendan Bracken, Minister of Information:

> I want you to leave England for three weeks, but I regret
> to say that I cannot tell you where you are going or what
> you will see when you get there.

It turned out that he, along with the novelist, Howard Spring, had been chosen by Winston Churchill to accompany him aboard the battleship *Prince of Wales*, to the Atlantic Charter meeting with President Roosevelt, at Placenta Bay, off Newfoundland. The result was Morton's work of instant history, *Atlantic Meeting*, published in 1943.

During 1942, Morton had brought out *I, James Blunt* and, in the October, *I Saw Two Englands*, in which he recorded a journey upon which he had set out in May 1939, before the war, and another upon which he had embarked in October 1939, after the outbreak of war.

Always a quiet, sensitive, unobtrusive man, as he grew older he came to dislike increasingly brash London, and he found himself out of sympathy with post-war England. When Field Marshal Smuts invited him and his wife, Mary, to visit South Africa, they gladly accepted it. And having written *In Search of South Africa* (1948), they liked the country so much that they decided to settle there.

He bought a farm, and half a mountain, 'Sheep Mountain', within sight of Table Bay, in the wine-growing district, 30 miles from Cape Town, and built himself there, as he wrote later, 'an English house, full of English things'. It was here, with the novelist Francis Brett Young as a neighbour, that all the books of his later years were written. Despite the fact that he became a South African, he actually seems to have spent most of his time in Europe.

In 1951, reverting to the old magical formula, he produced *In Search of London*. This was followed in 1954 by *A Stranger in Spain*. His last quintet of books were about Italy, the country that became his second home. He began with *A Traveller in Rome* (1957), for which he was awarded the coveted Cavaliere Order of Merit. Then, in 1960, *This is Rome*, followed, in 1964, by *A Traveller in Italy*, and *The Waters of Rome* (1966). His last book, *A Traveller in Southern Italy*, was published in 1969, when he was 77.

He died in South Africa on 25 June 1979, aged 86, leaving a widow, three sons and a daughter. His ashes were scattered on the little patch of England which he had created under the blazing alien African sun.

FELICIA, SILAS AND HER BENNY

The boy stood on the burning deck,
Whence all but him had fled;
The flame that lit the battle's wreck,
Shone round him o'er the dead.

Those lines, learned perhaps at school, from her poem *Casabianca* – commemorating a young boy of 13 years of age, Casabianca, son of the Admiral of the Orient, who remained at his post, in the Battle of the Nile, after the ship had caught fire, and all the guns had been abandoned; and perished in the explosion of the vessel, when the flames had reached the powder – are virtually all that are remembered today of the scores of thousands of lines written by Mrs Felicia Hemans (pronounced Hemmens), who, before the advent of Elizabeth Barrett Browning, was the most celebrated poetess of the nineteenth century. She was as, if not more, popular than Byron, who, incidentally, christened her 'Hewomans'. And, one hundred and three years after her death, Noel Coward was to parody her poem, *The Stately Homes of England* in his *Operette* (1938).

Born Felicia Dorothea Browne, at 32 (now 118) Duke Street, in Liverpool, on 25 September 1793, she was of mixed Irish, German and Italian blood.

Her maternal grandfather, Benedict Paul Wagner, came of a German Lutheran family, but was an Italian by birth. He was for many years consul to Austrian Tuscany. He was also a member of a German business house, Messrs Fahrer & Wagner, established in Liverpool in 1753. After Herr Fahrer's retirement, the firm became Messrs Wagner & Busch, with its office in Duke Street, and Wagner and his family living at 9 Wolstenholme Square. His two unmarried daughters, Elizabeth and Ann, continued to reside there in the square until their deaths. The last survivor, Ann, dying in 1852, having lived in the same house for some seventy-five years.

It was another of Benedict Wagner's daughters, Felicity Dorothea, who, in 1786, had married George Browne, an Irish wine merchant and banker, who also served as Imperial and Tuscan Consul, who had come to Liverpool from Cork around the time of the Irish volunteering demonstration of 1778. The couple had settled into a house in Duke Street, a few doors up from Mr Wagner's office, and it was here that Felicia was born.

Revolutionary France's declaration of war on Britain, on 1 February 1793, with its deleterious effect on credit, brought ruination to many merchant houses. George Browne had succeeded in surviving this crisis, but went under in the fiscal panic following the landing of French troops in Cardigan Bay in 1797. His financial disaster led George Browne to leave Liverpool in

1800, when Felicia was seven, and to take himself and his family to North Wales, where they lived first at Gwrych, near Abergele, in Denbighshire, their house standing upon part of the site upon which the Victorian Gwrych Castle was subsequently built. In 1809, when Felicia was 16, the family moved to a house named Bronwylfa, at St Asaph. These were the gentle, bucolic Welsh surroundings which she was always, in later life, to recall with great tenderness.

Her father left his wife and children in 1810, moving to Upper Canada. From her mother, a woman well qualified for the task of teaching her, she learnt Latin, drawing, music and modern languages, including German, French, Italian, Spanish and Portuguese, in several of which she was well read. She had also a great love of Shakespeare. Her memory is said to have been phenomenal. She was able, after only one reading, to quote lengthy passages from literature. Reginald Heber's 424-line poem, *Europe*, for instance, which she committed to memory and recited line-perfect within one hour and twenty minutes.

Thought by her family to be a child prodigy, Felicia had, at the age of eight, begun to write verses, and in 1808, when she was 14, she published a privately printed collection of these in a volume, by no means slim, *Poems by Felicia Dorothea Browne*, dedicated to the Prince of Wales. It was unexpectedly harshly received by the critics, which upset her very much, so badly, indeed, that she retired to bed suffering from strain and shock.

Recovering reasonably swiftly, she published another poem that same year, *England and Spain: or Valour and Patriotism*, in over 300 heroic couplets, inspired by her two elder brothers, who were fighting in Spain in the Peninsular War.

Her fugitive poesy having come by chance into his hands, and having heard tell of her personal beauty and charm through his friend, Thomas Medwin, who had met her while staying in Flintshire, Shelley wrote to her suggesting that they might correspond. This, however, she declined to do, and when he persisted, continuing to send letters to her, her mother, who regarded Shelley as a dangerous 'flatterer', stepped smartly in, firing off letters in all directions, persuading Shelley's friends to dissuade him from carrying on despatching unwelcome letters to her daughter. Later on, though, she did correspond with the Scottish poet and dramatist, Joanna Baillie, and with Mary Russell Mitford, poet, dramatist, and the author of *Our Village* (1832).

On 30 July 1812, after she had known him and corresponded with him for three years, having met him in 1809 through her brothers with whom he had fought in Spain, Felicia, aged 19, married, at St Asaph Cathedral, Captain Alfred Hemans, an Irishman, formerly of the 4th or King's Own Regiment. Captain Hemans, who had been appointed adjutant to the Northamptonshire Militia, took his bride off to Daventry, and it was here, in a fine Georgian house in the High Street, that her first son, Arthur, was born. The garrison was reduced, the captain became redundant, and he, his wife and son returned to Wales, making their home with Felicia's mother. Hemans gave Felicia five sons in six years, and then, in 1818, for no reason that has ever been revealed, left her. He journeyed to Italy, ostensibly for the sake of his health, and decided to stay there. Although he and Felicia continued to correspond sporadically concerning the children, they never met again. She remained back in her mother's home. After her mother's death in 1827, she is said to have offered to join Captain Hemans, and to have been refused.

However, it was Felicia Hemans' good fortune to live in an age when there was a great popular demand for poetry, and it was possible for her to support and educate her sons by bringing out a volume of poems a year. She was also able to earn some much-needed extra money by writing on foreign literature for the *Edinburgh Review*, as well as essays in many other magazines, and by winning a number of poetry prizes. She even tried her hand at the writing of plays, only one of which, *The Vespers of Palermo*, was ever acted. It was staged at Covent Garden, but even though Sir Walter Scott supplied an epilogue for it, it was not a success.

A prolific writer, she was flooded with editors' requests for her work, and by 1825, had achieved so wide a reputation that Andrews Norton issued an American edition of her poems. This brought in its wake an invitation to become the editor of a Boston literary periodical, which offer she gracefully declined.

She and her sons had been living in Bronwylfa, which the family had been renting, but which her brother had recently purchased, and when, in 1825, he married, Felicia with her boys, her mother, and her sister, Harriet, moved to a house called Rhyllon, a quarter of a mile away across the little valley of the River Elwy. They continued to live there up to the time of her mother's death in 1827, an event which upset her very severely, as they had been devoted, and it was then that, in order to secure a better education for her boys than was available in rural Wales, she decided to move back to Liverpool. As she herself confessed, so heartbroken was she at leaving the beautiful, inspirational scenery of her beloved Wales, that she covered her eyes when she finally drove away to Liverpool.

In 1827, she rented a fine Georgian house on the north side of Wavertree High Street, Number 17, the first in a block of three (17-21), set back behind a tall brick wall near the junction with Sandown Lane. So high had soared her reputation that it became a place of pilgrimage, visited by many famous people and autograph hunters, especially Americans, who valued her poetry highly, particularly her poem, *The Landing of the Pilgrim Fathers*, traditionally recited on Thanksgiving Day, and who used to carry off as souvenirs, pebbles from her path, or a spray from the trees in her garden.

The house was demolished in 1958.

During the four years that she remained in Wavertree she paid a visit to the local academy, which she celebrated in the poem, *On Visiting a Girls' School at the Hour of Evening Prayer*. She also did some travelling, which included two trips to Scotland, where she met Scott and Lord Jeffrey, and a visit, in 1830, to the Lake District, where she met Wordsworth.

She left Liverpool in April 1831, when she went to settle in Dublin with her younger brother, George, soon to become Commissioner of Police in Ireland. She was then in failing health, and her decline continued slowly but inexorably. She died in Dublin, at 20 Dawson Street, on 16 May 1835, at the early age of 41. She is buried in the vaults of St Anne's Church in that city.

Her demise was mourned by William Wordsworth, who hailed her as 'that holy spirit, sweet as the spring, as ocean deep'. Her work was admired and praised by such capable and eminent critics as Lord Byron, the Countess of Blessington, William Roscoe, Christopher North and George Eliot.

Although a daughter of Liverpool, she did not, it must be sadly admitted, much care for the place. In fact, she disliked both Liverpool and its residents. She longed to return to her hills in Wales, referring to Liverpool's:

> … waveless horizon! How it wearies the eyes … it is a dull uninventive nature all around here, though there must be some little fairy nooks, which I hope by degrees to discover.

Of the local Society, she wrote that it was, 'exclusively under the dominion of an aristocracy of wealth.'

~

Unlike Felicia Hemans, Silas K Hocking was not a native of Liverpool, unlike her, he was enchanted by the place.

> I liked Liverpool so much that I would gladly have settled down there for good. It was big enough to offer the fullest scope for one's energies and yet not so big that one was lost in the crowd. Also it was public spirited enough to meet all one's intellectual needs.

The Reverend Silas Kitto Hocking was a Cornishman, born on 4 March 1850, at Terras, St Stephen-in-Brannel, not far from St Austell. He was the third son of a farmer and overseer of a tin mine, James Hocking, and Eliza Kitto, and it was in his native Cornwall that he began his pastoral life.

From his early years Hocking had evinced an interest in public speaking. He would go anywhere, tramp for miles cross country to distant villages, through rain, wind, snow, frost and darkness, to listen to some 'temperance orator, returned missionary, political aspirant, or budding social reformer'.

He was not interested in the art solely as practised in the pulpit, but wherever he could find a public platform. It so happened, however, that his first invitation to speak came, when he was seventeen, from a little Methodist chapel about two miles from his home. He acquitted himself well, and the following year, 1868, his name appeared on the St Austell Circuit plan as a local preacher on trial. Six months later, he was taking services on the St Columb Circuit as an 'Auxiliary', the parish of his preaching extending from Newquay on the Atlantic seaboard to Mevagissey on the English Channel.

He had drifted into the ministry of the United Methodist Free Churches more or less casually. His real ambition, he confessed, had been to go abroad to join his eldest brother, who had settled in Los Angeles, and seek his fortune in the New World, but he knew how much it would please his parents if he were to become a minister, and his superintendent and the circuit authorities urged him to listen to the call of the Church – although, frankly, he had been conscious of no such call.

His first appointment as a fully accredited Methodist minister was at Pontypool, on the Newport Circuit, in 1870 – 'I never regretted the step I had taken.'

His salary was £55 *per annum*. Out of this, he paid six shillings a week for the rooms he rented in a small cottage in a mean street. After a couple of years he left Pontypool, an illuminated address and a complete set of the little green volumes of Bell's *Aldine Poets* in his modest baggage, directed by the Stationing Committee to pursue his good work in the heart of the Lincolnshire Fens.

He was immediately and acutely aware of the vast difference between the mountains of Wales, which he had grown to love, and the flatlands of the Spalding Circuit. His lodgings were in the market-town of Holbeach.

Two years of bitterly cold winter weather and somnolent summer afternoons, when not a breath of wind stirred the stagnant air over the dykes, and the wide stretch of fenland shimmered in the mud-cracking heat, passed. Then one morning he found a letter awaiting him on his breakfast plate. It proved to contain a gratifying invitation to move on to a country circuit in the north of England. The idea appealed to him greatly.

It was a Saturday, and he was leaving that afternoon to embark on one of his weekly rounds, and would not be back until the following Friday. He therefore lost no time in penning a grateful letter of acceptance, which, duly sealed and stamped, he placed standing against an ornament on the mantelshelf. He did not know it, but the hand of providence was about to deal him what he would in the fulness of time come to regard as a very considerable favour.

Only when he was on the train, well advanced on his way to Spalding, did he remember that he had forgotten to bring that vital letter with him to post. He was very annoyed with himself, but comforted by the thought that his landlady, good soul, would be sure to see it, and would post it for him.

His week of peripatetic pastoral duties passed, punctuated by alternatingly uneasy and duly eased thoughts about the letter. The first thing that he did when he got back home the following Friday, was to make a bee-line for the mantelpiece … and there was the letter, propped against the ornament, just as he had left it.

He stood still, transfixed,

> … feeling inexpressible things. I could have bitten my nails with chagrin and vexation. I had had my chance and missed it. By this time, I told myself, some other man had got the invitation.

At that precise moment, his eyes fell on a letter that had been delivered during his week's absence.

> I tore open the envelope without much interest, and then my heart gave a thump. It was an invitation from Liverpool. I could scarcely believe my own eyes. It seemed too good to be true. Liverpool of all places in the country! The very name awed me a little. Was it not the second city in the kingdom, and one of the greatest sea-ports of the world? To think that I, country born and bred, obscure and unknown, without any standing as yet in the denomination, should be invited to minister in such a city …

Liverpool was, indeed, to prove a place of tremendous importance in the life of Silas Hocking, for it was here that he was to find not only a wife, but the raw material for what was to become a best-selling book, and launch him upon a career of successful authorship.

When he first arrived in Liverpool in about 1875, he was cordially invited by Richard Lloyd, the Circuit Steward, to stay at his house until he could find suitable rooms. There he got to know the Lloyds' younger daughter, 18-year-old Esther Mary, and fell in love with her. They were married in 1876. She bore him two sons and a daughter.

There were five ministers on the Liverpool Circuit, each with his own centre for pastoral work. Hocking's was a 'down-town church' – in Grove Street, actually.

It had been a highly respectable neighbourhood in its day, but that day was before my time. My pastoral work took me into some of the poorest districts of the city, and it was here that I made the acquaintance of the originals of Joe Wragg and Little Nell and Her Benny; though I had no idea then that I should ever write a story about them.

Silas Hocking entered whole-heartedly into the life of the Liverpool of his day. He rode the ferry-boats – he had two small places to look after, one at Birkenhead, the other at Seacombe.

He used the city's library and free reading room, which proved an inestimable boon.

One could get almost any book one needed, and see all the latest magazines and reviews. In my previous circuits no such institution existed. If I wanted a new book, I had to buy it or go without, and as money was scarce it was generally a case of going without.

He had always been a lover of music, and in Liverpool he experienced,

… an enlarged conception of what music really meant, and to what magic heights it could climb. St George's Hall boasts one of the finest organs in the kingdom, and Mr Best was a very prince of organists. His recitals were a revelation to me. Then for the first time I heard all the great oratorios, performed by immense choirs and full orchestras, whilst the finest singers in the country were engaged for the solo parts. In addition scarcely a week passed that there was not a concert in the fine Philharmonic Hall."

Neither did he find Liverpool falling short in the matter of art:

Art was encouraged by a yearly exhibition of modern pictures as well as by the permanent collections in the Walker Art Gallery.

Crowning all this:

We had lectures on every conceivable topic. It was in St George's Hall I heard Mr Swan, and saw one of the first exhibitions of electric lighting. It was in the Mount

Street Institute I first saw and heard Mark Twain. He lectured on 'Our Fellow-Savages, the Sandwich Islanders', and as an encore told the story of *The Jumping Frog*.

Liverpool was not, he opined, a literary centre, and yet it could boast a number of able writers and journalists. He mentioned particularly Edward Russell, Ashcroft Noble and Hall Caine. He mentioned, too, those most distinguished Liverpool Noncomformist ministers, Hugh Stowell Brown and Mr Birrell, the father of Augustin Birrell. Liverpool, he averred:

> With its spacious squares, its splendid parks, its fine public buildings, its magnificent waterway, its miles of crowded docks, had a dignity all its own. Moreover, it breathed an atmosphere of culture, it encouraged the arts, particularly music and painting, it had its coteries of literary people, it was cosmopolitan.

In 1878, having passed all his examinations and been received into what was termed 'full connexion', Hocking was now entitled to a furnished house. One had become available at Burnley in Lancashire, and, this time with a wife for company, off went the itinerant preacher to what he described as:

> ... a big, dirty, over-grown manufacturing town lying along a deep valley, flanked by bleak and, for the most part, tree-less hills.

The Hockings' house was situated on the hillside above the town, and from their dining-room window they could count close on a hundred tall chimneys, all belching out a continuous cloud of smoke. The centre of the ministry was the Brunswick Chapel, a big, square building capable of seating a congregation of 1,600 dissenting souls.

It was all very different from Liverpool, and the couple had to grow used to new street sounds, such as that which, the first morning after their arrival, startled them out of their sleep – the immense rattle and clatter along the dawn-washed, cobbled streets of the iron-shod clogs of hundreds of men and women, lads and lasses, hurrying to the mills – the hum of machinery and the clacking of the looms, which, escaping from those mills, seemed to fill the air, and the all-pervading smell of oil and size and cotton-waste.

Hockings' workload in Burnley was not unduly heavy, and most evenings he was able to have to himself, reading or writing the occasional article for the *Connexional Magazine*. One particular evening he had planned to go out on a round of visits, but when he opened the front-door he was met by a deluge of rain accompanied by a raging wind. He hesitated momentarily, then turned back, hung up his hat and coat, and retired to his study.

> For a while I sat staring into the fire, listening to the wind rumbling in the chimney and the beating of the rain against the window. Perhaps it was the voice of the wind and rain that sent my thoughts trailing back and back to the days of my boyhood. Suddenly I had a picture of a little fishing village on the north coast of Cornwall, with the waves breaking on the rocks outside. Then I saw the beginning of a story. I turned at once to the table and began to write …

It was during the second year of his four-year stay in Burnley that Hocking wrote his story of 'two homeless Liverpool waifs, with only their courage and love for one another to keep them going' – *Her Benny*.

> I began to write [*Her Benny*] one Saturday evening after dinner. I had been distributing prizes to the successful competitors in an examination inaugurated by the Sunday School Union. Whilst the chairman was delivering a rather wordy speech, I glanced at the prize books which were laid out on the platform close at hand. One small volume arrested my attention. It was a story of street life somewhat on the lines of *Jessica's First Prayer*. I ran through it hurriedly … my feeling was that the story was not true to life or to fact … and the question that arose in my mind was, could I write a better story built on my own experience? As I made my way home I turned the matter over and over in my mind. The picture grew unconsciously. Before dinner was over it had obsessed me, I could think of nothing else. When the table was cleared I got out pen, ink and paper, and dropping into my easy chair before the fire with my writing pad on my knees, began …
> *It was getting dark, though the Town Hall clock had only just struck four. But a fog had hung all over Liverpool since morning, and everything was as damp and dismal as it well could be; and now, as evening came on, the fog had settled into a downright drizzle, converting the streets into what seemed to Nelly Bates (who was crouched in the shadow of St George's Church) to be endless puddles.*
> *"I wish Benny would come," said she to herself. "I wonder*

what has kept him? He said he'd be here when the clock struck four."

And she wrapped her tattered clothes more closely around her, and looked eagerly down Lord Street and up and down Castle Street. But no Benny appeared in sight.

My wife sat on the other side of the fireplace busy with her sewing. I wrote steadily until bed-time, by which time I had broken the back of the first chapter, and I scarcely altered a word of it before sending it to the press.

The subjects of the tale are:

> … two homeless waifs, with only their courage and love for one another to keep them going. Benny Bates and his sister, Nell, face the injustice and hardship of the Liverpool of the 1870s. While little Nell sells 'fusees' in Paradise Street, 'her Benny' earns a copper by carrying the bags of the gentlemen travellers at the Pier Head. Somehow, with the help of their old friend, Joe Wrag, the night-watchman, they survive … until one terrible day …

If there is any criticism to be levelled at what remains to this day an, albeit distinctly old-fashioned, but none the worse for that, tear-jerker, it is that Hocking's rendition of scouse betrays either an exceedingly inadequate ear, or an insufficient first-hand acquaintance with the Liverpool street arabs of the late nineteenth century, for his characters speak in what can only be described as a kind of bastard cockney.

The book, which appeared in 1879, was an immediate runaway success. It sold over 200,000 copies and was translated into many languages, and forty years on was still selling.

It did not, however, make Silas Hocking's fortune. He had been offered, and accepted, £20 for the copyright from the publishers, Frederick Warne & Co.

> On pressing for a more generous offer I was told that if by any chance the book proved a success, I should not be forgotten, but should have a share of the profits … In reply to a reminder [of that promise] I received a cheque for ten pounds. That was the end of *Her Benny* as far as I am concerned.

The original manuscript of *Her Benny* is now preserved in the Picton Library.

As lately as 1966 a new edition was published by the Gallery Press, Liverpool.

The circuit clock was ticking inexorably on again, and marching orders arrived once more, and the Hocking family was off to Manchester, where, his own specific ministry apart, Hocking did sterling redemptive work additionally, among the poorest of the poor lost sheep, with the Manchester City Mission.

Three years in Manchester, and then it was off again, in 1883, to Southport – 21 Scarisbrook Road – where they were to live throughout his time as minister of the newly-built Duke Street United Methodist Church chapel. He was to remain there for thirteen years.

By 1896, Hocking had published twenty books. They were selling by tens of thousands, and it was now that he took the decision to turn full-time author, and, at the age of 46, retired from the ministry. Between 1897 and 1917, he was to publish at least one book every year, and between 1919 and 1934, wrote another half-dozen, bringing his grand total up to 48 volumes. Literary ability seems to have run in the family, for both his younger brother, Joseph, and his sister, Salome, were prolific and successful novelists.

He also found time to travel extensively, visiting the United States, Canada, Egypt, Algiers and many parts of Europe.

Having witnessed at first-hand the injustices inflicted by the Anglican squirearchy in Cornwall, and how, late in life, his father lost everything, a victim of the county's archaic and unjust system of land tenure, Hocking understandably turned to both social and land reform.

He stood, unsuccessfully, twice for Parliament. In 1906 he contested (Liberal) Mid-Bucks, and in 1910, Coventry. His radical stance in relation to such issues as Sunday cinema, golf and divorce reform, did not endear him to many of the voters.

He spent his later years in North London in a house named Heatherlow, in Avenue Road, Highgate. He died aged 85 on 15 September 1935.

THESPIAN
ECHOES

TO MEET MR HARRISON

There could be no mistaking the tall figure in the velvet-collared, camel-hair overcoat and smart brown trilby that unfolded itself from the first-class carriage of the London-Liverpool express and stepped out on to the platform at Lime Street Station. I was there to meet Mr Harrison, returning that day in September 1954 to the very same platform from which, accompanied by his doting mother, he had set off twenty-seven years before to London to seek his theatrical fortune.

Today, Rex Harrison was arriving back in his home town a very rich and very famous man, a totally different person from the 19-year-old lad who had left with the discouraging words of William Armstrong, the resident director of the Liverpool Playhouse, ringing in his ears.

> He begged me, in his very short, precise Scottish speech, to give up acting. He said the profession was overcrowded and only people with exceptional talent could get to the top. And he said: 'Please, Rex, why don't you try and do something else?' Ironically, in later years William Armstrong claimed to have discovered me.

With his wife, Lilli Palmer, he was back for the British premiere of John Van Druten's play, *Bell, Book and Candle*, at the Royal Court. We arranged to meet at the theatre that evening.

When I got there, I hardly recognised him. He was sitting alone in the middle of the stalls still wearing his hat – I gathered that he was self-conscious and sensitive about his baldness – and a pair of thick horn-rimmed glasses. He looked stressed, and was alternately snapping and shouting bad-temperedly at the members of the cast.

Always a perfectionist, he was taking the rôle of director very seriously. Not once was the faintest shade of the suave, charming, amused and amusing character that Harrison presented so delightfully on stage and screen, even remotely discernible. Here was just a nasty, sarcastic, ill-humoured, difficult, if not impossible, to please, bully. And, most surprisingly, he presented, personality-wise, as being simply a disagreeable nonentity; not an iota of charisma. The off-stage transformation was literally unbelievable.

Sitting there close to him in the near-dark for well over an hour, I began to sort out in my mind the sequence of events in his life that had led up to this moment.

He was born, into the Edwardian age, on Thursday 5 March 1908, at

Derry House, a fairly imposing, double-fronted, middle middle-class residence, with a large lawn stretching in front of it, and a fine laburnum tree overhanging the gate, in Tarbock Road, in what was, ninety-four years ago, the tiny Lancashire village of Huyton. It was a difficult birth, and his mother, who had already had two daughters – Marjorie, born in 1900, and Sylvia, born in 1904 – was advised that she ought not to have any more children.

The Harrison family had, a generation back, been extremely wealthy. Whence precisely their fortune had derived, no one ever elected to disclose. Although it was not told in Gath – or Gateacre – the whisper was that the family money had been minted by the slave-trade.

Rex's father, William Reginald Harrison, known in the family as Bill, was the third of a characteristically large Victorian brood of seven sons and one daughter. They had been reared in a very grand Georgian property, Belle Vale Hall, at Gateacre. The hall, with its magnificent stable, that looked like a small mansion – into the clock tower of which the young Rex once climbed, and, sitting in the clock's works, waited, hands over ears, for it to sound the hour – was surrounded by acres of grounds. They included lakes, croquet lawns, hard and soft tennis courts, and a cricket pitch and pavilion. Together with Rex's father and his six brothers, there were enough stable lads and gardeners to field a cricket eleven. The family, who boasted a crest and the motto, 'Courage through fear', also owned a yacht, and held the shooting rights on a Scottish grouse moor.

Rex recalled being taken on visits to Belle Vale Hall as a child. He was all his life to remember the great staircase, the gun room, the huge dining-room, the wonderful views across fields and orchards, the splendid rookery, and the lovely noise of the rooks. His grandfather, who had gone bankrupt, was dead by then. His somewhat eccentric Grandmother Harrison was, however, still very much alive. She spent her waking hours in a very large, electrically-driven Bath chair, in which she would tear around at a spanking pace intoning the while like a mantra: 'Have to eat hash. Have to eat stew. No money, no money, no money.'

Belle Vale Hall had eventually to be sold. It was converted into a jam factory for a while, but was subsequently demolished, and the site is now Belle Vale Housing Estate.

William Reginald had been educated at Harrow School. He was there at the same time as Winston Churchill and John Galsworthy, incidentally, Rex's favourite playwright and novelist. He went on to the University of Hanover to study mechanical engineering, there being at that time no faculty of the kind at Oxford or Cambridge. He returned to England, and met and promptly fell in love with Edith Mary Carey.

She came from a Baptist background. Her grandfather had dedicated himself to the conversion of the heathen in India. Among her progenitors, ministers, parish clerks and dominies predominated. Her father, Eustace

Carey, had not, however, felt the call of the clerical cloth, preferring to train as an analytical chemist, and finished up as an industrial chemist in the lucrative position of secretary of the United Alkali Company. He married Mary Jane Picard, and raised a family of three sons and one daughter, Edith Mary. She had played a good deal of tennis with her brothers, and with Bill Harrison when he was courting her.

It was shortly after their marriage that Bill's father went into bankruptcy, and Bill Harrison very soon abandoned engineering in favour of a humdrum and not especially remunerative job as a produce broker at the Liverpool Stock Exchange. He and Edith were, however, sufficiently well off to employ a cook, a housemaid and a nanny, and to run a car. The house at Huyton, staid and Edwardian in atmosphere, was furnished with good, heavy, inlaid wood furniture, some of which had descended to them from both sides of the family, and exuded a feeling of modest prosperity.

Reginald Carey, as Bill and Edith Harrison's new-born baby was christened, although he was, as we shall see, to become Rex, was a rather puny, sickly-looking infant, and indeed, in his top-floor bedroom a large kettle was often to be seen boiling on the grate, billowing forth clouds of steam to relieve his congested lungs. It has been reported that also, unknown to his parents, the young Rex suffered from intestinal tuberculosis. Cosseted and tenderly nursed by his mother, petted and coddled by his sisters, who treated their baby brother like a new doll, Rex grew into the typical spoilt and self-willed child.

At the age of four, Rex was taken by the hand and led by his mother up the lane running past Derry House to Huyton College. Although it was founded in 1892 as a school for girls, there was a kindergarten which accepted boys between the ages of four and seven. The year was 1912, and, oddly enough, at that time my mother was a pupil at Huyton College, but, some years older than Rex, she would have been in one of the higher forms.

Thoroughly accustomed to manipulating females and getting his own way at home, Rex tried his tricks on with his fellow-pupils. They did not work. They signally failed. The little girls ganged up against him, and bullied him quite harshly.

Summer holidays at this time were taken either with a multitude of cousins at the seaside, on the beaches of Penmaenmawr, in North Wales, where, after swimming in the often bitterly cold Irish Sea, Rex would have to be fed sugary buns by his parents to warm him up, or in the Lake District, at his maternal grandfather's house, Ferney Green, at Bowness-on-Windermere.

Back home in Huyton, the six-year-old boy, who was later to be known world-wide as 'Sexy Rexy', embarked upon his first romance. The object of his extravagant affection was a little girl of eight named Sheila Brunner. The nursery at Derry House overlooked the far larger grounds, which amounted to an estate, of the Brunners' much grander house, opposite. It was Sheila's home. She had lovely long, dark hair, which, Rex decided, compensated for her undeniably skinny figure. On hot summer days the two children would take their clothes off and swim together in their birthday suits in the ornamental pools in Sheila's grounds.

Describing it years later, Rex wrote:

> The water was black with mud and tadpoles, but to me
> it was crystal clear as I watched Sheila swimming about,
> her long hair trailing in the water.

When one day their innocent aquatic antics were discovered, there was bilateral parental turmoil. The two children were hauled off home. It was further discovered that Rex had been playing truant from the kindergarten, hiding in the coal-hole until lessons had begun, and then sloping off to the Brunners' – and Sheila. As a punishment, he was locked up and forbidden to see Sheila.

His reaction was to smother himself in black grease as he removed the chain from his tricycle, to strand himself up a tall tree, and finally, in a petulant fury, to hit himself on the head with a hammer, so hard that the claws stuck in his forehead, leaving deep scars which remained faintly visible for the rest of his life.

As things turned out, he was to be separated from Sheila anyway by irresistible force of immovable circumstance. It was while the Harrisons were on holiday at Penmaenmawr in August 1914, that the First World War broke out, and late in 1915, or early in 1916, the family moved across the Pennines to Sheffield. Rex's father's war effort was to enter the Rigby steel factory there, owned by a friend with whom he had studied engineering in Hanover, to design armour plating for battleships. They settled into a rented house at Sharrow Bottom, near the steel mills.

Rex, Sheila-less and unhappy, caught a bad dose of measles. He was kept in a duly darkened room for the duration of the illness, but, that standard precaution notwithstanding, he still lost most of the sight of his left eye.

He definitely did not like Sheffield. No trees to climb. No ponds to swim in. Attending as a day boy, Birkdale Preparatory School, where he was one of about 60 pupils. The rare occasion standing round the piano with his sisters trying to sing Gilbert and Sullivan airs to their mother's inaccurate accompaniment. His greatest excitement, a few Zeppelin raids that sent them all scuttling to the cellars.

The war ended. He'd begun to think it never would. At last they could leave Sheffield. They went first, and briefly, to stay in modest lodgings at Southport. And then they returned to Liverpool, not Huyton, but to a smaller house at 5 Lancaster Avenue, Sefton Park, and Bill Harrison resumed his not too taxing duties as a produce broker.

Rex was now ten years old, and had reached an important decision. He had never liked the name Reginald. He hated it. When he had first started to talk he had not been able to pronounce it, and had called himself 'Baa'. After that he had been Reggie, and then Bobby. But now he had made up his mind. Henceforth, he would be Rex. He didn't know where he'd first heard the name. Someone calling their dog, perhaps. It didn't matter. He liked it. And the whole family went along with his request.

Now, cycling wildly into Rex's life, came Cynthia Miles, blonde and shapelier than Sheila. A close neighbour, she lived only a few minutes away, and it was not long before he and she were whirring at breakneck speeds around Sefton Park on their bicycles. The susceptible Rex was once again smitten.

In 1919, eleven years old, Rex was sent to Liverpool College, a fairly well-known minor public school. He was not given to intellectual pursuits. In his own words: "I felt fairly convinced that Einstein had not made a second coming." He frankly despised things academic. He admitted that his knowledge of literature was, and remained, minimal. His father, whom he regarded as exceptionally well read, used to help him with his homework.

He did, however, delight his father with his athletic prowess. Bill Harrison had been quite a sportsman in his time, running the 100 yards in 10.05 seconds, and playing hockey for England as a member of the West Derby Hockey Club. Indeed, it was under his father's patient tuition that Rex had developed into a good enough left-handed bowler to be selected for the school's First XI. He played a lot of cricket, and was to remain a cricket addict all his life. He played rugby, too, and sufficiently well to get a place in the school's Second XV. He also joined the school's Officer Training Corps, and although he heartily hated the after-school-hours square-bashing, he quite enjoyed taking part in the military manoeuvres.

But what interested Rex far more deeply than anything else was the Junior Dramatic Society, which was run by the classics master, Mr Fred Wilkinson, and in which he hastened to enrol.

His first appearance in any theatre was in the annual school play, *A Midsummer Night's Dream*, as Flute, the bellows-mender, who doubles as Thisbe, a fair maiden, for which part his mother made him a large corn-coloured wig of straw, that went on like a basin, and a long dress. He played it with an ample bosom and – deciding to go for laughs, which he got in plenty – a lisp. There were two performances at the Crane Theatre, in May 1922.

His second stage rôle at Liverpool College was in Maeterlinck's *The Blue Bird*, in which he played the Cat. His mother again made his costume for him – a clinging black velvet suit, with a hood with ears on it, whiskers fashioned from waxed pipe-cleaners, and an enormously long tail. Lacking as yet the necessary stage experience and expertise requisite for convincing tripping on his tail, he nevertheless won laughs with his opening, and only, line: "Miaow-are-you?"

His parents, his sisters, and, most importantly, his sweetheart of the moment, Cynthia Miles, were in the audience to witness his triumph, and they all complimented him on his performance. The next day, he and Cynthia bicycled furiously round Sefton Park, Rex screaming out his "Miaow-are-you?" entrance line, and she responding to every repetition with piercing shrieks of delight.

At the end of five years the time had come for 16-year-old Rex to leave Liverpool College to make a start at earning his own living. But what to do? That was the question. His father toyed with the idea of his joining him at the Stock Exchange. Rex didn't think so. Sister Sylvia's fiancé, a young Scots barrister, David Maxwell Fyfe, who was to become Home Secretary and end up as Lord Chancellor and Earl of Kilmuir, suggested that he should train as a solicitor. Rex didn't think so. Said Sylvia: "He hadn't the brains." What Rex *did* think, what he absolutely positively *knew*, was that he was going to be an actor. And that is what he now told his parents.

It wasn't much of a surprise really. In a sense, they had only themselves to blame. Since the time that he was little more than a toddler they had been taking him regularly to pantomimes and to the theatre. He had seen the Liverpool appearances of such giants of the time as Gerald du Maurier, the one whom ever after he always yearned to emulate, Ralph Lynn, Charles Hawtrey and Seymour Hicks, at whose performance he had laughed so loud, long, and heartily that his parents had been requested to remove him from the theatre.

The young Rex had for years been coming home from his visits to the theatre, dragooning his family to sit themselves down on a row of chairs in the drawing-room, while he drew the thick curtains over the bay window, in order to emerge from behind them bowing deeply, acknowledging his parents' rapturous applause, and taking curtain calls innumerable, without considering it necessary to give any prior performance!

Nevertheless, his father, tall, straight-backed, wearing his usual Norfolk jacket with a cornflower – the Harrow School flower – in his buttonhole, wasn't too sure about the idea of having his son go on the stage. But his mother, the dominant member of the family, was, in fact, rather pleased. It had long been evident to her that Rex had an artistic temperament and ability. She herself had studied music in Stuttgart, and, frustrated in her own ambition to become a concert pianist – for which she definitely did not have the ability – she was determined that Rex should be allowed to follow his talent to the limit of its stretch. And she convinced her wavering husband that their son should be encouraged every step of the way, that they should do all that lay in their power to further his ambition.

Thus persuaded, Harrison *père* promised that he would have a word in the ear of one of the members of the board of the Liverpool Playhouse whom he knew, and see what could be done.

What was done was that an interview was arranged with the Playhouse's resident director and producer, William Armstrong, a tall, energetic, Scot, from Edinburgh, with thinning red hair, and a dour manner. He scanned intently Rex's face and body. "He looked at me with obvious distaste. Clearly, he would have liked me to be prettier." Perhaps. Nonetheless, Armstrong said that he would see if he could fit him in, and would let him know when a vacancy occurred.

After months of waiting and hoping, the call came. A postcard dropped on to the hall mat at Lancaster Avenue. It bore, printed along the top, the magic words 'The Playhouse, Liverpool', and read simply: 'Please attend rehearsals, 10.30, 30 May 1924', and was signed, 'William Armstrong'.

In addition to its resident company of seventeen actors and actresses, the Playhouse also took on about ten students every season. Rex ranked as a student, and was paid ten shillings and sixpence a week. Fortunately, he lived at home with his parents, so salary was not of great moment. He began his theatrical career doing odd jobs backstage and watching rehearsals. He had "scarcely found his clothes hook in the communal dressing-room", when, at the end of the third week in June, the Playhouse closed for its ten-week, unpaid, summer break.

Rex duly reported back in September, and made his first professional stage appearance on 17 November 1925, in a half-hour curtain-raiser, *Thirty Minutes in a Street*. Cast as an anguished father-to-be, he had to rush across the stage, distraught and dishevelled, shouting distractedly, "Fetch a doctor! … Baby!" In the excitement, confusion, and novelty of his situation, on the opening night he hurtled out of the wings and pelted across the stage yelling at the top of his bent, "Fetch a baby! … Doctor!" And that was his first ever stage utterance!

After that, three months elapsed before he was given the chance to appear again. This was as 'Another Footman', a tray-carrier you could say, in John Galsworthy's *Old English*, which opened on 15 February 1926. The rôle did not require much of him, merely to pour more port into his glass when the star, Herbert Lomas, gave the order, "Fill up, fill up". But, by some malignant mischance, Rex found himself stage-struck, petrified, unable to move. Lomas, the great professional, paused. Then, smoothly, delivered the line again. The audience laughed. Music to Lomas' ears, who set great store by audience interplay. This time Rex poured the port. Lomas decided that he liked the bit of business, and they kept it in for the rest of the run. That was Rex's last rôle of his first season.

He started his second season with a brief appearance in *Doctor Knock*, by Jules Romain, on which the curtain went up on 11 October 1926. Following the departure of several of the actors and actresses the previous June, he found himself promoted to the status of resident member of the 1926-1927 season company, and in receipt of a correspondingly increased stipend.

On 9 November 1926, he played the native, Jimmy Kanaka, in Eugene O'Neill's *Gold*. This was very exciting, for it was the first time that he had been entrusted with a part big enough to see his name as an actor on the call board inside the stage door.

It was a part that required him to 'black-up' and wear only a loincloth. He had to climb to the top of a palm tree in the centre of the stage and pretend to sight a ship. He took up his position on the stage among the other sailors on the desert island, then began his ascent of the fake palm.

Unfortunately, no one had taken the trouble to warn him that the palm tree was still wet with the flame-resistant chemical with which it had been fire-proofed, too soon, as it turned out, to dry properly before the performance. And the consequence was: the native who shinned up the tree descended piebald.

> Instead of making an exit like a Noble Savage, I slunk off
> like a whipped cur, still trying to cover the white spots
> with my arms.

Having played in JM Barrie's *A Kiss for Cinderella*, which was the company's Christmas 1926 offering, he was cast in *Milestones*, by Arnold Bennett and Edward Knoblock, which brought him his first critical notice. Opined the *Liverpool Echo*: 'Mr Rex Harrison was nicely in the picture in a minor part.'

What was to be his last, and most important, rôle, was that of a messenger in the final production of the season, John Drinkwater's *Abraham Lincoln*. Rehearsing, Rex decided, in the interest of verisimilitude, to give method realism to the part of a man absolutely exhausted and incredibly out of breath. He was in mid-representation when out of the obscurity of the stalls there issued forth a voice.

"You all right, Harrison?"

"Yes, Mr Armstrong, yes. I'm *acting*."

"Oh, I thought you were having a heart attack."

Whatever William Armstrong may have thought, the *Liverpool Echo* once more brought praise to bear:

> Two of the younger members of the cast, Mr Basil Moss
> and Mr Rex Harrison, again showed themselves to be the
> possessors of definite talents. Mr Harrison's dumb show
> as the messenger from Fort Sumter was finely effective.

Now aged 19, Rex had decided that this was to be his final appearance with the Liverpool Repertory Company. He felt that he had learnt a great deal at the Playhouse during his two and a half years there, but he was impatient to try his luck in London. On 18 June 1927, he came officially off the Playhouse payroll.

When the time came to say farewell, William Armstrong, in his very short, very precise and clipped Scottish accent told him bleakly that he strongly advised him to give up any thought of a career on the stage:

> The theatrical profession is overcrowded, and only people with exceptional talent can get to the top. Oh, Harrison, for God's sake don't go on with this. It's no good. I do beg you to give it up. Go into your father's business. Why don't you try something else? Do anything, but don't go on with acting.

"Ironically," said Harrison, "in later years William Armstrong claimed to have discovered me!"

Hardly surprisingly, Rex left the Playhouse with no regrets. Having decided to ignore Armstrong's gloomy predictions, he went off to London to seek fame and fortune. And his mother came too! The pair of them caught a train from Lime Street Station, and his mother saw him safely settled in with her widowed sister-in-law, his Aunt Evelyn Carey, and his cousins, at her flat in Leinster Gardens, Notting Hill Gate. From there he began the round of the West End agents, looking for work.

~

It was getting on for midnight when, at last, Rex Harrison felt that the *Bell, Book and Candle* cast had had as much rehearsing as they could take for the moment, and he invited me to come along with him to his dressing-room.

"Strangely enough," he said, "one of my first recollections is of being brought as a child to a matinée at the old Royal Court to see Fred Terry and Julia Neilson in The Scarlet Pimpernel. "

I was particularly interested to discover how he was affected by his return to the scenes of his youth and early struggles, and as we sat there, he told me over a glass or two of whisky, something of his Liverpool days.

The years between, he said, seemed to have diminished.

> When you travel all over the world meeting different people you tend to forget the places and folk that you left behind when you were very young, but whenever I return to Liverpool I have found that all those things have remained tucked away in the back of your mind until some little thing suddenly releases a flood of memories.

His four great friends in his Liverpool days had been Basil Moss and Jack Minster, like himself junior members of the Rep company; Christopher Thomas, who was employed at the Leverhulme soap works; and Arthur Barbosa, a lanky Anglo-Portuguese student at Liverpool Art School.

'Art', as Rex always called him, and who, in sardonic response, called him 'Sir', was to remain one of the very few friends in his life whom Rex did not lose or alienate. They lived on the same Number 15 tram route, and their homes were quite close. Rex would drop in, just push past the maid as soon as she opened the door, or, if he found it unlocked, open it himself, stand at the foot of the stairs and yell up them, "Art! Art!" Art's mother took a dim view of his conduct, and used to say, "That Harrison boy … no manners at all."

Theirs was, of course, the Liverpool of the Roaring Twenties, the Liverpool of the economic depression. The streets were very different from the way they are today. There was the odd omnibus, but the trams, rattling and rocking along their ordained lines, literally held sway. There was a local legend that an hour's unbroken journey on the top deck would unfailingly bring about any ardently desired miscarriage! Motor-cars were jostled by horse-powered delivery vans and pony traps. A rough, tough, exuberant air blew, like the perpetual-seeming draught straight off the Irish Sea, through the toddlin' town.

Out into the galvanic night air Rex and his sensation seeking friends would sally forth. Most likely the local dance halls would be the main objective of the evening. Rex recalled with a twinkling eye "the crazy flappers with bandanas and short skirts" doing the Charleston and the Black Bottom. "I loved them all, and I loved my own lovely beige Oxford bags. I was very dressy then."

He was, indeed, gradually transformed into an extremely dapper young man-about-town, with a predilection for plus-fours. He used to borrow his racecourse tweeds from his Uncle Stanley Harrison, who owned and trained racehorses, and had himself ridden in the Grand National, falling off, breaking his collarbone, and remounting to finish sixth.

For a time, Rex wore his hair, greased to a patent leather shine, parted in the middle. Very lounge lizardy. An impression further embellished by the wearing of a monocle, an affectation which he subtly explained away on the ground of his afflicted left eye. In practical terms, the monocle was used to great effect in the appreciative scrutinising of Liverpool's pretty girls; and in line with this aristocratic pose, he used to pretend that he had been educated at Uppingham, a public school that was generally regarded by those in the snob know, as rather more socially impressive than Liverpool College.

He was also an expert exponent of the latest dances – Charleston and Black Bottom – and would teach the young Liverpool maidens, among other things, how to dance them. One of the most favoured rendezvous was the tea dance, the *thé dansant* as it was fashionably called, and here, on afternoons when he was not required to be in the theatre, the light-fantastic-tripping Rex could most frequently be found.

The great meeting place for all the Playhouse actors and actresses, and also for the members of the touring companies who came to Liverpool, was the Lyceum Café, at the bottom of Bold Street. It was there that Rex met Carol Reed, who, not yet transmogrified into a cult film director, was then still an actor, carrying a spear in Sybil Thorndike's touring company, which was bringing Shakespeare and Shaw to Liverpool.

Rex mused wistfully:

> Places like the Lyceum Café don't exist any more. I don't know what young hopefuls do without them. It was a large room full of smoke; in those days everyone used to smoke away like chimneys. There were lots of tables, milky coffee and tea, and those cakes that broke your teeth, aptly named rock cakes, with currants and raisins in them, little fairy cakes with icing on top, and cream puffs. The waitresses were very old or very young, and wore black uniforms with white aprons. You could sit there for hours over one coffee without them disturbing you.

As a matter of fact, it was from Carol Reed that Rex plucked away his girlfriend, a very pretty young actress, Primrose Morgan. He took her out to dinner, then home for a drink, and to meet his parents. But by the time they reached Lancaster Avenue, the entire household had retired to bed. Rex put Primrose up for the night in the spare room, and broke the news of her presence in the house to his parents at breakfast.

For all his undeniable charm, there was quite a significant downside to the Harrisonian character. He had a very nasty temper. He was excessively inclined to swearing and the use of really bad language, which he gave forth with freely and disgustingly in front of women. He was also, as my Aunt Brenda, who knew him well in those days and used to meet him with his ukulele at parties, testified, very mean in petty ways, always, for instance, cadging, and never offering, cigarettes. And although an enthusiastic beer toper, with the merry rallying cry, "Bung ho, troops!" his stinginess in the matter of standing his corner was a byword among his drinking cronies, whose rallying cry was, "Your shout, Harrison!" His sexual adventurings were also regarded as somewhat quaint, and he developed a frankly confessed liking for the ladies of the streets, especially black ones. This may have been a trait inherited from his father, for, according to one of Rex's cousins, old Bill was "known as a womaniser by all the relatives, and disliked because of it."

A friend of both Rex and Art's was Stuart Jeans, whose uncle, Frank Jeans, the well-known Liverpool surgeon, was at his happiest spending his non-working hours with non-operating theatre folk, whom he loved to entertain at his house in Rodney Street. If the light was burning in the big, round, high-up, cornice window, that usually meant that there was a party in progress, and it was at parties thrown by him that Rex met many a London star who happened to be in Liverpool touring the provinces – Jack Buchanan, Ronnie Squire, Binnie Hale – as well as a sprinkling of what were to prove in the none too distant future, very useful West End managers.

~

It was getting really late now. People were very obviously wanting to close the theatre down and go home to bed. We shared a taxi to the Adelphi, and a last drink.

The old hotel brought another flood of memories …

> Back in the 'twenties, the Adelphi, which was a popular place for music and dancing, opened a night spot called the Bear Garden. They had an unbelievably noisy band there of what used to be described as the 'washboard' variety. They played blues with a man scraping a piece of wood rhythmically along a wooden washboard. It was a form of New Orleans jazz to which Art and I were at that time particularly addicted.

Sometimes, in the less august terpsichorean haunts of the rowdier local dance halls, Rex and Art would take turns at conducting, and Rex, in partnership with Basil Moss, had formed a ukulele duo. Some nights, after the safety curtain had descended at the Playhouse, the pair would hare off to fill the Sandon Club, at the Bluecoat School, with their string-twanging renditions of the latest transatlantic rhythms.

It was time for me to leave. We drained our glasses. Rex gave me a rather curious, searching look and said sadly:

> Now that the old house in Hartington Road has been sold, the last of my Liverpool roots has gone. My mother remained there right up to the time of her death in 1952. Unfortunately, I was in America when she died, so I wasn't able to attend her funeral.

Then, very quietly, he told me:

> I'm not going to have much time to look round Liverpool
> this trip, but one thing I am going to find time to do is
> visit my mother's grave.

We shook hands. The last I saw of him was his back disappearing in the direction of the lift.

Rex Harrison was to live on for another forty-six years, enjoy the runaway success of *My Fair Lady*, go through four more marriages, and end up a multi-millionaire, before dying, of cancer, in New York, at the age of 82, on 2 June 1990.

He died as he had lived, with a foul obscenity on his lips, his last word addressed to his son by Lilli Palmer, Carey, on his deathbed. But when, shortly before 5am that Saturday morning, he made his final exit, it was in complete silence.

FILM STARS DO DIE IN LIVERPOOL – VIRTUALLY

They are light years away now, the days of the weekly injection of sustaining unreality in a workaday world provided by a visit to the pictures.

The local cinema could have been a stylish modern palace, like the Plaza at Allerton, or the Abbey at Wavertree, or what we used, with snobbish inaccuracy, to call a flea-pit, like the Grand on Smithdown Road. But, palace or flea-pit, the local cinema was the gateway to a world of wonder: the rich-beyond-dreams world of chocolate-box-handsome men, like Clark Gable, and breathtakingly beautiful women, like Greta Garbo. The Hollywood world of perpetual Californian sunshine, the singing and dancing world of Fred Astaire and Ginger Rogers, and the hosts of elegant, long-limbed, sensationally-coiffured young women dancers, descending on twinkling feet the wide golden stairway from Paradise to the waiting arms of the cane-twirling, quicksilver-footed young men in top hats and tails, in those brilliant, wonderfully extravagant musicals.

It was another, a parallel, universe that lay behind the silver screen, its citizens such remotely god and goddess-like figures as Spencer Tracy, Katharine Hepburn, Bette Davis, Humphrey Bogart, Lauren Bacall, Cary Grant and James Stewart. You entered this Never-Never-Land through magnificent portals, perhaps with a plashing fountain in the marbled foyer, after paying your one-and-nine, and were escorted to your comfortable plush seat by a smartly uniformed kinematographic minion, known as an usher or usherette. Your exit, two or three hours later, was invariably a sobering, depressing anticlimax. Out you went from the candyfloss world of glitz and glitter, through a down-to-earth door with a clanging iron push-bar into a dreary brick back-alley behind the nobly-fronted picture-palace, where it always seemed to be drizzling with rain.

Film stars were only visiting celluloid shadows. Film stars did not come to live or die in Liverpool. But one did – virtually. Her name was Gloria Grahame, and her story is told in a remarkable book by a Liverpool-born actor, Peter Turner.

It is a tender story. A love story, really. Very subtle. Very on and off. Told originally and most fully by Peter Turner himself, one of the protagonists, in his delicately haunting book, which contrives very cleverly to be almost – but not quite yet – set in a time warp, *Film Stars Don't Die in Liverpool*.

The curtain rises, as one must surely say since the 'players' are both actors, in an apartment house in Camden Town, North London, in May 1978. Gloria Grahame was in London rehearsing the part of Sadie Thompson in a revival of the play based on a Somerset Maugham short story, *Rain*, at the Palace Theatre, Watford. She was a well-respected Hollywood film actress.

Did you see *The Bad and the Beautiful*, Lee Marvin's movie *The Big Heat*, or Humphrey Bogart's classic, *In a Lonely Place*? If so, you saw Gloria Grahame. She played an Oscar-winning rôle in *The Bad and the Beautiful*. In an unforgettable performance as a gangster's moll, she mixed drinks for Lee Marvin before having scalding coffee thrown at her in *The Big Heat*. She was Ado Annie, 'the girl who can't say no', in *Oklahoma*, and the wise-cracking elephant girl in De Mille's *The Greatest Show on Earth*. If you didn't remember her name, you'd certainly know her face.

Off-screen she achieved renown for her real-life rôle as a bride in a Hollywood series of glittery marriages. Her fourth, and last, was to her stepson, Tony Ray, who was the son of her second husband, the film director, Nicholas Ray – thus making him her husband and her son-inlaw.

Liverpool-born Peter Turner was a 26-year-old fledgling actor. His romantic entanglement with the cult film star – the legendary floosie, the epitome of the tart with a heart – twenty-odd years older than himself, blossomed. They became lovers.

The affair started modestly enough. Peter was quartered in a small room at the top of the large Edwardian house near Regent's Park. Miss Grahame was renting the spacious ground-floor apartment. Pouring herself a gin, his theatrical landlady told him with more than a touch of pride to whom it was that she had let her best apartment. Everybody, she insisted, had heard of Gloria Grahame, adding with spirited hyperbole that she had been in every, but *every*, Hollywood film.

It was when, having quietly descended the stairs one morning, he was in process of passing through the hallway, that Gloria suddenly opened her door. She directed a bright smile at him. It hit target. She invited him in. Then smilingly confided that she had to take a dancing class. They danced in time to the music of *Stayin' Alive*.

That very hot day in the spring of 1978 sealed their partnership. On and off over the next couple of years the pair were to be living together under the same roof – in New York, California, and during visits to Liverpool, a place she loved, and where she met Peter's parents and most of his cohort brood of eight brothers and sisters.

By the August of 1980, the relationship had taken on an unexpected, but mutually happily accepted, seeming permanency. Then, out of the blue, as these things so often seem to happen, Gloria turned a warring face on Peter. He searched memory and conscience, but could uncover absolutely no reason to account for this staggering *volte-face*. The rambling old apartment they shared in Manhattan became an emotional ice-house.

When Peter's agent telephoned from London to tell him that he had been offered a part in an upcoming television series, he was glad to be able to utilise it as an appropriate exit line, envisioning Gloria expressing sadness at their splitting up, but pleased and excited for him that he had landed a good part. Not a bit of it. There was an almighty row. Terrible things were said on both sides. Next morning his key to the apartment was handed in. The door closed behind him. A silence the width and depth of the gelid Atlantic finally descended upon them both.

Sic transit Gloria.

That chilly silence was suddenly, and chillingly, broken by the ringing of a telephone in a Liverpool house one late September's morning in 1981.

For Peter Turner, Actor, the week beginning Monday 28 September 1981, was special. Very special. It was the first time that he had been asked to work at his home town theatre, the Liverpool Playhouse. It meant, too, that he could stay at his parents' home with them. The couple, in their seventies, had just celebrated their 50th wedding anniversary, and were excitedly preparing to make their first ever trip abroad, the holiday of a lifetime, flying out to Australia to visit Peter's brother, Billy.

The telephone call was to precipitate a bizarre train of events. It came from Lancaster, where Gloria was rehearsing for a play. Peter had known that she was in England, but the Big Silence still lay distancingly between them. He had half expected, half hoped, that she would contact him, but she had not, until now. And now it was bad news with which she approached him. There was something wrong. She had collapsed. She was ill. She wanted him to come to her.

Peter's brother, Joe, and his wife, Jessie, both of whom knew and liked Gloria, sprang to his aid. There and then they took Peter up to Lancaster in their car.

The trio went straight to Gloria's hotel. There they were told that Miss Grahame had been having pains in her stomach ever since she arrived, but she had made light of them and carried on working. But on the Saturday (26 September) she had collapsed in rehearsals, and was taken to the hospital, where she was admitted and put to bed. The next day, (Sunday), against the strong advice of the doctors, she had signed herself out and returned to the hotel.

Escorted by the hotel's proprietor up to Gloria's room, Peter was told that she had been lying there like this for two days, and the manager just didn't know what to do.

Peter went into the room. It was small. The curtains were half-closed, making it almost dark. At first all that he could see of Gloria was a tangle of blond hair. The rest of her was covered by a blanket. She emerged from beneath it, and he saw with a shock that her face was thin and grey, smeared with old make-up. The Gloria of their Manhattan days was practically unrecognisable.

She put up a characteristically brave show. She said that she had fainted, and they had promptly whisked her off to hospital. All that was the matter was that she had had gas in her stomach, but the doctor had given her an injection of something or other. Now she couldn't even stand up. The medic had made her ill.

Just then, Peter was told that there was someone on the telephone who wanted a word. It was a consultant from the Lancaster hospital. Making no bones about it, he told Peter that Miss Grahame had cancer. The tumour was, he said, about the size of a football, and she should have an immediate operation.

Returning to Gloria's room, Peter told her that she really needed to be looked after, and could not go on staying alone there at the hotel.

She didn't argue, just nodded agreement. Asked him to take her to Liverpool, adding that it was a place where she would really like to live.

Peter had to be back in Liverpool by half-past six to be onstage at the Playhouse, so he took grateful advantage of the offer of a lift there in a fast car. Joe and Jessie, travelling more slowly, with Gloria lying in the back seat of their car, brought her to Peter and Joe's parents' Liverpool home.

When he got back to the house from the theatre, Peter's mother told him that Gloria was up in the middle room – which was situated in a kind of no-man's-land, halfway up the stairs leading off a landing at the back of the house, and directly above the kitchen. Tired out after the journey, she was asleep.

His mother said that she had realised the very minute she opened the door to her that this was a very sick girl. She had seen that look before. She recognised it. She knew what was wrong with her.

There were only a few of Gloria's things scattered about the room, but, to Peter, it seemed as if she had always been there. She certainly did not look out of place. It was almost as if she had finally come home.

That Tuesday night, or rather, in the early hours of the morning of Wednesday (30th), he tried to telephone Gloria's daughter, Paulette, in California. Nobody answered.

By now, all the Turner family, Peter included, were anxious to get Gloria into hospital or a nursing home, where she could be properly looked after medically – but she absolutely refused to go.

Meanwhile, later on the Wednesday, Peter managed to get in touch with Paulette. He asked her to telephone Gloria's sister, Joy. And a call came through from a doctor at the Lancaster hospital. He was grave. He said that Gloria had only 48 hours to live. Peter's mother started to cry.

Gloria was also refusing even to see a doctor. But, for their own protection, the Turners decided that a doctor must be called in. Dr Casey, Irish, semi-retired, and in private practice locally, came. He tried to persuade Gloria to go into hospital. She was having none of it. He left defeated. Before departing, however, he told the family that Gloria was beginning to lose her body fluids, and that he wouldn't be surprised if she were to slip into a coma. It would begin by her going into what looked like a very deep sleep,

If that happened they must let him know.

When Peter got back from the theatre that night Joy was on the telephone. He did not mince words. He told her that her sister was desperately ill. She was unable to eat. She had cancer of the stomach, was about to go into coma, and was, in fact, dying. He asked Joy to come over to Liverpool immediately. She said that she would try to.

Peter's mother, by now thoroughly worried, said that *somebody* had to come, because if they didn't she wouldn't be going to Australia on holiday She wasn't prepared to go away and leave somebody sick in her house. She just couldn't do that. She'd have to stay and look after Gloria.

Then, alarmingly suddenly, unbelievably, Gloria appeared downstairs. Wraith-like, in a long white nightdress, her hair hanging limp around her face, she looked bewilderedly about the kitchen. You could see her struggling to control her breathing, to speak. Then, pathetically, her eyes seeking out each face, she appealed to each in turn, to tell her that she was not sick, was not "gonna die".

Peter helped her back up to her room. She whispered to him that she was getting better. She must be getting better. She had made it downstairs on her own, hadn't she?

He sat her on the bed. She turned her face towards him. She had put on her make-up. The browns and greens were smudged. The red was on aslant. She asked him to tell her how she looked. He told her that she looked beautiful.

From the floor above, which was rented to students, came the plaintive sound of a girl singing prettily a song from *The Pirates of Penzance*. They were practising for their end of term production.

> Poor wand'ring one! Tho' thou hast surely strayed,
> Take heart of grace, Thy steps retrace,
> Poor wand'ring one!

On Friday 2 October, Dr Casey paid the Turners another visit, and, noting how stressed the family were – Gloria had been with them four days now – suggested that they ought to get a nurse to come into the house to help them.

It was then that Peter thought of Nurse Barbara Brawnsley. She worked at the Vasectomy Clinic. He had met her when, appearing in a play that was set in a vasectomy clinic, he had decided, in search of local colour to bring verisimilitude to his performance, to go along to see the real thing in action, as it were. He telephoned her now, explained the circumstances to her, and she expressed herself perfectly willing to come along and lend a helping medical hand.

Thus it was that, in all good faith, with all good intention, the final grotesquerie was precipitated.

Clad in her old gaberdine mackintosh, a plastic headscarf bound securely over her startling orange hair, Nurse Brawnsley duly arrived at the house. Once they had recovered from the initial shock created by her appearance, and were all sitting around the kitchen table chattering, smoking, and drinking cups of tea, the family seemed to take to her. Peter's mother thought her a bit strange to look at, but decided that she was probably a very nice woman, and anyway appeared to know what she was doing.

Nurse Barbara supplies a positively Shakespearean touch of comedic relief to what is otherwise unmitigated tragedy. Peter, grateful for her at-the-drop-of-a-hat help, and happening to know that she was partial to a spot of gin, went out and bought her a bottle of Gordon's to regale her during the course of her less than pleasant task. Then, feeling comfortably reassured, he went off to the Friday night performance at the Playhouse.

Arriving back home later, he was met at the door by his worried mother and father. They told him that, try as they might – and they had been trying for some considerable time – they could not get Nurse Brawnsley out of the house. She just would not go home, and to make matters worse she was drunk. Peter's mother had thought that Nurse was upstairs giving Gloria a bedbath, but when she had gone up to the room to check on how things were going, she found poor Gloria lying on one bed and "that woman" on the other with the bottle.

At that precise psychological moment, Nurse Brawnsley, a veritable Mrs Gamp, came staggering down the stairs. Her voice slurred from too liberal an imbibement of Peter's gift, she began to protest how difficult a woman her patient had proved to be. Gloria would not let her do a thing for her. Then, sagely nodding her orange-topped head, she opined that what Miss Grahame needed was "Miss Euphoria".

Pressed for an explanation, she informed the assembled company that Miss Euphoria was a cocktail of morphine and gin. It was very nice and, better still, Gloria wouldn't have known – or overly cared – what was happening to her.

A horrified Peter instructed his mother to call a taxi for the irremovable Nurse Barbara. And, somewhat unforgivingly, they bundled the 50-year-old Florence Nightingale of the Vasectomy Clinic off into the forgiving darkness of the Liverpool night.

Liverpool, the sensitive city, played her part in the Gloria Grahame epic, providing the appropriately dreadful climatic background to the drama.

I know, I know, the pathetic fallacy! But fact is fact. Ceaselessly fell the terrible rain, the wind lashed out in savage bouts of blind fury. The world beyond the weeping window-panes reflected the tears and melancholy within the darkened room.

Peter sat down and cried.

It was on Saturday evening (4th) that at last Paulette and her brother, Tim, arrived from America. They were here to make decisions. Gloria was no longer the Turners' responsibility. They were upstairs with Gloria. The door was fast closed. Peter was excluded.

The solemn, echoing sound of ringing church bells filling the empty Merseyside sky proclaimed the dawn of Sunday morning. The bells stopped. But, mercifully or unmercifully, Time does not stand still. Its clock was tick-tocking to the hour of irreversible decision.

Tim spoke. He had decided to take his mom back to New York. He had talked to her and spoken to Joy, who had not been able to make it to England, and he had found out that there was a doctor in New York whom Gloria trusted. He had persuaded his mom to let this doctor take a look at her. Tim was sure that his mother – a determined lady he called her – would make it back to New York, and that to return there was her best and only chance.

In the dark, misty light of dawn the taxi arrived. They carried Gloria's living body down to it. She was still breathing on the aeroplane that, at 6.20am, bore her from Speke Airport to Heathrow. Still breathing as she was winged over the grey, yawning expanse of the Atlantic. Still breathing when they carried her into St Vincent's Hospital, in New York City. A few hours later, though, her breathing stopped.

But, for sure, her heart, so long as it continued to beat, remained, I am quite certain, in a house of refuge in Liverpool. And it is here, in this strange, lovely, out-at-elbows city of the North, that the spirit of Gloria Grahame, film star of the now vanished Hollywood of her high noon, will eternally hover, a ghost gracefully restored by affection's memory to her old-time beauty.

MELODIOUS
ECHOES

DOCKLAND NOCTURNES

They are unmistakable. Washed by the waters of the moon. The Liverpool paintings of the Victorian artist, Atkinson Grimshaw. Nocturnes. Widely reproduced of latter years, you will find them gracing the walls of many a native-born Liverpudlian's home, from Lancashire to Melbourne, Acapulco to Zanzibar. All painted in the 1880s. All night scenes. All moonlit vistas of Liverpool docks and dockland.

Typical of his work is what is perhaps the most famous of his pictures, *Salthouse Dock, Liverpool*, painted in 1880, exhibited at the Royal Academy in 1885. In it, Grimshaw allowed full play to his lifelong fascination with the contrast between moonlight and artificial light → the yellow coronas of the rakish gas-lamps; the lanterns, sparkling like fireflies in the rigging on the ships' masts; the soft shine of the cabs' lamps; the glowing shop windows; the moon-ridden, scud-shawled sky; all mirrored in the glister of wetted cobbles.

Here, where land and water meet, is Foster's Ilyssos Ionic Custom House, Durandu's superior tobacconist's (at the Exchange Street branch of which my grandfather used to buy his boxes of cigars and have his special blend of pipe tobacco mixed), the poulterer's with its dependant frieze of stark dead fowl, the landward roofscape of flagstaff and spiky telegraph poles, balancing the seaward forest of intricate masts and spars and dusky tracery of Tissot-like riggings.

There is an enormous sense of quiet busyness about the scene. The people may be only silhouettes, but they prompt questions and invite speculation. Glimpsed in the flaring dark, they are so patently flesh and blood, poised in the frozen act of so many and varied activities. Father and child, calotype-black against the orange gas-glow of the well-stocked shops, the trundling man with the handcart, the crowded horse bus load, the smudged lurkers in the waterfront shadows, the hailed hansom … on what errands were they, one hundred and seventeen years ago, all bound?

It is a painting, like those of Frith, that draws us right into the time and place that it depicts. We can almost feel the warmth seeping out of the bright shops into the raw and gleaming street, sense the secret worlds locked away behind the dark façades of the houses, and the cabined life pulsing below the murky hulls of the docked ships. The artist has somehow succeeded in capturing the very essence of long since swept away Sailortown, the Liverpool of *Her Benny*, of Mrs Maybrick, the prosperous merchants of the Exchange Flags, the salty shellbacks, and the proud old sea-captains.

Let us then see what we can discover about the invisible man behind these fascinating Liverpool canvasses, an artist whose *A Wet Road, Knostrop,*

Yorkshire, sold at Sotheby's in November 1995 for £90,600, and his *Scarborough Bay by Moonlight* fetched £151,500 in 1997. A painter for whom the moon was made not of green cheese, but of pure gold.

To start with, John Atkinson Grimshaw was not a Liverpudlian. He was a Yorkshireman, born in Leeds, on 6 September 1836, the son of a policeman, David Grimshaw, who lived at 9 Back Park Street.

Six years later, the Grimshaws moved to Norwich, where David Grimshaw found a job with Messrs Pickford's, the carriers, and young John was a pupil at the King Edward VII Grammar School.

In 1848, when John was 12, the family returned to Leeds. David Grimshaw took up a position as a collector for the Great Northern Railway Company, and his wife opened a grocery shop, in, it is believed, Brunswick Row.

The lad began his working life at the age of 16, as a clerk, working, like his father, for the Great Northern Railway Company, a position which was anathema to him, as his consuming and unwavering ambition was to become a professional artist. This, however, was something of which his mother and father, strict Baptists, disapproved. His mother's nonconformist conscience was particularly opposed to his artistic inclinations, her objection being expressed actively by her throwing his paints on the fire, and turning off the gas in his room.

In 1858, he married his cousin, Frances (Fanny) Theodosia Hubbarde, the daughter of James Hubbarde, editor of the *Hampshire Advertiser*, and the couple settled into a house in the Leeds suburb of Wortley. He was still employed at Leeds railway station, but he was painting in his spare time and selling his pictures to a Leeds bookseller, Thomas Fenteman, who, an exceedingly religious man, bought them only on the strict understanding that they had not been painted on a Sunday! These paintings were mainly still-life studies of dead birds, blossoms, moss-grown rocks, ferns, and foliage, and they were signed 'JA Grimshaw'.

It was not until late 1861, or early in 1862, that, encouraged by his wife, the 25-year-old Grimshaw exchanged the distasteful security of the pen for the congenial precariousness of the brush. Although entirely self-taught, his capabilities were fortunately to prove the equal of his courageous optimism, and within five years he was to find himself established as a successful artist. So much so that, in 1864, he could afford to take an attractive Regency house in Cliff Road, at Woodhouse Ridge, to the west of the town.

By the late 1860s, he had developed a distinctive style of his own, and, discarding the Pre-Raphaelite manner in which he had painted his earliest still-lifes, he adopted a simplified technique, still meticulous as to detail, but abandoning his previous use of bright colours and employing a considerably subdued palette.

A strict Baptist by upbringing, in 1867 Grimshaw – and his wife –

converted to Roman Catholicism, and in 1868, he tried his hand at a large scale religious painting, *The Seal of the Covenant*, based on the *Book of Revelations*. It was about this time, too, that he began to paint moonlit landscapes, and painted them so superlatively that it has been said that moonlight was his trademark. He was now signing his paintings 'Atkinson Grimshaw'.

Throughout the late 'sixties and 'seventies Grimshaw was producing imaginative and romantic landscapes, and benefiting from the prodigality of a number of local Leeds collectors who were keen to acquire for themselves the very latest in contemporary art. Never at his best with figures – a problem with which he coped by depicting people in silhouette – he painted scenes, atmospheres almost, with a distinguished subtlety, distilling the *genius loci*, snaring the effects of rain and mist, or the last bright-burning end of autumn afternoons in suburban streets and rural lanes, with a feeling and precision which no one has surpassed. He worked in dark tones and yet contrived to make even the mud glow. He put October on canvas, hovering damply about the hollows of the rutted and mock-rural suburban roads.

There are those who see Grimshaw's work as a sort of extension of the 'moonlight Pether' tradition. Others think to descry significant correspondences between his pictures and calotype photographs. They instance the solid blackness of objects contrasted with the preternatural effulgence of background, and conclude that in Grimshaw's paintings photography and painting achieved their most intimate fusion. It is said, too, that Grimshaw resorted to a method whereby a master drawing was projected through a photographic enlarger on to a canvas – rather as Baron Corvo employed magic lantern slides to assist him with the figure drawings for his religious banners.

During the decade 1870-1880, Grimshaw's moon-drenched nocturnes became exceedingly popular. People were buying his pictures faster than he could paint them, a state of affairs which provoked from the 'Stinging Butterfly' of Chelsea the Whistlerful observation: "I considered myself the inventor of nocturnes until I saw Grimmy's moonlights".

As a result of this new-found prosperity, he was able to rent a large Jacobean manor-house, Knostrop Old Hall, which stood two miles east of Leeds by the River Aire. He furnished the place lavishly, and, in his lamplit study there, he would of an evening muse over the works of Dickens, of whom he was an avowed admirer, and the poetry of Shelley, Keats, Browning and Tennyson. His reading of the poets is believed to have exercised considerable influence upon him. Indeed, many of his paintings have been described as 'poems in paint'.

He was also by this time, 1876, deep enough in pocket to be able to rent also, in Mulgrave Place, overlooking Scarborough's North Bay, a large and elaborate cliff-top house, crenellated, turreted, and completely surrounded by a conservatory, which he called Castle-by-the-Sea, after Longfellow's poem.

His life did not pass unscathed by the breath of Bohemian scandal. *Post-mortem* rumour titillates with behind-hand whisperings of 'nocturnes' of a different kind with Miss Agnes Leefe. She was an actress whom in all probability he had met through his friend Wilson Barrett, actor-manager of the Leeds Grand Theatre, where she was employed. Grimshaw imported her into his household as his studio assistant and model, who posed for him nude. The subsequent rumours of impropriety were very likely baseless, for actually Agnes became a companion to both the children – Fanny bore him 15 assorted boys and girls over the years, only six of whom survived to adulthood – and to his wife. Aggnes Leefe died, deeply mourned, of tuberculosis at Knostrop, in 1890.

Grimshaw made his only trip abroad in 1878, escorting his children's governess, Mrs Ruhl, back to her home in Germany, and, taking advantage of the occasion, ventured into brief painting forays in France and Germany.

The following year, at the age of 43, he was to sustain a most grievous financial setback. The exact cause of it remains, even all these years later, mysteriously uncertain. Family tradition has it that he had backed a large bill for a friend, who let him down. In any event, Grimshaw was ruined, and although his work continued as popular as ever, he was to remain burdened with debt to the end of his days.

He was forced to relinquish his Castle-by-the-Sea, install his wife and family at Knostrop, where they were frequently harried by bailiffs, and spend long periods working alone in London. At first he stayed at Anderton's Hotel, in Fleet Street, that same hostelry which was later to be patronised by that terrible Victorian bogey, Dr Thomas Neill Cream, lethal distributor of pink pills to pale prostitutes. From there, Grimshaw moved on to rented rooms in Trafalgar Studios, in Manresa Road, Chelsea. He was to remain here for two years – 1885-1887. During this period he painted many scenes of Battersea, Wandsworth, Putney, and Hampstead, and became a friend of Whistler.

It was from about 1880 onwards that Grimshaw had virtually abandoned the conventionally romantic landscape. He set up his easel in the town, and made a kind of scenic poetry of the Victorian streets and docks of London, Leeds, Liverpool, Hull and Glasgow, in a series of townscapes which were to set the seal upon his reputation. Liverpool remained his favourite location for his dockside views.

Artistically, Grimshaw is difficult to place. He was pre-eminently a landscapist, but, like Lowry, his talent was so pronouncedly individual as to defy precise categorisation. He was *the* painter of the Victorian street scene. Yet, while faithfully delineating in scrupulous detail the quintessential material world, he brought to that portrayal a glazing of transcendant romance, conjured up from within himself. In the last three years of his life he painted some small-scale views of the docks at Liverpool. These were sold to a dealer who had specially commissioned them, perhaps to sell to Americans, as the transatlantic liners docked at Liverpool in those days.

His main Liverpool paintings are six in number – *Liverpool from Wapping* (c 1875), *Salthouse Dock, Liverpool* (1880), *The City Docks by Moonlight* (1882), *Liverpool Quays by Moonlight* (1887), *The Custom House: Looking North* and *The Custom House: Looking South*.

In 1890, he returned to live at Knostrop, and there, on 13 October 1893, aged 57, he died of cancer. His last words, addressed to Fanny, were: "No sun. No moon. No stars."

But the moon he had bequeathed to us in enduring perfection.

THE DAPPER DRAPER

For a lad born at Cwmrhaiadr – a place as difficult to locate geographically as it is to pronounce correctly – amid the green valleys of Wales, young Owen Owen, brushing the farmyard mud from his boots, was to travel, both distance-wise and socially, a long, long way.

He left home on 27 September 1860, as he was approaching close to his 13th birthday. His destination was his Uncle Samuel Evans' small drapery shop at Bath, where it was all arranged that he should become an apprentice. Safely stowed in his small tin trunk was the suitably inscribed Bible which it was a Welsh family tradition to present to young sons who were leaving the Cymric nest to venture forth into the harsh, devil-haunted English world of work.

Home in 1860 was a 600-acre farm at the end of the valley of the River Llyfnant, two miles south of the market town of Machynlleth. Owen's father, Owen Owen, Senior, had lived at Cwymrhaiadr since 1841, when, as a result of Owen Owen Senior's drink problem, he and his father, Thomas Owen, unable to pay a mortgage when it fell due, had been forced to sell the family ancestral home of Bwlch to an Aberystwyth banker, and to take up the tenancy of Cwymrhaiadr.

There was, in the good old days of Queen Victoria, and on into Edwardian times, a fairly steady flow of young men and women from the more remote areas of Wales into England. Statistics disclose that in 1861 some 150,000 Welsh people were living in England, nearly 50,000 of whom had settled in London, Liverpool and Manchester. So far as trades were concerned, the Welsh builders were famous. Apart from that, the two other businesses traditionally established by the Welsh were milk rounds and drapers' shops.

Young Owen Owen's apprenticeship went well, and by 1867 he was becoming increasingly restless, determined to strike out and go into business on his own account. His future, he had decided, lay in Liverpool, a city which he had visited a couple of years previously, and where, before his death at the age of 33 in 1856, his father's brother, Robert, had had a thriving drapery shop at 93 London Road.

Owen was still eight months short of his twentieth birthday when, on 24 February 1868, financially backed by his Uncle Samuel and his half-brother, Tom, he arrived in Liverpool. In the loneliness of his room in his new lodgings, he sat down at eight o'clock on his first evening and scribbled what he called 'A few thoughts on arriving in Liverpool'.

He wrote, with appropriate maritime imagery:

Who can tell what I am now laying the foundation of? Is

this the time and tide that leads to fortune, or is it a ship sailing on the world-wide ocean, without compass to guide, or an anchor to steady?

To the dictates of his deep Wesleyan Methodist upbringing, and a natural unease concerning the configurations of his future, he then proceeded to pen

A few rules to guide me to the Harbour of Best Success which under the providence of God, with my own industry, I hope to make succeed.

His list of nine commandments ran:

1. Rise very early, and live very well and very cheaply.
2. Be honest to my customers and just to my creditors – this will give confidence.
3. Pay debts as soon as possible so as to owe no man; and give no credit to anyone for longer period than two months; this can't be thought of at first.
4. Work myself and be as much as possible in the shop. Help, hands, for I have no lands.
5. Be civil to everyone.
6. Time being money, waste none; for now is the time to work, read and make a fortune.
7. Do not frequent theatres, music halls, or anything to neglect the business.
8. Policy, policy, policy, policy. Think again, reflect, be of the same mind for some time together. Don't change your mind; think first and think twice before you act.
9. Keep the stock low and always fresh.

His first practical task was to find a suitable shop premises – one small enough for him to run by himself, but in a position where it would attract a steady stream of customers. He settled on 121 London Road, which had previously been a druggist's. London Road was not exactly the smartest of areas, but it was a populous and busy one.

The shop had only been open a day or two when he acquired his first assistant. Her name was Mary Lewis. She herself was later to recall:

I was examining some merchandise that was on display. I observed Owen Owen trying to sell some item or other to another customer. The customer eventually walked out without buying the goods. I told Owen Owen that I would have sold that garment to the customer. After discussion, I was offered a job as an assistant at the shop. I accepted and was with the company for thirty-one years.

Five years on – 1873 – and the small shop had extended to nearly a quarter of an acre of business flooring, with a frontage of 120 feet, stretching from London Road round the corner into Audley Street, and a staff of more than 120 people. Owen's avowed policy of supplying 'the public with the newest and cheapest fancy goods at the lowest possible prices', had paid off handsomely.

Owen's sister, Jenny, came to Liverpool to keep house for him. The arrangement did not last long. She met here a Wesleyan minister, the Reverend James A Barrowclough, and they married in 1875. Another of Owen's sisters, Margaret, arrived to replace Jenny as her brother's housekeeper. She contracted tuberculosis and died on 6 February 1880. Greatly distressed, Owen purchased a family vault at Anfield Cemetery. For many years subsequently he was looked after by a housekeeper whom he employed, Mrs Sarah Sawtell.

It is uncertain exactly where it was that Owen stayed when he first came to Liverpool, but he was for some time living at 3 North View, Edgehill, which, oddly enough, is listed in *Gore's Liverpool Directory* of 1868 as a seminary. Subsequently, he moved to live, not over the shop, but very close to it, at 57 Pembroke Place. From there, he was, in September 1887, to set up a more splendid residence at 82 Prince's Road, beside the tree-lined Boulevard. Here, in addition to Mrs Sawtell, he kept several servants. He had also a four-wheeled Victoria carriage and a brougham.

Away from the counter and the counting-house, Owen's spiritual life was just as devout as it had always been. In his first Liverpool years he had attended the Wesleyan Brunswick Chapel, in Moss Street, but by the mid-1880s he was veering from Wesleyan Methodism toward Unitarianism, and was regularly joining the congregation at the Unitarian Church in Hope Street.

Neither was he neglectful of his physical well-being. Believing in muscular Christianity, he maintained a fervent interest in physical fitness and sport. He was a member of the Liverpool Gymnasium, in Myrtle Street, founded in deference to the exemplar of a Liverpool gentleman who rejoiced in the classical title of *Gymnasiarch*, and which Owen would visit in the evenings. He also made regular pilgrimage to Smedley's Hydropathic Centre, at Birkdale Park, Southport, as well as to several of his other Hydros.

In 1884, he became a keen cyclist, having bought himself a tricycle from the Royal Machine Manufacturing Company of Bold Street, for £22, and invested in a bell for 4s.6d. In 1885, he joined the Cyclists' Union. He was also an enthusiastic tennis player; a member of the Bohemian Lawn Tennis Club, the Anfield Lawn Tennis Club, and, later, the Victoria Social and Lawn Tennis Club. As he grew older, golf was gradually substituted for tennis and became his favourite sport.

Politically, he was, as befitted an adopted son of Liverpool, a Gladstonian Liberal.

Although a Welsh exile, Owen always remained loyal to his native land, remembering how green was his valley. He was a dedicated member of the Liverpool Welsh National Society and was to be seen at many of their functions in the city. He gave generous donations to the National Eisteddfod of Wales, and when this was held at the Haymarket in Liverpool in 1884, was prominent in what was one of the greatest events in the history of the aforesaid Liverpool Welsh National Society.

Since about 1881, Owen had, over the years, been making considerable purchases of property in the vicinity of his, as it had now become, department store. He acquired premises in Shaw Street, Stafford Street, Audley Street and Irvine Street. His anxiety to acquire local property stemmed from the ambition which he had long secretly nurtured, to do everything in his power to assure that his staff – and especially, remembering his own experience as a young man of the loneliness of a strange city, his youthful apprentices, many of whom had left home in North Wales at an early age – should live as a large family, in a place near the store that they could call home, and with a matron to take care of them.

In 1884, at a cost of almost £11,000, the erection of a hostel in Stafford Street was completed, and Miss Mary Lewis, whom we have already met, was installed to play the rôle of matron, which she did until her retirement in 1899. A second hostel, for women employees, was opened in Shaw Street.

Owen's interest in the welfare of his staff extended beyond the matter of mere accommodation. His concept of them as his extended family was well illustrated by the various benefits which he devised for them.

Every year, in January, a tea-party and ball was held for the staff, paid for out of Owen's own pocket.

The state of their health was a prime concern. For this reason, he encouraged them to take part in various sports in their free time. He was exceedingly proud of his staff tennis and cricket teams, for whom he hired a sports ground. He saw to it that in times of sickness his employees were well looked after. And Mr Owen Owen's own holiday home, Plas Mariandir, at Penmaenmawr, was freely opened up to anyone who needed rest and convalescence. Staff, and friends, whose health had broken badly, or who were just in need of a complete change, were financially helped to go abroad for a rest on the continent. It was, moreover, his firm which, by its example, led the movement towards shorter hours of work in Liverpool's stores, and his was the first to introduce a weekly half-holiday.

As the century wore on and Owen's fortune grew, he was increasingly paying visits to London, where he was not only becoming involved with his brother William's drapery business in Westbourne Grove, but was also occupied with various other business activities of his own. Every month he was staying for a week, or even a fortnight, at Woods Hotel, Furnival's Inn.

It was in London that, still a bachelor at the age of 44, he met and fell in love with a young woman named Ellen Maria Richards. She was a close friend of Mrs Sawtell's daughters, Emily and Annie, with whom she worked as a shop assistant at Gorringe's. She and Owen were married on 19 December 1891, at St John's Parish Church, Weymouth, and, after a honeymoon in Italy, settled into 82 Prince's Road, early in February 1892. And it was there that, on 28 March 1893, she presented him with his first child, a daughter, Muriel Gwendolen Owen Owen.

The following September (1893), after 25 years, Owen Owen left Liverpool, never, apart from brief business visits, when he stayed at the Adelphi Hotel, to return.

The success of Owen Owen's Liverpool store continued unchecked. Always immaculately turned out in a tail-coat and striped trousers, a floor-walker would sweep silently up to conduct the customer to the required department, where a chair would be rapidly drawn up for her – or him. In wet weather, one of the many page boys on duty would meet customers at the shop door to shelter them from the rain, and, if they bore a dripping umbrella, they would be removed and carefully guarded for the duration of the customers' stay. There was now a staff of 400 to look after Sir or Madam's needs, and the shop normally remained open until 8pm.

In 1899, the small draper's shop, opened 31 years before, became a public limited company, with the farmer's son from the valleys its highly respected chairman.

Owen was to father four children. A son, Harold, was born on 13 September 1895, at the London home to which he and his wife had moved from Liverpool – Woodlea, 41 Grove End Road, St John's Wood. A second daughter, Eira Dilys, was born there on 27 July 1898. And, fourth and finally, on 23 April 1902, at The Manor House, 37 Fitzjohns Avenue, Hampstead, where the Owens had moved in February 1901, a second son, Arthur Lloyd.

Two of the greatest triumphs for the Owens *qua* a family were, first, the purchase, in October 1896, by Owen's half-brother, Thomas Owen, of the Cwmrhaiadr Estate, where Owen Owen had been born, and whence the family's somewhat ignominious banishment in 1849 had ended their hundreds of years presence in the beautiful Llyfnant valley. The second triumph was when, ten years later, in September 1906, Owen was able to buy back Bwlch, thus restoring it to the family after an absence of nearly 66 years.

But between the two triumphs there had been tragedy. On Sunday 10 July 1898, Thomas Owen, walking on his recouped land near Cwmrhaiadr, had slipped on the slimy rocks while trying to cross a stream, and, stunned, fallen into the water and drowned. He was fifty-eight.

By the turn of the century, Owen Owen had bought his way into an interest in many metropolitan and other department stores, and had become a considerable London property owner and developer. Indeed, for many years his bust could be seen above the entrance to one of his properties, Kingsway House, in Great Queen Street. He had achieved great wealth and was noted for his many gifts to charitable causes. He had become a well known and well respected captain of industry.

In March 1906, he sailed from Liverpool to North America, for the purpose of observing the American methods and practices of retail trade. He returned from the States in the following May.

By the second half of 1909, Owen's health was plainly deteriorating. He and the family spent Christmas for the first time ever away from home, at the Riviera Palace Hotel, at Penzance. Early in 1910 cancer was diagnosed, and in the March he underwent an operation which was performed in a room at 37 Fitzjohns Avenue which had been converted into an operating theatre. It was not a success. On Easter Sunday 27 March 1910, Owen Owen, aged 62, died. After a funeral service at the Rosslyn Hill Unitarian Chapel, in Hampstead, he was cremated at Golders Green.

He never was laid to rest in the vault which, all those years ago, he had prudently purchased at Anfield Cemetery. No matter, his memory remains alive in Liverpool, where generations have made their way to the vast department store where his name was writ large in stone above its ever-welcoming portals. And that is how he would have wanted it.

PERSONAL
ECHOES

BEL' ARRIVO – MYSELF WHEN YOUNG
For Clare Whittington-Egan

Like a scene viewed diminuendo through the wrong end of a telescope, I see it now – the landscape of my lost childhood. It seems a kind of *Alice-in-Wonderland* world, where everything looks larger than life, as if I had nibbled, like Alice, a sinistral fragment of magic mushroom, or swallowed a draught from the little 'Drink Me' bottle. I suppose dogs and cats and trees and people appear bigger because I am smaller, and I am being trundled, hand-held, through this Brobdingnagian region – actually Princes Park – by my nurse, Nanny Brown, and delivered to a huge, forbidding brick fortress, bearing, although I cannot yet read it, the legend 'Bellerive Convent'.

To adopt and adapt to my own purpose TS Eliot, I sit here on the escarpment of the Malvern Hills, an old man in a dry month, writing of being a boy; a very small boy, some seventy years ago, being subjected to his first alarming taste of life outside the safe and cosy confines of the family nest, at that time in the high rafters of Princes Park Mansions; or was it still in Upper Parliament Street, where I used to watch from the first-floor drawing-room window the trams go by, always begging to be allowed to wait to see just one more bearing the bright blue tin advertisement with the red and white striped Mr Punch on it, curving round the open cage end of the front of the top deck? I am, frankly, not sure. And, sadly, there is no one left to ask.

In the not very certain eye of memory, I behold this small boy, who, far away and long ago and in a different part of the forest, was me, being delivered into the hands of the enemy; black and white penguinish figures called, I was told, nuns, whom I was puzzled to address as 'Mother' and 'Sister'. They were surely no relatives of mine. Anyway, with their flapping robes and floating veils, and the way they moved, as though on wheels, with hidden feet, they frightened me.

I vaguely recall launching myself at one of them – Mother Blanche – who struck me as a fierce, cold, disapproving, hostile figure, grabbing at, and tearing off, her veil. Twenty-odd years later, when I published my first book about Liverpool, it came to my ears that, with laughter and charity, *les bonnes mères* of Bellerive – including, if I mistake not, the object of my attack herself, by then verging into her nineties – remembered in its author that horrid little boy who had molested *Bonne Mère* Blanche! And I am happy to be able to report that I had long since been forgiven my infant peccadillo.

It was at Bellerive that I first embarked upon what was to become a tedious later life habit – falling in love. I think that memory does not play me false in supplying me with the name of my first love as Sheila. I have tried, but I cannot summon back her little face; unless she is, perhaps, the pretty sprite who sits beside me holding my hand in one of those long, panoramic school photographs, taken in April 1929. What I do, with guilty clarity, remember, is that Sheila lost one of her front teeth – and that was the end of the affair. As, I think it was the Scottish poet, Thomas Campbell, shrewdly observed, 'Coming events cast their shadows before!'

What else do I recall of antediluvian Bellerive? Was there not a long, mosaic-floored subterranean corridor, leading beneath the road from one convent house to another? I see it with a delicate blue and white statue of the Virgin Mary standing somewhere, I think at one end of it. And always the statue is surrounded for me by a galaxy of spring flowers – yellow daffodils, pink tulips, blue hyacinths – a perpetual feast-day display. I felt, and feel, that the highway to heaven must surely be furnished so.

But the devil was in me even then! There was, I recollect, another little boy, his name is gone, but I remember his iron-callipered leg and his unaffected ferocity. He was the son of the Liverpool consul of one of those Catholic South American countries. I found his very existence a challenge, and I can recall, his physical handicap notwithstanding, his immense tigerish strength, and how we would roll about on the floor locked in the fiercest mortal combat. And then, when it was all over, decided for the nonce one way or the other, how we reverted diplomatically to being the superficially best of mutually-respecting friends.

Another name from friendship's roll which springs warmly and ineradicably to mind is that of Joseph Marmion, the son of Dr Marmion of Elmswood Road. I have never clapped eyes on him since those 1920s days, when there were less motor-cars on the roads, and what was to become Liverpool Airport was just a big field at Speke, where, looking over the wooden barred gate, I saw amateur pilots in those old-style leather helmets and goggles, taxiing off for flips in pre-Noachian, open-cockpitted flying machines, and the Liverpool Zoo, hard by the Marmions', home to Mickey the chimp, brought exotic excitements to the quiet purlieus of enchantingly lovely, leafy Mossley Hill.

On a somewhat wilder, and, to be honest, inexplicable note, I can call back to memory's inner eye the image of my young and boisterous self, newly arrived from the delights of watching the old men in the thin, watery sunshine filtering through the bare branches of gaunt trees, playing their recondite games of ollies on the olly pitch in Princes Park, leaping on to one of the tree-stumps in the Bellerive playground, and standing there bellowing to the world at large, and my playmates in particular, that I was "The Bishop of Rum-ti-Foo". God and I alone knew what I was talking about then. Now, God alone knows! I cannot imagine that at that tender age I had familiarity with The 'Bab' Ballads of Sir William Schwenck Gilbert and his balmy island of Rum-ti-Foo.

I remember making my first communion, and the ribbed texture of the starched, white linen blouse-like garment, with affixed white linen tie, which I wore that day instead of my usual soft wool jersey. Thick and shining fringed, deceptively innocent-faced, my time-fixed shade wears it still in the regulation cabinet photograph by Mowell & Morrison.

It was in the Bellerivean Groves of Academe that I was initiated into the mysteries of reading and writing; good and worthy skills which have stood me in bad stead for the rest of my scrivening life!

Then, suddenly, the page turned … the fairy-tale beginning was over. *My* teeth began to drop out. The baby in the Duchess' arms was transmogrified into a sneezing piglet. Real-life came knocking with rough knuckles at the nursery door. Nanny Brown and her much-loved successor, Ethel Blundell, who, before I came along, had been my mother's personal maid, faded before the advent of the stern figures of the pedagogues into whose less tender hands I was about to be consigned.

The clock, that despotic ruler of all our lives, had made its loud tick heard. It was time to move on. Time – to parodise the pious intonings of those old-fashioned, innocently cliché-bound travelogue commentators that one used to hear at the pictures – to say farewell to Bellerive as the westering sun of my childhood bathes it in the golden after-glow of that Wordsworthian 'light that never was, on sea or land'; time to move on, round the corner into Belvedere Road, into the, comparatively speaking, calloused hands of Fathers Cullen, O'Donovan and Murphy, and ear-clipping Mr Kerr, rulers of 'St Vincent's Academy for the Sons of Gentlemen', where life took off the gloves.

The Middle Passage

Scanned from the breezy summit of Hill 21, the dark and shadowed valley labelled 'Age 40-50' on the life map, seemed an impossible, immeasurable distance away. The plateau of nineteen years, stretching between now and then, was surely limitless ... infinite.

The odd thing is that now, nudging the half-century, I do not feel any different. When I look in the mirror I can still see the schoolboy cap on my – grey-edged – locks.

It's true, though, policemen *do* seem to look younger. And, wistfully, I think of Alexander Gray's poem, *On a Cat Ageing*.

> He blinks upon the hearth-rug
> And yawns in deep content,
> Accepting all the comforts
> That Providence has sent.
> Only – the thought disturbs him –
> He's noticed once or twice,
> The times are somehow breeding
> A nimbler race of mice.

Listening in the anxious dark to the muffled echo of my heart-beats, relayed through the pillow, I ask myself, am I less physically fit? Have thirty-five years of smoking and downing 'strong drink' (I started young) seriously damaged the bright, clean body with which I began?

My doctor is either very optimistic, or a very tactful man. At any rate, he has given me neither ill news, nor fell warnings.

Exercise. Having disdained it all my youth, in the mid-forties I took up riding. A bicycle and a horse. No car. The riding of horses I embarked upon at 44, never previously having been on anything livelier than a New Brighton donkey.

I am no three-day-eventer, but one thing I have proved. I am tough. You have to be to put up with half a ton of horseflesh standing on your foot. And when he wasn't crushing me with his iron-booted hooves, Big Bunny was doing his best to buck me off as we go over the jumps.

My other horse, Little Bunny, would vary the procedure. He would fall down with me, and contrive to roll right over me. I've been concussed, bitten in the stomach, and kicked in the spinney (very painful!) Still, as the St John's ambulance man said as he bent over me after one particularly dolorous fall, "Riding keeps you fit".

My arteries may not yet be hardening, but, if I am honest, I have to admit that my mind is. I do take less kindly to innovations. Decimal currency, for instance. I know all the mathematical arguments for the incalculable superiority of the system, but for me it remained – incalculable. I grew up in the days of farthings, half pennies, pennies, threepenny bits, tanners, bobs, florins and half-crowns … and they did have a bit of purchasing power.

Sex. No longer frantic, like a furtive fag puffed behind the woodshed. A leisured affair. No need to prove anything. All is proved by the simple fact of one's acceptance in the amatory rôle.

The same with ambition. Nearing 50, you are either a roaring success, with three ulcers to prove it, or a man with a great future behind you. Or, if you're sensible, inured to whatever position or level in life your capacity has brought you. Whichever, that most disturbing of all emotions, competitiveness, is likely to be on the wane. And what a relief that is. Consolation, should you feel the need of it, is always available in the study of the lives of Great Men who proved to be late developers.

But, success or failure, there is reason for self-congratulation in mere survival – like a batsman who has knocked up 50 not out, and is still there at the wicket slogging for six the googlies that Fate keeps bowling up.

One looks back at the vicissitudes weathered, the dangerous corners turned. One has all the faded charm of a survivor.

And the advantages of half-centenarian achievement? Well, you begin genuinely to care less about what other people think. I don't mean that loss of self-awareness which can afflict some folk in their dotage, that disconcerting disregard for vital zips and buttons, but the pruning back of self-consciousness.

You can wear what you like. You have entered the Comfort Zone. The Peacock Years are behind you. Comfort is coming to count for more than cutting a dash. You can still look smart when necessary, but not as a full-time fetish.

I find, too, in my anec-dotage, that I am able to give up pretending. If I don't like something, I say so, politely of course, whereas ten years ago I wouldn't have dreamt of it.

I don't read the books I *should* read any more. I read the books I *want* to read.

This valley isn't at all a bad place. Things are no longer so black and white, clear-cut, as they were. Perhaps the greyness comes from me. People used to be good or evil. Now I see that, as a rule, they are neither exclusively, but a mixture of both. I suppose you could call this new tolerance 'charity'. I hope so. For, God knows, I have need of it myself.

A great capacity, lately developed, is the ability truly to stand in other people's shoes. You do not necessarily approve of their attitudes and avowals, but you understand them.

It is only when you have discovered charity that you can acquire hope.

At 40-plus, one feels perhaps less passionately, but, I think, more sincerely. The friendships that remain, canonised by the years, have become infinitely more precious.

Suddenly one day you wake up, rub your eyes, and realise that every one of us is a fellow-traveller, progressing, whether by Rolls Royce, or upon two painful, broken-booted feet, to the identical one-way terminus. It is the last piece of good sense that makes nonsense of everything else. We are all condemned men under indefinite reprieve.

In my twenties and thirties I used to take things for granted. Not any more. And there is a certain sweetness in uncertainty.

I no longer have any favourite season. I am grateful for each as it arrives – and I am there to see it! Spring, with skippety lambs and crocus spears; summer, bee-loud and drowse-laden in the pastures; autumn, the golden, stocktaking time; winter, holding all life in white hostage.

And, in my case at least, there is a curious blending of past and present. It is as if a third eye has opened. I see with my two eyes, but, superimposed, I also see the scene with the eye of memory.

As 50 approaches, there is just one thought that gives me pause. I could be a grandfather – and the great trouble about that is waking up to find yourself married to a grandmother!

Looking back, I realise that the years are great levellers. They pick the bones out of old contentions; they iron-out the creases and wrinkles that disfigure youth. Clichés shine with the sudden truth that begat them. Age is only something that happens to you with Time. It may wither … but it need not condemn.